Personal Virtues

Introdu [D0745170]

Edited by

Clifford Williams

First published 2005 by
PALGRAVE MACMILLAN
Houndmills, Basingstoke, Hampshire RG21 6XS and
175 Fifth Avenue, New York, N. Y. 10010
Companies and representatives throughout the world

PALGRAVE MACMILLAN is the global academic imprint of the Palgrave Macmillan division of St. Martin's Press, LLC and of Palgrave Macmillan Ltd. Macmillan® is a registered trademark in the United States, United Kingdom and other countries. Palgrave is a registered trademark in the European Union and other countries.

ISBN-13: 978–1–4039–9454–7 hardback
ISBN-10: 1–4039–9454–4 hardback
ISBN-13: 978–1–4039–9455–4 paperback
ISBN-10: 1–4039–9455–2 paperback

This book is printed on paper suitable for recycling and made from fully managed and sustained forest sources.

A catalog record for this book is available from the Library of Congress.

10   9   8   7   6   5   4   3   2   1
14   13   12   11   10   09   08   07   06   05

Printed and bound in China

Contents

Sources and Acknowledgements

The editor and publishers wish to thank the following for permission to use copyright material:

Joseph Kupfer, "Generosity of Spirit," *The Journal of Value Inquiry*, 32 (September, 1998), 357–368. Copyright © 1998 Kluwer Academic Publishers. Reprinted with kind permission from Springer Science and Business Media and the author.

Patrick Boleyn-Fitzgerald, "Gratitude and Justice," *Ethics*, 109 (October, 1998), 119–137, 152–153. Copyright © 1998 by The University of Chicago. Reprinted with permission of The University of Chicago Press and the author.

Nancy E. Snow, "Humility," *The Journal of Value Inquiry*, 29 (June, 1995), 203–216. Copyright © 1995 Kluwer Academic Publishers. Reprinted with kind permission from Springer Science and Business Media and the author.

Tara Smith, "The Practice of Pride," *Social Philosophy and Policy*, 15 (Winter, 1998), 71–90. Copyright © 1998 Kluwer Academic Publishers and Social Philosophy and Policy Foundation. Reprinted with the permission of Cambridge University Press and the author.

Martha Nussbaum, "The Cognitive Structure of Compassion," in *Upheavals of Thought: The Intelligence of Emotions* (Cambridge: Cambridge University Press, 2001), 304–327. Copyright © 2001 by Cambridge University Press. Reprinted with the permission of Cambridge University Press and the author.

Robert C. Solomon, "Reasons for Love," *Journal for the Theory of Social Behavior*, 32 (March, 2002), 1–28. Copyright © 2002 The Executive Management Committee/Blackwell Publishers Ltd.

Reprinted with permission of Blackwell Publishing and the author.

Luc Bovens, "The Value of Hope," *Philosophy and Phenomenological Research*, 59 (September, 1999), 667–681. Copyright © 1999 *Philosophy and Phenomenological Research*. Reprinted with permission of the publisher and the author.

Eamonn Callan, "Patience and Courage," *Philosophy*, 68 (October, 1993), 523–539. Copyright © 1993 Royal Institute of Philosophy. Reprinted with the permission of Cambridge University Press and the author.

Robert C. Roberts, "Forgivingness," *American Philosophical Quarterly*, 32 (October, 1995), 289–306. Copyright © 1995 *American Philosophical Quarterly*. Reprinted with permission of the publisher and the author.

Karen Jones, "Trust as an Affective Attitude," *Ethics*, 107 (October, 1996), 4–25. Copyright © 1996 by The University of Chicago. Reprinted with permission of The University of Chicago Press and the author.

Every effort has been made to trace the copyright holders but if any have been inadvertently overlooked the publishers will be pleased to make the necessary arrangement at the first opportunity.

Contributors

Joseph Kupfer, Department of Philosophy and Religious Studies, Iowa State University

Patrick Boleyn-Fitzgerald, Department of Philosophy, Lawrence University

Nancy E. Snow, Department of Philosophy, Marquette University

Tara Smith, Department of Philosophy, University of Texas at Austin

Martha Nussbaum, Law School, University of Chicago

Robert C. Solomon, Department of Philosophy University of Texas at Austin

Luc Bovens, Department of Philosophy, Logic and Scientific Method, The London School of Economics and Political Science

Eamonn Callan, School of Education, Stanford University

Robert C. Roberts, Department of Philosophy, Baylor University

Karen Jones, Department of Philosophy, University of Melbourne

Introduction

During the last several decades virtue ethics has enjoyed a revival among philosophers. Most of the revival has dealt with theoretical features of virtue ethics and little of it has treated specific, everyday virtues. Perhaps this theoretical focus has been necessary so that virtue ethics can gain a secure foundation. Perhaps, too, it has sprung from the predilection of philosophers for abstract thinking. Whatever the cause, not nearly as much attention has been given to generosity, gratitude, patience, and other virtues as has been given to such issues as whether virtue ethics is superior to other ethical theories or whether virtue is rooted in human nature.

Nevertheless, some philosophers have thought deeply and well about a number of particular virtues. Enough have done so, in fact, to produce a good collection of their articles. My aim in getting together this collection is to balance the theoretical side of virtue ethics with the practical. It is also to show that philosophers have as many illuminating insights about the particularities of everyday life—where life actually gets lived—as they do about more abstract issues.

In this introduction, I will explain why virtue ethicists have thought virtue is an important moral category. I will then discuss the connections of studying virtues to acquiring self-knowledge and gender issues. Last I will go through the virtues that the authors in this book treat. Along the way I will explain why I believe it is important to study individual virtues.

Why virtue?

The recent revival of virtue ethics began as a critique of what has been called "modern moral philosophy." Modern moral philosophy consists of two major strands: the duty ethics of Immanuel Kant and the consequentialism of John Stuart Mill. For Kant and Mill the important question was, "What gives an action moral worth?" To see why virtue ethics regards virtue as important, we must look briefly at Kant's and Mill's answers to this question.

Kant thought that for an action to have moral worth, it must meet two requirements. The first is that it must conform to duty. By this Kant meant that it must not violate any moral principle. Moral principles, for Kant, enunciate our duties. These duties, Kant thought, derive from a single, supreme duty, which is expressed in what he called the categorical imperative. The categorical imperative states, in one of its versions, that we ought always to act so as to be able to "universalize" the moral principle on which we act. This means that we must be able to regard the moral principles on which we act, such as "We ought to keep our promises," as applying to everyone without exception. If we cannot, then the moral principle is wrong and we should not act on it. If we can, the moral principle is right and we should act on it.

Duty also enters into Kant's second requirement for an action to have moral worth. It is that an action must be done from duty. By this Kant meant that the motive for an action must be that we conceive it our duty to do it. When we keep a promise, we must do so with the motive that it is our duty. If we keep a promise only because we think we will gain in some way by doing so, such as acquiring more wealth or keeping a friendship alive, then doing so has no moral worth. But if we keep a promise because we believe it is our duty to do so, then what we do has moral worth. This motive is the only one that gives an action moral worth, according to Kant.

Mill thought that the way to judge whether an action has moral worth is by looking at the consequences of performing it. We cannot decide what is right or wrong simply by applying a moral principle to a contemplated action. Mill tied this claim to hedonism, the thesis that happiness is the only intrinsic good—somebody or other's happiness, not necessary one's own. The result is that for Mill the supreme criterion of morality is the Greatest Happiness Principle, which says that an action is right in proportion to the happiness it produces, and wrong in proportion to the unhappiness it produces. There is no further requirement for an action to have moral worth, according to Mill. The motive for an action does not play a role in its worth. Of course, a particular motive may produce actions that have moral worth according to the Greatest Happiness Principle, in which case it will have worth on its own, but it does not directly enter into the moral worth of an action, as it did for Kant.

Most of what has passed for normative ethics among philosophers since the time of Mill until the latter third of the twentieth century has consisted of discussions of these two ethical theories. Is Kant's categorical imperative sufficient to justify moral principles, or is it just necessary? Is it even necessary? Does Mill's Greatest Happiness Principle apply to individual actions or does it apply only to moral rules? Does Mill's consequentialism account for justice? Is there some way of combining Kant's focus on principles with Mill's focus on consequences? These and other questions were the substance of modern moral philosophy until a philosophical voice here and there questioned some of the basic assumptions on which that substance was built.

One of the first voices was Michael Stocker's, who wrote a landmark article titled "The Schizophrenia of Modern Ethical Theories."[1] His main claim in this article was that modern ethical theories contain a "split between one's motives and one's reasons," a split, he says, that is properly dubbed "moral schizophrenia." The ultimate reason that Kant's duty ethics and Mill's consequentialism give for the rightness or wrongness of what we do, Stocker claimed, does not fit the motives we ordinarily have. "What motivates us," he wrote, "is irrelevant so far as rightness, obligatoriness, duty are concerned." And this means that there is a basic disharmony in these two ethical theories. For, "at the very least, we should be moved by our major values and we should value what our major motives seek." Modern ethical theories, therefore, make harmony in the moral life impossible.[2] Let me expand on this some.

Consider the virtue that Joseph Kupfer in his article in this book calls "generosity of spirit." With generosity of spirit, we give favorable judgments or impart positive attitudes to others via complimentary remarks. Our giving is conceptual and emotional instead of material. If Kant's claims about moral worth are right, then in order for our compliments to have moral worth, some moral principle would have to require us to give compliments, and we would have to give our compliments with the motive that we are fulfilling that requirement. Stocker's charge against Kant is that the motive we actually have in being generous of spirit does not fit with the motive Kant says actions with moral worth must have. We are generous with our praise, not because we conceive it our duty to be generous, but simply because we value something about the person whom we praise or because we value something the person has done. We conceive of our praise as a gift, which we give without imagining that we must do so.

The same charge can be leveled against Mill's consequentialism. When we are generous with our emotions, we do not calculate the consequences of being generous. What moves us is not the thought of the happy consequences of our generosity, but simply the goodness of the person we praise or the goodness of what the person we praise has done. So there is a split in Mill's consequentialism. It says that the only thing we should value, ultimately, is happy consequences. But that value does not move us to be generous. Conversely, what we value in the generosity is not what Mill's Greatest Happiness Principle says we should value. This disharmony in Mill's and Kant's ethical theories, Stocker claims, is a grave defect.

But why, one might ask, is it a defect? Why can't Mill, at least, reply that the motives of our actions need not involve their justification, and vice versa, that the justification of our actions need not involve their motive? What moves us to act need not be what justifies the action, and what justifies the action need not be what moves us to perform the action. The question Mill began with, after all, was what gives an action moral worth. And we can answer this question without mentioning what makes us want to do the action. Mill is concerned only with justification and not also with motivation.

The trouble with this answer—here I think Stocker's critique is right—is that the justification of an action should state what we value in the action. And what we value in an action should be what motivates us to perform the action. The logic is clear and simple. The justification of an action is, by definition, what we value about the action. For Mill it is the happy consequences of what we do. This is our ultimate end in life, according to Mill, and, by implication, what gives our lives meaning. So naturally we should want to do things because they fulfill this ultimate end. And this desire should not be just a second-order desire, one that moves us to have action-producing desires, but a first-order desire, one that immediately moves us to act as we do. Since some of what we do is legitimately done without this desire, as writers on virtue have shown, Mill's consequentialism contains an illegitimate split.

Another way to get at this critique of modern moral philosophy is to see that there are significant features of the moral life that are not accounted for either by Mill's consequentialism or by Kant's duty ethics. As Annette Baier remarked in discussing the concept of obligation, "there is a lot of morality *not* covered by that concept."[3] And, we might add, there is a lot of morality not covered by the idea of consequences, either. Although the concepts of obligation and consequences play a role in our lives as moral beings, they do not account for every part of the moral dimension of our lives, or even the largest role. In particular, neither obligation nor consequences account for virtues. Baier says, again, "The virtue of being a *loving* parent must supplement the natural duties and the obligations of justice."[4] In other words, we do not conceive our being loving parents as a duty, but as a virtue, something that would make us deficient if we did not have it, but not something that duty constrains us to be. We need the concept of virtue if we are to understand our moral selves rightly. A number of points need to be made here.

Understanding the moral life Although the question Kant and Mill asked is entirely legitimate, and even necessary, a host of other questions about the moral life press in, because there is much more to the moral life than justification. There are motives and emotions, loves and hates, striving for excellence, moral indifference, resistance to goodness, and ideals. To ask only Kant's and Mill's question is too narrow. The right question to ask is, "How shall we understand the moral life?" To answer this question we need to discuss virtues and vices, for they are central to the moral enterprise. As John Steinbeck wrote in *East of Eden*, "Virtue and vice were warp and woof of our first consciousness, and they will be the fabric of our last."[5] Modern moral philosophy restricted its role to answering the justification question, and by implication, intended or not, restricted the conception of the moral life. Once that conception is widened, moral philosophy becomes widened as well.

Motives One of the wider dimensions not adequately covered by Kant's duty ethics and Mill's consequentialism is motives. As we have seen, Kant thought that the only motive that gives an action moral worth is the sense of duty. But once one surveys the virtues that are warp and woof of our daily consciousness—gratitude, hope, patience, forgivingness, trust—one sees clearly and immediately that there are many other morally valuable motives. Although the sense of duty is a legitimate moral motive in certain contexts, to say that it is the only moral motive worth having is to restrict the moral life to an unrecognizable dimension. Once we admit into the moral arena the motives involved in gratitude, hope, patience, and other virtues, moral philosophy fits the moral life much more closely. What we value is what moves us, and what moves us is what we value. The split is overcome.

With Mill, the matter regarding motives is different. He said that motives play no role in the moral justification of an action. Only consequences do. Kant, however, is surely right in saying that an action must have the right motive in order to have moral worth. Mill needs to have recognized this. Consider the action of expressing gratitude through a simple, spoken "Thank you." If Mill is right, we are to consider this action as having moral worth solely because of the consequences for its recipient. But suppose the speaker is a practiced actor who can induce gratitude-like responses in others without actually feeling gratitude. Would we say then that the "Thank you" has moral worth? Decidedly not. To express gratitude is essentially to impart a sentiment, and the imparting of that sentiment is part of what makes saying "Thank you" have moral worth. The motive involved is simply a desire to express the sentiment.

Mill is right to the extent that consequences play a role in evaluating actions. For some actions this is a high degree, but for other actions it is a low degree. These other actions we evaluate largely, if not exclusively, by the motives that prompt them. This is because these other actions are conceptually tied to having the motives. Possessing gratitude just is to be motivated to express a certain sentiment. With this, the split between what we value and what moves us is overcome.

The inner life This point about the importance of motives means that there is more to the moral life than action. Kant's and Mill's principal question, "What gives an action moral worth?", was too restrictive in still another way, for our inner lives are as important to us morally as the actions we do and the actions that are done to us. Our inner lives contain a wealth of emotions, desires, and concerns that we value highly. We value hope over despair, self-acceptance over self-hate, contentedness over anxiety. We value the desire to love over indifference, and concern for others' distress over insensitivity. And these valuings are moral, not just individual preferences. They are moral virtues. It is a moral virtue to be able to hope instead of succumbing to despair, and to be able to accept ourselves as we are even though we want to hate ourselves. It is morally virtuous to want to love rather than to be indifferent to love. Possessing certain emotions, desires, and concerns in the right way, with the right intensity, the right object, and in the right circumstances makes us better moral creatures. The realm of the moral is far wider than what is allowed in a morality of right and wrong actions. As Michael Stocker wrote in another important essay, "Emotions are central to the nature, meaning, and value of a great deal of human life.... Much of our ethically important life ... involves emotions."[6]

It would, however, be unfair to charge Kant and Mill with neglecting the inner life entirely. Kant's sense of duty is certainly an inner state, and so is Mill's happiness. The correct charge against Kant is that there is more in the inner life that is morally valuable than the sense of duty. And these other morally valuable inner states do not derive their value either from conformity to a moral principle or from being motivated by a sense of duty. If it should turn out that Kant is right in saying that we have a duty to possess inner virtues, then the charge against him would be, as we have seen, that this divorces what we should ultimately value from what moves us. The correct charge against Mill is that there are other intrinsically good inner states besides happiness, namely, virtues such as hope and self-forgiveness. If it should turn out that Mill is right in claiming that these inner virtues are justified by their production of happiness, then the correct charge against him would be that focusing on the question of justification, as Mill does, ignores the richness of the inner life and also, again, splits what we should value from what moves us.

Character Widening the domain of the moral life has another implication as well. With Kant and Mill, the basic unit in the moral life is actions. That is, it is actions that are right or wrong. But if we allow virtues into the moral arena, then persons will be a basic unit of the moral life, either in addition to actions or instead of actions. It is persons who trust and forgive. Persons hope and express gratitude. When people trust and forgive consistently, we say that they are trusting and forgiving persons, that is, that they possess the virtues of trustfulness and forgivingness. These virtues are part of their moral character, which consists of the set of virtues and vices that they consistently exemplify.

Again, we cannot fairly charge Kant and Mill with neglecting moral character entirely. For them, moral character depends on the rightness and wrongness of actions, and for Kant it also depends on possessing a sense of duty. With virtues, however, the concept of moral character includes more than actions and the sense of duty. It includes an abundance of inner states and goings on—motives, desires, emotions, dispositions to act in certain ways, and habits. Some of these are connected tightly to actions and some are connected loosely. Whichever it is, they are all part and parcel of what makes us moral creatures. How we feel and what we desire are as at least as important features of our moral character as what we do. It is the same with our dispositions and habits. Virtues, in fact, have often been identified with dispositions or habits. We possess the virtue of patience, for example, when we have the disposition to act in a patient way or the habit of acting in a patient way. It is clear that including virtues in moral character opens up a vista of concepts to analyze, rich veins for philosophers to explore, while making moral character depend only on actions and the sense of duty compresses our understanding of the moral life.[7]

Moral enrichment Perhaps by now it will have become evident that with virtues moral enrichment is the main aim of the moral life instead of acting rightly. To be enriched in the moral life is to exemplify as many of the virtues as one can, both in one's inner life and in one's overt actions. It includes having a rich emotional life, having an array of good desires and feelings, and acting on one's dispositions to be patient, kind, and generous. There is more to a person's moral character when it contains a network of virtues. The morally richest persons display virtues in all aspects of their lives, private and public, and they display them consistently and to a maximal degree.

This concept of moral enrichment fits our moral intuitions about what is important in life better than the concept of fulfilling one's duty. One who simply fulfills her duties would have a morally poor life—not bad but not rich either. It would be lacking in the virtues we conceive the best persons to have. This is not to say that duty has no place in the moral life, but it is to say that if it were the only feature, life would be bleak indeed.

The duty ethicist may respond by saying that without the concept of duty, there can be no explanation of the demandingness of morality. Virtues are like ideals—states we can strive for if we choose, but not something we must exemplify. In order to account for the demandingness of morality, it must be our duty to exemplify virtue. It cannot be that virtue is simply added to duty; rather, duty must underlie virtue so as to give it its moral force. Moral enrichment is not sufficiently demanding.

To this it may be said that demandingness is not the only attribute of morality. Striving for moral ideals is a prominent feature as well. But it is not the case that this striving for moral ideals is optional in the way striving for nonmoral ideals is optional. Though it does not have the same moral force that duty has, it still has a drawing power that goes beyond the optional character of nonmoral ideals. To be merciful, for instance, is not a duty, but it is not purely optional either. We would judge a person who is not merciful in the right circumstances as morally deficient. And "morally deficient" is a strong reproach, just as "moral enrichment" is a strong commendation.

To account for the optional character of some actions, duty ethicists often introduce the concept of supererogatory actions—good actions that go beyond duty. But doing so does not capture all the distinctions that are needed, for supererogatory actions are optional in a way that striving for moral ideals is not. The moral force of striving for moral ideals goes beyond the moral force of supererogatory actions but is less than that of duty. Thus, the concept of virtue accounts for a feature of the moral life that is missed by the distinction between duty and supererogatory actions. John Steinbeck picturesquely captured the moral force of virtue in *East of Eden*: "A man, after he has brushed off the dust and chips of his life, will have left only the hard, clean questions: Was it good or was it evil? Have I done well—or ill?"[8]

For these reasons, then, virtue ethicists have insisted that the concept of virtue be reintroduced into moral theory. Virtue accounts for the value we attach to motives and other inner states. It fits with the fact that persons and their character, not actions, are the basic items of moral predication. It explains why we regard enrichment as significant. Overall, it helps us to understand our moral lives better than does the concept of duty or consequences, or even both duty and consequences.

These considerations also generate an interest in investigating particular virtues. They prod us to examine the virtues that make for a rich moral life. They move us to acquire extensive descriptions of particular virtues so as to get a fuller picture of that life. They cause us to distinguish virtues from their near neighbors, between, for example, hope and wishful thinking, between good pride and bad pride, the right kind of humility and the wrong kind of humility. Because emotions and motives matter to us, we will want to describe the connections of various virtues to our emotions and motives. What emotions do we have when we pity, or want to overcome when we forgive ourselves? What motives are connected to wanting justice as opposed to wanting revenge?

Self-knowledge

In describing particular virtues, we gain another benefit— self-knowledge. Because virtues are tied to motives, desires, and emotions, we must analyze these inner states when describing particular virtues. Doing this gives us insights into what we care about and what moves us. We uncover hidden motives and desires. "A deeper understanding of the good life, the truly valuable, and the requirements of decency depends on our knowing something about the soul's complexities. Ethics is inseparably tied to psychology," declares John Deigh.[9] The articles in this book contain a wealth of insights about the psychological states connected to the virtues they treat; reading them expands our perceptions of our own inner moral terrain considerably.

One way in which reflecting on individual virtues leads to self-knowledge is by discovering that we actually have the emotions connected to the virtues. If we are trying to describe the differences between pity and compassion or between the courage required for mountain climbing and the courage required for trusting, we may find that we have engaged in the identification with others' concerns that compassion involves, or possessed the condescension that is associated with one form of pity, or had the fear of rejection that we must overcome in order truly to trust, but not had much of the fear of heights that might block mountain climbing.

Another way in which reflecting on individual virtues results in self-knowledge is by uncovering the causes of our being less than virtuous. We may discover that we pay insufficient attention to particular virtues, that is, do not hold them in our consciousness sufficiently long or with enough vigor to move us to act. Perhaps we will discover that we possess distorted perceptions of moral situations. Or we may uncover ambivalence—we want to exemplify virtues yet also do not want to do so. If we did come to this last conclusion, we would find ourselves in the company of numerous analysts of the human interior, beginning with Plato and going through Augustine, Kierkegaard, Freud, and Ernest Becker, who have claimed that we are fundamentally divided. We strive to be virtuous, they say, but at the same time resist it. Although the articles in this book do not directly concern themselves with such causes, they impel us to reflect on them.

It may be objected that psychology has no place in normative ethics. Normative ethics consists of judgments about what we ought or ought not to do or about what is good or bad, but psychology, even moral psychology, consists only of descriptions, and descriptions cannot be turned into moral judgments.

This is quite right. A description of the anger that we must set aside in order to forgive is not the same as the judgment that anger is bad, nor is a description of the emotional state of trust the same as the judgment that trust is good. Nor do virtue ethicists assert that moral judgments can be derived from descriptions of inner states. The point of such descriptions is not to turn them into moral judgments, which in any case cannot be done, but to come to a fuller understanding of what is involved in being virtuous. We would have a meager understanding of compassion and trust if we did not grasp much of the emotions connected with them.

The virtue ethicist can also rightly point out that an understanding of the inner states that are involved in living well is not stimulated as much by either Kant's duty ethics or Mill's consequentialism. Because they are act-based theories, they do not spawn much interest in describing inner states, and so do not engender much self-knowledge. This is a liability. If ethics does not stimulate knowledge of what matters most to us, namely, the inner states that are connected to living well, it contains a split similar to the one Michael Stocker lamented in modern moral philosophy. It is a decided virtue of studying individual virtues in depth that it does stimulate such knowledge.

To be good

Because studying individual virtues stimulates self-knowledge, it can also stimulate us actually to be good. It can do this in several ways. First, we can become more vividly aware that certain motives, desires, and emotions are good for us to have. In exploring the complexities of gratitude, for example, we can become more aware of the desirability of having gratitude. Second, the mere fact of attending to a virtue can draw us to it. It can do this even though the description of the virtue is impersonal, systematic, and precise. Exhortation and emotional pleas need not be present to move us toward virtue. Perhaps this was Plato's assumption behind his contention that the philosophers in his ideal state, the ones who most love the good, become good by contemplating it. Third, by studying individual virtues, we can gain moral sensitivity. We can become affected more readily by the presence or absence of particular virtues, and because of this may be led to lament their absence and take pleasure in their presence. We can also become more sensitive to our own progress toward virtue.

This feature of studying virtues goes back to Socrates and Plato. Socrates declared at his trial that the reason he went about asking questions of his fellow Athenians was that he cared for their souls. In *The Republic*, Plato ties his conception of the four virtues needed in the ideal state to a discussion of how to train people to exemplify those virtues. The thought continues in Aristotle's *Nicomachean Ethics* with his remark that the aim of studying ethics is not simply "to know what virtue is, but to become good."[10] And it is hard to imagine Aquinas not concurring with Aristotle with his extensive descriptions of individual virtues.[11] These philosophers understood that exploring virtues can enlarge one's vision of what life can be, and can move one toward that vision, within a context of clear-headed thinking, conceptual precision, and well-supported argumentation.

The point here, vis-à-vis Kant's duty ethics and Mill's consequentialism, is not that virtue ethics encourages us to live well whereas these do not, but that virtue ethics does this better. Knowing what our supreme duty is or what the sole intrinsic good is may go some way toward encouraging us to live according to it, but knowing the intimate details of the moral life goes much further. Of course, neither may have a high degree of influence on how we actually live compared to practices such as associating with the virtuous (or the not so virtuous) or becoming involved in volunteer activities. But there is higher degree of influence when studying virtues than there is when studying theoretical ethical theory.

Gender issues

The recent rise of feminist philosophy has raised the question of whether virtue ethics is preferable from a feminist standpoint. Are the reasons for preferring virtue ethics over Kant's duty ethics and Mill's consequentialism feminist reasons? Is virtue ethics neutral or biased with respect to gender? The short answer to these question is, "It depends." It depends on which feminist philosopher is doing the talking, and it depends on the nature of the virtue ethics under consideration.

Some feminist philosophers have criticized duty ethics on the grounds that it is oriented too much to abstract and universal principles. In duty ethics, duties are expressed in principles that are said to apply to people without regard to the particular, concrete situations they are in. But doing this, say these feminist philosophers, is not true to what really is the case. We are, all of us, all the time, in concrete situations. The male philosophers who have put forward an ethics of abstract and universal principles have insufficiently recognized this fact, simply because of their proclivity to the abstract and universal over the concrete and relational. In order to include the concrete and relational in ethics, some feminists have adopted what they call an ethics of care. An ethics of care does not prescribe universal principles regardless of particular situations, and it recognizes the relational nature of people, especially women. In an ethics of care, caring is said to be either the fundamental virtue or a primary virtue. If it is the fundamental virtue, then all other virtues are derived from it; if it is a primary virtue, then it displaces the emphasis male philosophers have placed on obligations and public virtues, such as justice and civic responsibility.[12]

Virtue ethics does seem to be more congenial to an ethics of care than to a duty ethics. The de-emphasis on duty in virtue ethics fits the care-ethicist's claim that the best caring is not motivated by a sense of duty. The focus in virtue ethics on emotion fits well with the analysis of caring given by advocates of care ethics. However, the contrast between acting out of care and acting on the basis of principle may not be so great as care-ethicists maintain. As

Rosalind Hursthouse observes, virtue ethics contains a large number of rules—each virtue generates a prescription and each vice a proscription.[13] So adopting virtue and care in place of duty in order to get rid of moral principles may not succeed. Nor may care and justice be so contrasting as is alleged. Care may require justice, and justice may require care. Or care may need to be supplemented with justice and other virtues. Or, more generally, care, justice, and other virtues may need to be based on duty, or at least supplemented by duty. If any of these is true, then a simple ethics of care would not be a viable option. However, this fact would not undermine a virtue ethics in which both care and justice play a role, or in which duty underwrites or supplements virtue. Some feminists, though, may not want these modified types of virtue ethics.

There is also the question of which virtues are to be included in a virtue ethics. Feminist philosophers would not be disposed to adopt a virtue ethics if the virtues emphasized in it were ones typically associated with men. Susan Okin, for example, asserts that Aristotle's "account of the virtues takes the perspective of the free, educated, and leisured male members of society."[14] For virtue ethics to be adequate, she says, it would "need to include as human virtues (not just as adjunct 'feminine' virtues) the qualities needed to nurture, to take care of those who cannot take care of themselves, and to raise children to adulthood."[15] This consideration does not undermine virtue ethics for feminists, though it does mean that they will want to look at the particular form it takes.

Accordingly, the question of whether virtue ethics is preferable from a feminist standpoint has no simple answer. Most current feminists seem to favor an ethics that looks more like virtue ethics than duty ethics or consequentialism. But more work needs to be done in order to nail down some of the issues I have mentioned.[16] The virtues included in this book are ones, I hope, that both feminists and those who do not consider themselves to be feminists will regard as significant. We have here a further reason for studying individual virtues—to find those that do not discriminate against particular segments of humanity.

The virtues

There is one more reason for studying specific virtues—to discover anything about virtue in general, we must study particular virtues. "The way to study virtue is to study the virtues, and to do so rather in depth," Robert C. Roberts asserts.[17] The point seems so obvious as not to need mentioning. The way to study the formation of mountains is to study the formation of individual mountains. The way to become knowledgeable about schizophrenia is to become acquainted with persons who are afflicted with it. For it is only by so doing that "a fund of insight out of which any generalizations that are possible may emerge."[18] This collection of articles is designed to provide that fund of insight.

I chose the articles for several reasons. I looked for articles that possess the unique combination of being philosophically substantive yet highly readable. I excluded virtues that are more closely connected to civic, legal, and political contexts, such as justice, and selected virtues that are more personal. I did not include any intellectual virtues. I passed over older articles so that the book could contain the best of relatively recent thinking. Other virtues could have been included, but that would have made this book too long. Lines had to be drawn somewhere.

It might be argued that no virtues are purely personal—all virtues are social in the sense that they require other people as their objects or are conducive to a well-ordered society or involve other people in some way. It might be thought that there is no sharp distinction between personal and public virtues, for all virtues can be exercised by individuals in public or political contexts. These are all true. Compassion and forgivingness are directed toward others. A society in which higher amounts of generosity of spirit, gratitude, and patience are exhibited is more desirable than one in which these are absent. Humility and hope affect how we treat others in some way or other. And all the virtues we would classify as personal can be exemplified by persons in civic and political contexts.

Despite these facts, there is a sense in which some virtues are primarily personal. As Tara Smith put it, "an individual might cultivate [personal virtues] apart from her specific role in some institutional structure," and they are "not rooted in conventional roles and responsibilities."[19] Personal virtues can be exhibited in one's "private dealings with others; no reference to any formal social structures is necessary."[20] They are not like the laws of justice that are codified in a legal system and woven into legal and civic interactions.

The distinction between personal and public virtues may not be clean and neat; there may be borderline cases or ways in which personal virtues are connected to the maintenance of formal social structures. Nevertheless, it is a useful distinction, especially since much of the attention that has been given to specific virtues has focused on ones that are clearly connected to institutional structures. This last fact makes it important to study virtues at the other end of the spectrum, partly to balance the material available for philosophical scrutiny and partly to provide a balanced account of the moral life, which includes both public and private arenas.

The writers of the articles in this book cross philosophical boundaries. Argumentation and conceptual analysis are characteristic of Anglo-American analytic philosophy, and description is characteristic of European phenomenology. These writers do both. In good Anglo-American style, they furnish reasons for thinking that their viewpoints are correct, criticize different viewpoints, and defend their viewpoints against objections. In good European style, they describe extensively. They use examples drawn from literature and real life to clarify inner states. They cast about for flashes of insight. In Wittgenstein's words, they "look and see"; in Husserl's words, they go "to the appearances."

These articles also demonstrate that good philosophy can be both astute and accessible. They are sophisticated, but they can also be understood by those with little or no background in philosophy. Both the beginner and the advanced philosopher will profit from them.

Generosity of spirit The book begins with Joseph Kupfer's "Generosity of Spirit," which treats a different kind of generosity than the material generosity that has been considered paradigmatic by philosophers since the time of Aristotle. In material generosity, one gives money or material goods. In generosity of spirit, however, one gives thoughts, emotions, or character. Being generous in giving thoughts—generous-mindedness—means that one gives favorable judgments in situations where they are not owed. One expends more mental effort than normal, perhaps by giving the benefit of the doubt or simply by praising someone's achievement when normally one might not do so. Being generous in giving emotions—generous-heartedness— means that one goes beyond duty in expressing good emotions. Forgiving someone when one has a right to be angry is an example. So is loving someone who has given one cause to stop loving them, as is being gracious in the performance of duty. The physician, for example, who shows that she feels the suffering of her patients and who looks into her patients' eyes with kindness is being generous-hearted.

In being generous with one's character, one goes beyond duty in helping others develop the virtues one possesses. When, for example, two people are in a harsh situation, one of them might buoy the other up with hope or courage or strength to endure. Nietzsche apparently had this kind of giving in mind, Kupfer remarks, in his conception of the overflow that is characteristic of the *Übermensch*. The *Übermensch* has a superabundance of vitality, a fullness, that floods out to others. Unfortunately, Kupfer points out, this giving is clouded by Nietzsche's contention that the *Übermensch* gives to others in order to assert his will to power. Kierkegaard's conception of agape love that builds itself into others is not clouded in this way, Kupfer notes.

Although what is given in generosity of spirit differs from what is given in material generosity, the two share common features. In both, one intends to benefit the recipient, and in both one gives what one values. So in describing generosity of spirit, Kupfer is treating ordinary generosity. But he is also expanding our concept of generosity significantly. He is showing that generosity extends a good deal further than philosophers have hitherto noted. He is surely right. Psychological giving is as legitimate a form of giving as material giving. And we are presented with numerous opportunities to give psychologically every day, far more, no doubt, than opportunities to give materially. What

Kupfer has done, then, is to show that generosity plays a larger role in the moral life than we might have thought.

Gratitude Patrick Boleyn-Fitzgerald does the same with gratitude. Current philosophical treatments of gratitude, he says, restrict it to a minor role in the moral life. They uniformly state that the occasions on which gratitude is appropriate are those in which it is a response to a benefit, a benefit that is given with the right motivation, usually benevolence, and that is either wanted or accepted by the beneficiary. Boleyn-Fitzgerald claims that gratitude is appropriate in situations that do not meet any of these three conditions. He discusses two such situations at length: occasions on which we are harmed and occasions on which we benefit another person. In neither of these cases are the three conditions met—there is no direct benefit from either the person who harms us or from the person whom we benefit, no benefit is intended by either of these persons, and the person who is harmed or confers a benefit does not accept any benefit. Yet gratitude is appropriate in both of these cases because we are given opportunities to exercise virtues we would not otherwise have exercised. In the case in which we are harmed, we are given the opportunity to practice love and patience. In the case in which we benefit someone, we are given the opportunity to practice compassion. In these situations, then, we are presented with opportunities to develop our moral character. This role for gratitude is much larger than the customary one of exercising it simply in cases in which we are given something. Gratitude is, in fact, at the center of the moral life and not at the fringe, Boleyn-Fitzgerald concludes.

The reason current treatments of gratitude are so narrow, Boleyn-Fitzgerald says, is that they focus only on cases in which justice is a reason for possessing gratitude, cases, that is, in which we owe gratitude. But there are other reasons for possessing gratitude. It can combat undesirable emotions, such as anger. It can promote caring in special relationships. It can aid in the development of other virtues. It can preserve community among acquaintances. It can also preserve peace. The proper question philosophers should be asking is, therefore, "When do we have a good moral reason to be grateful?", and not simply, "When is gratitude owed?"

If Boleyn-Fitzgerald is right, current ethics has an imbalanced conception of what is important in the moral life. Gratitude is more important than it has been thought to be. What Boleyn-Fitzgerald demonstrates, then, is that virtue ethics is not simply an exposition of individual virtues. It is also appraising their worth and showing their connections to emotions we value. It is ranking priorities and reflecting on what matters most to us.

Humility The central cognitive element of humility has often been said to be refraining from exaggerating one's importance, or avoiding thinking of oneself more highly than one ought to think. Nancy Snow claims that this does not get at the essence of humility, since refraining from exaggerating one's importance rests on knowledge of one's limitations and deficiencies. This knowledge is cognitively central to humility, she says, and she offers a number of cases to support this claim. She also distinguishes two senses of humility. One of the senses, the narrow sense, involves being aware of the limitations of one's specific traits. The other sense, the existential sense, involves being aware of human finitude in general.

In addition to this awareness of our limitations, one must also care about the limitations, and the care must be commensurate with the seriousness of the limitation. In narrow humility, this means that one must be appropriately pained by one's limitations. In existential humility, it means that one must appreciate to the proper degree the value of the reality that extends beyond one's limitations, such as the grandeur of nature. Thus, those who are humble have an awareness of their limitations plus a concern about them, and they allow both to influence their attitudes and behavior.

Humility is intrinsically good, Snow says, because we value self-knowledge independently of its effects. Humility is also good because it fosters other virtues, such as compassion and forgivingness. To the objection that humility can curb ambition and undermine self-respect, self-confidence, proper pride, self-esteem, and autonomy, Snow replies that although humility can have these effects, it need not if these positive traits are fully formed and firmly entrenched. Humility can, in fact, lead to the formation of these traits, because the accurate assessment involved in humility will cause one not to attempt more than one is truly able to accomplish.

Snow's reference to self-esteem and proper pride raises the question whether, despite what she says, humility really does undermine self-respect and self-confidence. In order to maintain a constant sense of humility, we must continually remind ourselves of our limitations. But doing this may well cause us to lose respect for ourselves or destroy our self-confidence. These in turn may make us become discouraged, not just with respect to everyday living but also with respect to moral achievement. Is there a way to retain humility and these positive traits, or must we jettison humility in favor of them?

Pride Tara Smith believes that we must jettison humility. In "The Practice of Pride," she critiques Nancy Snow's view of humility and defends pride against its detractors, which have included a large number of philosophers and non-philosophers. Pride, she says, has been misrepresented as arrogance or ostentatious self-congratulation or an exaggerated conception of oneself. And it has been thought that either a person is a boaster or a self-effacer. But these are false alternatives, she maintains. True pride is a positive self-evaluation that is based on one's moral character. A person with pride takes one's character seriously and regards the values one holds to as important. So, Smith says, a person with pride is ambitious—she pursues values tenaciously. Because she believes in herself, the person with pride strives to be a better person. This in turn nourishes a healthy love of oneself.

The difference between Smith's view and that of pride's detractors, Smith says, is not just terminological, for it involves a difference in what is valued. Pride involves valuing oneself whereas humility does not. The humble person does not want much and is content with little, whereas the person with pride is ambitious in a good way. The humble person regards her concerns as insignificant, but the person with pride values her concerns.

Humility, moreover, has harmful effects. Because it requires us to be aware of our limits, it encourages us to aim low and erodes our ambition. With humility, we lower our sights and do not make as much moral effort as we otherwise would. We should, indeed, be realistic in our self-appraisals, but this comes from honesty, not humility, Smith claims.

Despite Smith's declaration that the difference between her view and Snow's view is not terminological, we must ask whether it really is. There may be a sense of humility that does not subvert a positive self-evaluation and is consistent with a healthy love of oneself. If there is, then there could also be a sense of pride that is consistent with an awareness of our limits. Contrary to Smith's claims, one could have both humility and pride.

Still, Smith is right to point out that there is a difference between properly valuing oneself and undervaluing oneself. And she is right to notice that this difference has often been associated with pride and humility. However, if we can distinguish between a humility that involves proper valuing and a humility that involves under-valuing, in the same way that Smith has distinguished between a pride that involves overvaluing oneself and a pride that involves proper valuing, then pride and humility will not contrast with each other but will complement each other.

Compassion Martha Nussbaum claims, as does Robert Solomon in his article on love, that emotions are not simply blind passions. They contain, or are grounded in, cognitive content. To show this for love, Solomon argues that love is based on reasons. To show this for compassion, Nussbaum gives an extensive description of the beliefs that are necessary for and give rise to compassion. These descriptions are based on Aristotle's analysis of pity in his *Rhetoric*.

The first belief is that the suffering of the person on whom one has compassion is serious. We do not have compassion on one who has lost a toothbrush or pencil, or at least not much compassion. The judgment that the suffering is serious, Nussbaum says, is made by the one who has compassion and not by the one who suffers, for someone who is suffering seriously, by living in poverty or being battered by a spouse, for example, may not regard it as serious.

The second belief is that the suffering is not caused by the sufferer's culpable action, or at least is disproportionate to the sufferer's culpability. When people are responsible for their own harm, we blame them. If we also have compassion on such people, Nussbaum notes, it is because their suffering is brought about by something in their general condition over which they have no control.

The third belief that is necessary for compassion, according to Aristotle, is that the one who has compassion must believe that she could suffer in the same way as the one on whom she has compassion. Nussbaum objects to this requirement because a divine being can have compassion even though it is not vulnerable to the same kind of sufferings that humans experience. What is really at issue here, she says, is whether the suffering of other people is a significant part of one's own "scheme of goals and ends." The belief that one could also suffer can provoke one to regard others' suffering as important, but if one antecedently cares about the good of others, one does not need it in order to exercise compassion.

Those who regard emotions as independent of concepts or beliefs will claim that we can have these beliefs without having compassion. If compassion is a painful emotion directed at another person's misfortune or suffering, as Aristotle asserted, then, these objectors say, we can have these beliefs without having the pain. Nussbaum's reply is that the pain of compassion just is a way of seeing the victim's distress with concern. This means that compassion arises when we have the thoughts she has described. It is an "upheaval of thought"—in the same way, Nussbaum contends, that other emotions are also upheavals of conceptual content.

How shall we adjudicate between Nussbaum and the objectors? That depends on whether her claim is conceptual or empirical. If it is conceptual, we will need to analyze the idea of pain directed at another's misfortune and see whether it is contained in or analytically connected to the beliefs she describes. If it is empirical, we will need to turn our attention inward and see whether we actually have the pain when we have the beliefs.

Love Many people regard love as something one gives without having reasons. If one had reasons for love, these people believe, it would not be real love. In real love, one simply loves; one does not have ulterior motives, nor does one love because of the beloved's characteristics.

Robert Solomon claims, though, that love has reasons. The reasons must, of course, be good ones. If one loves because the beloved satisfies neurotic needs, or because of unconscious motives for revenge, or out of fear, resentment, or contempt, one does not have a good reason for love, and therefore one does not have good love, perhaps not even any love.

Distinguishing between good and bad reasons for love would not, however, satisfy those who think love has no reasons. For they would say that the having of any reasons undermines love, for several reasons. For one thing, the features of the loved one on which the reasons are based could change. The beauty of the loved one may fade or the wit of the beloved may deteriorate. But love should not languish when the loved one changes. For another thing, to have a reason for loving someone is to have an ulterior motive. Those with true love, however, do not have ulterior motives. They love the person herself, not simply what they get from the beloved. Last, someone other than the beloved could have the same characteristics as the beloved. If this were the case, one would have the very same reasons to love that other person, and would consequently be just as justified in loving that person. But one should not transfer their affections to someone else just because they have the same characteristics.

Solomon replies to the first of these objections by saying that reasons for love can change—love develops through a lifetime of experiences and memories. To the second he replies that though some reasons for love involve wanting to get something from the beloved, other reasons do not. One that does not is the way each partner in a love relationship inspires the other. This certainly would be a good reason for loving someone, Solomon maintains. And to the third objection, he replies that the best reasons for love do not involve characteristics of the beloved. They involve, rather, the relationship between the lovers. This relationship involves the shared history of the lovers and the shared identity that develops because of this history.

It may be that part of the debate between Solomon's reasons-for-love view and the no-reasons view can be resolved by getting clear about what counts as reasons. Solomon has certainly clarified the kinds of reasons involved in love. But there are substantive issues in the debate as well. Would love be arbitrary if there were no reasons for it? If so, would we still want to call it love? Could one even love if one had no reasons for loving? Is "unconditional love" really unconditional? To these questions we can imagine Yes and No answers, though, as Solomon's astute discussion demonstrates, they will require a complex analysis of the nature of reasons.

Hope Though hope is commonly regarded as an important everyday virtue, like many of the other virtues in this anthology it has received little attention from philosophers. Luc Bovens' article helps remedy this lack. He argues against a sceptical challenge to the value of hope, first, by showing that hope has several salutary effects. With hope, events occur that otherwise might not, because hope helps to bring about those events. The sceptic fails to notice that certain desirable events are causally dependent on hoping. Hope aids in countering our fear of taking risks, because it causes us to focus on the gains we can acquire instead of the losses we might incur. Though we need fear in order to avoid taking unwarranted risks, we need hope to encourage us to take some risks. If we took no risks, we would miss out on a good deal of what life offers. In addition, hope can cause us to rearrange our priorities. It does this by causing us to think about the value of what we hope for, which in turn can cause us to direct our hopes in different directions. Hope also brings increased self-understanding, because, again, it causes us to reflect on our values.

The sceptical challenge to hope is mistaken as well, Bovens claims, because hope is intrinsically valuable. In times of hardship, hope involves anticipating relief of one's troubles, and the pleasure of this anticipation is intrinsically good. Hope is intrinsically good for another reason—hope is part of love, for in loving others we hope for their well-being. Since love is intrinsically good, so is hope. The same reasoning applies to the sense of self-worth—we hope for our own well-being when we have a sense of self-worth, and because this sense is intrinsically good, so is hope.

The sceptical challenge is correct, Bovens concedes, in pointing out that hope can increase our frustration and easily become wishful thinking. To guard against these, and to determine the right amount of hope, we need to evaluate both the good-making features and the bad-making features of the situations in which we find ourselves. We may not be able to evaluate these well enough to be exact about the amount of hope that meets the sceptical challenge, but this is no defect of Bovens' account. For, as Aristotle remarked, the one who studies virtue should expect no more precision than its subject matter allows. Bovens has said enough to mitigate the sceptical challenge.

Further inquiry into hope could investigate its connections to other virtues. In what ways, for example, is hope involved in generosity or trust? Could one respect oneself or forgive oneself without hope? One could also investigate the connection of hope to epistemic rationality. Bovens has illuminating things to say about this connection, which shows that the study of moral virtues may be connected to epistemology more than epistemologists have hitherto thought.[21]

Patience and courage Patience, too, has been neglected by philosophers even though it ranks high on just about anyone's list of important everyday virtues. It is central to child-rearing and teaching, Eamonn Callan observes in "Patience and Courage," and it is at least as important as courage. This latter claim, however, is not widely accepted, Callan notes, for if we had to choose which vice we would rather have—impatience or cowardice—most people would choose impatience. This means that they think that cowardice is worse than impatience, which in turn means that they value courage more than patience. Most people also think, Callan says, that there is a tension between the two virtues, that is, that those who possess courage are not likely to have patience, and that those who possess patience are not likely to have courage. This tension is not conceptual, but motivational; it involves psychical discord, not conceptual incompatibility.

One way in which this psychical discord would occur, according to the conflict view, involves valuing courage highly. When people value courage highly and also value egalitarian justice, they are often moved to take prompt action. But this disposition to take action appears to conflict with the endurance required by patience.

You cannot exercise courage while waiting patiently for justice to be done. This psychical discord is produced by the tendency of what is valued highly to become imperialistic, to "conquer the psychological territory," which means that other values become marginalized and are thrust into the psychical background. So if courage were valued highly, it would tend to push out patience; impatient courage would then be dominant.

Callan's response to this version of the conflict view is to argue that the habits that go with courage can cohere with the habits that go with patience. The aim of moral development is to expand one's sensitivities, and when this is done with respect to a particular virtue, one understands and appreciates other virtues better. Callan's unity thesis, then, is that both courage and patience can be developed in a person without causing inner conflict in that person. Though this modest thesis is far from a traditional unity of virtue thesis, it is important, Callan believes, because it restores value to patience and resists talk of the fragmentation of values.

Callan's argument for the unity thesis also shows that our conception of particular virtues is affected by our dispositions and emotional makeup. If a virtue has become imperialistic in us, we are likely to view it as conceptually incompatible with certain other virtues when in fact it is not conceptually incompatible. Exploring the psychology of a virtue, then, is often necessary to becoming accurate about its conceptual content.

Forgivingness Robert Roberts makes a number of conceptual distinctions based on psychological observations. He does this in his discussion of the emotion that forgiveness typically overcomes. According to Roberts, this emotion is anger. When we forgive, we set aside our anger toward one who has wronged us, without, however, giving up the judgment that we have been wronged. The emotion we set aside is not typically indignation, he says, because forgiveness is appropriate when resentment or anger that is milder than indignation is present. The emotion is not always resentment, either, because one who resents normally has a gnawing, brooding anger, whereas forgiveness is fitting when explosive, sharp anger is present. Nor is the emotion typically moral hatred, because hatred is too strong for many cases of forgiveness. Anger, then, is the common element in all cases of forgiveness. And, Roberts indicates, different cases of forgiveness involve different ways of being angry.

Not all writers have made the distinctions Roberts makes, and the terms used by other writers on forgiveness sometimes have a different meaning. Joram Graf Haber, for example, defines resentment simply as "anger that one might properly feel at having been personally injured."[22] It looks as if Roberts' anger may be Haber's resentment.

A number of conditions dissipate the anger of forgiveness, Roberts argues. These include the repentance of the offender, excusing conditions in which the offender is situated, the weakness and suffering of the offender, the moral commonality the offender has with the offended, and the relationship the offended has to the offender. These conditions also serve, Roberts states, as considerations favoring forgiving, or as reasons for forgiving. The forgiving person will be moved by the repentance and suffering of the offender to give up her anger toward him. When these conditions are not present, however, even the forgiving person will be likely to withhold forgiveness and hang on to her anger.

Roberts' talk of reasons for forgiving raises the question of whether forgiveness needs reasons. If it possesses a gift-like quality, as it seems to, then the presence of a reason for one's forgiving would undermine the gratuitous character of the forgiveness. It could not be a gift if there were a reason for extending it to the offender.

Roberts could reply, rightly I think, that gifts can be given for a reason without undermining their gratuitousness. We give gifts on special occasions and for special reasons without detracting from the free character of the gift. The giving person is freely moved by the occasion to give. Similarly, the forgiving person is freely moved by the repentance and suffering of the offender, whereas the unforgiving person is not. Because the forgiving person's concern is to be in benevolent, harmonious relationships, she looks for, and accepts, reasons to forgive.

Trust Interpersonal trust, says Karen Jones in "Trust as an Affective Attitude," consists of an optimistic attitude and an expectation. The optimistic attitude is the hope that the goodwill and competence of others will encompass our interaction with them. The expectation is that those whom we trust will be favorably moved by the thought that we are counting on them. This expectation is grounded in the attitude, that is, we have the expectation because of the attitude. And the attitude is a distinctive way of seeing others, which means that it is at once both cognitive and affective. The affective component is central, though; trust is not primarily a belief, Jones maintains.

She argues that this account of trust explains several facts about trust. Because the attitude of optimism is at the center of trust, trust and distrust are contraries, not contradictories, for there is a middle area in which one neither trusts nor distrusts. Also, because trust involves an affective component, it cannot be willed, for we cannot simply decide to have an attitude, though we can cultivate it. Last, trust can produce beliefs that are resistant to evidence, because with trust we will interpret evidence about the one trusted in certain ways.

Here one might wonder why the cognitive component of trust could not account for these facts. Some beliefs are contraries, not contradictories; beliefs can no more be simply willed than can affections, though we can cultivate them; and some beliefs are resistant to evidence. These possibilities, however, do not entail that Jones is wrong about trust consisting primarily of an affection. Our intuitive convictions seem to point in that direction.

Jones points out, rightly, that trust is not the same as reliance, for we can rely on machines to act in certain ways, and we can rely on unvirtuous people to act in unvirtuous ways. Because no goodwill is involved in either of these cases, there is no trust.

Are there guidelines we can use to determine when trust is appropriate? Jones says that we can make no generalizations about the appropriateness of trust, because too many variables are involved. We must consider the social climate, the consequences of our trusting, and our own tendencies to be trusting or untrusting. We cannot say, therefore, that the default attitude toward people is either trust or distrust.

This survey of the articles in this anthology, and the articles themselves, show that the moral life is extraordinarily rich and complex. It is a decided virtue of virtue ethics that it incites us to recognize this richness.

Notes

1   Michael Stocker, "The Schizophrenia of Modern Ethical Theories," *The Journal of Philosophy*, 73 (August 12, 1976), pp. 453–66; reprinted in Roger Crisp and Michael Slote, eds, *Virtue Ethics* (New York: Oxford University Press, 1997), pp. 66–78.

2   Stocker, pp. 453, 454.

3   Annette Baier, "What Do Women Want in a Moral Theory?" *Moral Prejudices* (Cambridge, Mass: Harvard University Press, 1994); reprinted in Roger Crisp and Michael Slote, eds, *Virtue Ethics*, p. 266. Her italics.

4   Baier, p. 268.

5   John Steinbeck, *East of Eden* (New York: Penguin Books, 1952), p. 475.

6   Michael Stocker, "How Emotions Reveal Value and Help Cure the Schizophrenia of Modern Ethical Theories," in Roger Crisp, ed., *How Should One Live? Essays on the Virtues* (New York: Oxford University Press, 1996), p. 183.

7   For a treatment of character in virtue ethics, see Christine McKinnon, *Character, Virtue Theories, and the Vices* (Peterborough, Ontario: Broadview Press, 1999), especially Chapter 3, "The Role of Character in Virtue Ethics."

8   Steinbeck, p. 475.

9   John Deigh, "Introduction," in John Deigh, ed., *Ethics and Personality: Essays in Moral Psychology* (Chicago: The University of Chicago Press, 1992), p. 1.

10 Aristotle, *Nicomachean Ethics*, 1103b28–29, trans., Terence Irwin (Indianapolis: Hackett Publishing Company, 1985), p. 35.

11 Thomas Aquinas, *Summa Theologica*, II–II, Questions 1–170.

12 See Nel Noddings, *Caring: A Feminine Approach to Ethics and Moral Education* (Berkeley: University of California Press, 1984), for an exposition of one version of an ethics of care. See Marilyn Friedman, "Feminism in Ethics," in Miranda Fricker and Jennifer Hornsby, eds, *Feminism in Philosophy* (Cambridge, England: Cambridge University Press, 2000), pp. 205–211, for an account of how Carol Gilligan's *In a Different Voice* influenced the development of an ethics of care.

13 Rosalind Hursthouse, *On Virtue Ethics* (New York: Oxford University Press, 1999), p. 36.

14 Susan Moller Okin, "Feminism, Moral Development, and the Virtues," in Roger Crisp, ed., *How Should One Live?*, p. 228.

15 Okin, p. 229.

16 Okin writes, "There has been, so far, little progress towards a specifically feminist account of virtue ethics." Okin, p. 229.

17 Robert C. Roberts, *Emotions: An Essay in Aid of Moral Psychology* (New York: Cambridge University Press, 2003), p. 3.

18 Roberts, p. 3.

19 Tara Smith, "Justice as a Personal Virtue," *Social Theory and Practice*, 25 (Fall, 1999), p. 361.

20 Smith, p. 361.

21 For a development of this possibility see Linda Trinkaus Zagzebski, *Virtues of the Mind* (Cambridge, England: Cambridge University Press, 1996).

22 Joram Graf Haber, *Forgiveness: A Philosophical Study* (Lanham, Maryland: Rowman & Littlefield, 1991), p. 35.

1 Generosity of Spirit

Joseph Kupfer

I

Early in *Pride and Prejudice,* Elizabeth Bennett tells Mr. Wickham that for disinheriting him, Mr. Darcy should be publicly exposed. Wickham replies that he would not be the one to expose Darcy's dishonorable treatment of him, "while I remember the father, I could never bring myself to disgrace the son."[1] Because Elizabeth has yet to discover the perfidy of Wickham, Jane Austen's heroine is impressed with the morality of his avowed self-restraint. She says, "I admire your generosity, Mr. Wickham."[2]

Mr. Wickham has given no one money or anything of economic value. What generosity does Elizabeth think he is exhibiting? I will clarify the nature of the generosity which is imputed to Wickham by locating it within an account of psychological giving, characterized here as generosity of spirit. It is a valuable form of generosity, largely obscured, at least from philosophical view, by Aristotle's influential analysis of generosity. Aristotle treats economic or material generosity as paradigmatic, and says: "By 'material goods' we understand everything whose value is measured in money."[3]

As important as economic giving is, focusing on it has kept us from paying attention to generosity that involves personal endowment, thought, emotion, and character. Because these are dimensions of our personality or selves, I refer to the virtue in which they are incorporated as generosity of spirit. The term also calls attention to the manner in which truly generous people give, whether the giving is economic or psychological.

In investigating generosity of spirit or personality, we may check our bearings with reference to those features of economic generosity which define the virtue in general. For example, from economic generosity we learn that generosity is a species of benevolence. It demands that we give with the intention of benefiting the recipient, out of a concern for his or her welfare.[4] If we give without this intention, then we are just going through the motions. However, benefiting another person is not sufficient for our giving to be generous.

If I give away some old furniture which I would just as soon throw out, I may be making the recipient better off but I am not being generous. The beneficiary of my largesse is but a human substitute for my garbage pail. I must value what I give. Although Aristotle says that the generous individual "sets no store by material goods," other of his remarks indicate that generous people value their possessions.[5] Generosity requires giving up, depleting our store of wealth. The more we value what we give, the more generous we are. Giving what is valued and intending to benefit the recipient of what is given are two of the constraints on economic generosity which will be reinterpreted in generosity of spirit.

The first dimension of generosity of spirit to be considered is generous-mindedness. We are generous-minded when we make judgments that reflect giving. As James Wallace notes, generous-minded people see merit where others tend not to.[6] What is then given that parallels the material things bestowed in economic generosity? What is given is a favorable judgment, although it is not given up the way economic goods are. Generosity of mind occurs, for instance, when we employ the principle of charity to interpret a text or philosophical argument. Adopting the interpretation which gives another person's ideas the best chance of success is generous-minded. In turn, this enables us to do the best we can for and with the text's meanings. We are then in a position not only to think better of the text but to think more about it.

Thinking more about a text suggests a secondary sense of generous-mindedness: giving more mental effort than is usual on behalf of another. Expending mental energy on matters that are important to others is like economic generosity in that we are spending a valuable resource for another person's sake which we could keep for ourselves. When we use our mental energy for someone else, we are being generous *with* our intellectual powers. When we give a favorable judgment, we are being generous in *how* we use the powers. The two are combined when reaching a favorable judgment about someone requires exercising our powers of discrimination and interpretation more vigorously than the situation typically calls for.

The recipient of generous-mindedness is given the benefit of a doubt, or more emphatically, the benefit of a favorable judgment. What is valuable in this is itself a valuing or valuation. A positive valuing gives the beneficiary the chance to shine and make good on the faith conferred. The opposite of generous-mindedness is a hyper-critical eye or mean-spiritedness which disposes us to overlook merits, ferret out flaws, and delight in nit-picking. The extent to which it pains us to notice faults is a measure of generous-mindedness, as is the ease with which strengths capture our attention.

Lester Hunt mentions an editor of an anthology who chooses someone else's essay over his own when his essay is "obviously superior."[7] The editor is generous-minded because he judges the other person's article better than his own when it did not deserve to be so judged. Those who are generous-minded give other people's work a positive interpretation, overlooking defects at their own expense.

The generous-mindedness in Hunt's example fulfills another general condition of generosity by providing a benefit which is not due another because of duty, obligation, or desert.[8] Generosity requires going beyond duty or satisfying the demands of justice. We must give more than is owed. If an editor publishes someone else's essay when it is better than his own, the editor is being just, not generous. Because the editor has to be doing more than rewarding merit, he must mistakenly believe the other writer's article deserves to be published. The editor must think he is merely being just. At this point, Hunt's example requires a qualification if it is to serve our purpose. To result from generosity of mind, the editor's decision cannot rest mainly on defective judgment. A generous view of others has to be the guiding force.

In our version of the example, the editor must think more highly of the other individual's essay because his generous-mindedness subordinates how he appraises his own work. Perhaps the editor's generosity of mind works in tandem with his humility. He would have no problem, then, accurately comparing the work of two other writers. Moreover, the disparity between the two essays cannot be so glaring as Hunt's "obviously superior" implies, or we might suspect a serious lack of judgment.[9]

One danger in this, as in all cases of generosity, is harming the self by overextending it for other people. Another worry might be that the editor's choice of the inferior essay is unfair to the readers of the anthology. After all, they are not getting the best material to read. But this is less a difficulty with the example of generous-mindedness than an irritating truth about moral life. Being generous is no guarantee of fairness, and may even deflect an individual away from it. More broadly, the operation of one virtue is compatible with failure in other virtues or duties, and sometimes disposes individuals to such failure.[10]

Hunt offers his example simply to illustrate generosity as giving more than is someone's due. He is not concerned with generous-mindedness in particular. Consequently, Hunt may have had in mind a case in which the editor accurately judges his own essay obviously superior, but still publishes the other writer's article. Although this would not be generosity of mind, because not the result of expansiveness in thought or judgment, it could be another form of psychological giving—generous-heartedness.

II

The second dimension of generosity of spirit is generous-heartedness, an emotional giving. James Wallace offers as an example the virtue of forgiving trespasses against us.[11] What is given then? We give up our claims against other people, or the right to make demands on them. Generosity of heart here resembles material generosity in that the giving does involve a giving up. But forgiving differs from material generosity in that what is given up is not itself what is given. When we forgive, we give trespassers surcease from a burden, release from a claim against them and a chance to begin anew. Something of non-material value is given in the interest of other people's emotional well-being.

When we are generous-hearted, our feelings are the source of our giving. The generous-hearted forgive for the sake of offenders from more fellow-feeling or love than the wrong-doers are entitled to. Letting go of resentment and relinquishing claims against other individuals is generous-hearted only if it comes from a source such as goodwill or compassion. To forgo a claim against someone from prudence, to spare ourselves turmoil or anguish, for example, hardly bespeaks a generous heart.

Consider again Elizabeth Bennett's response to Mr. Wickham in *Pride and Prejudice*. Wickham claims that he could never bring himself to disgrace Darcy because he remembers Darcy's father with so much love and respect. Elizabeth responds by praising Wickham for his generosity. On the account offered here, Elizabeth is praising Wickham for being generous-hearted. She believes Wickham to be sparing the feelings and social standing of someone who has supposedly seriously wronged him. Wickham is sparing Darcy, moreover, because of Darcy's father, a person Wickham loved and remembers fondly. Wickham is inviting Elizabeth to view him as a man whose affection for the elder Darcy has been stretched to include the son, not with affection, perhaps, but with a merciful regard.

Generous-hearted individuals are big-hearted, able to enter into the psychology of other people. The ability to encompass other people's travails or hopes, needs, or expectations, comes from an experience enlarged through identification with their lives. Largeness of emotional range often requires generous-mindedness to supply a corresponding largeness of view. The forgiveness or mercy we show wrongdoers usually takes a mental effort issuing in appreciation for the details of their individual histories. Martha Nussbaum notes how the merciful attitude "entails regarding each particular case as a complex narrative of human effort in a world full of obstacles."[12]

The work of the imagination is underscored by the similarity between our appreciation of real people's lives and the experience of literary narratives. As with literature, taking a merciful attitude toward an actual person requires putting ourselves in the offender's place, with his or her history of hardships and resources. A supple, energetic imagination vivifies for us another person's predicament, distorted experience, and harmful choice. A lively sense of what another human being's life is like makes possible the expansive emotional response of generous-heartedness found in mercy.

Nussbaum describes how imagination and feeling are wed by the structure of the novel. "It is a form of imaginative and emotional receptivity," she says, in which the life of another penetrates "into one's own imagination and heart."[13] The narrative underpinning of mercy and forgiveness shows how generosity of heart can depend on generosity of mind. In addition to uncommon mental effort, generous-mindedness can provide creative synthesizing of another individual's life into a coherent, revealing story.

Being disposed to feel about and for others in beneficient ways can extend beyond compassion for suffering or mercy for wrong-doing to more positive feelings. It can include, for example, loving someone who has given us ample cause to stop. We could also be genuinely happy for a friend who gets the promotion we wanted for ourselves. As in generous-mindedness, generous-heartedness often results in giving way to others. We give up what is our due to meet the emotional needs of other individuals.

We demonstrate such deference when we let another person take credit for something we have accomplished. By our inaction, we indirectly pass on credit to which we are entitled, as if it were wealth that we stood to inherit. Something similar occurs when we do not ask for credit for being right or demand that someone acknowledge our better judgment—which stock to buy or team to bet on—when we have it coming. We give the other person relief from having to admit being wrong or having to praise us. It is like being a gracious winner. We often think of a gracious person as one with humility, but generous-heartedness can be a component of it as well.

Recall Lester Hunt's example of an editor who chooses to publish another writer's article over his own. The editor is generous-minded because he judges the other person's article superior when his own could plausibly be appraised as better. However, the editor would be generous-hearted if he thought more of his own article, but gave up his chance for publication. The other person's self-esteem or vulnerability would then be placed above the editor's need for accomplishment or recognition. Where the generous-minded give another person's work a stronger interpretation at their own expense, generous-hearted individuals put another person's emotional needs or well-being before their own.

In the film *Chariots of Fire,* the aristocratic runner gives up his place in an Olympic footrace to enable a teammate, who is a Scottish missionary, to run on a non-Sabbath day. In giving up his rightful opportunity, the aristocrat is generous-hearted. Out of sympathy for his fellow runner's feelings of frustration and disappointment, the generous runner not only puts another person's interests above his own, but he waives an entitlement to pursue his interests. Would his act have been more generous had he not already run and won a silver medal? Not having run, and succeeded, the aristocratic runner might well have valued his position in the upcoming race more, making his gift greater.

We are generous when we relinquish opportunities, choices, and prerogatives even when they are not our due. Generous-heartedness disposes us to be deferential, regardless of our entitlements. We are generous-hearted, for instance, when we defer to another person's taste. Allowing a friend to decide which movie the two of us should see gives her preference priority. Relinquishing our prerogative, we enable the other individual to meet an interest or satisfy a desire. To the extent that we do not care about the choice of movie, we are less generous because the object of our deference is less valued.

The deference may regard generosity itself. We can be generous when by receiving a gift we permit someone else to be generous. Allowing another individual to give to us brings her the joy of having her choice or labor please us. This is why we happily eat the birthday pie grandma bakes specially for us when we would prefer something else. By gratefully receiving, we are generous in making ourselves the object of another's generosity.

Our gratitude itself could be the result of generosity. Generosity of mind can lead us to ascribe benevolent motives to those who bake us pie or otherwise try to do us favors. We are also generous-hearted in that we do not see ourselves as entitled to what we receive. Because we view what we receive as freely bestowed, we are grateful for a gift instead of simply satisfied that we have received our due.

Inhibiting our tendency to give may also give someone else the opportunity to be generous. By not giving to Smith, we may provide Jones the chance to show generosity toward Smith. We subordinate our delight in giving to the satisfaction another person takes in being generous. Although we might take pleasure in this indirect generosity, the pleasure of giving through self-restraint seems itself restrained when compared to the enjoyment derived from directly expressing a generous nature.

Generous-heartedness can lead individuals to restrain their impulses to more overt acts of generosity in order that potential beneficiaries may keep their self-respect. The dignity of other people may be maintained by sparing them incursions on it. Enlarged sensitivity to the affective life of other people is woven into the fiber of this generosity of the heart. The examples of self-restraint reveal a further connection between being gracious and generous-heartedness. The ease with which our inclination to act directly on generosity gives way to the importance of other people's feelings is another strand of graciousness.

III

As noted earlier, the virtue of generosity prompts us to give more than is required and to do more than fulfill obligations. But the concept of generosity of spirit enables us to see how it is possible to perform duties and yet be generous in their performance. Generosity of spirit includes acting in the spirit of generosity, a spirit with which even actions demanded by duty may be invigorated. People who act in the spirit of generosity perform duties graciously, with the ease that comes from absence of psychological resistance or obstruction. A generous attitude mitigates against a sense of duty as onerous, making it seem as though doing the dutiful thing has been freely undertaken.

In contrast are people who perform their duties perfunctorily or with much effort. Their lack of a generous spirit makes them feel the weight and constraint of duty. Of course, few people are consistently able to fulfill their obligations so seamlessly and effortlessly. But whenever individuals are able to meet their duties happily, generosity of spirit is liable to be responsible.

Another way in which generosity is consistent with meeting obligations lies in the fact that some obligations exist only because the people are generous in the first place. Individuals take on extra obligations, more demanding or numerous than the usual requirements of beneficence, from a generous character. For example, people who work in homeless shelters are obliged to provide for the homeless. Because obligatory, the tasks performed by shelter workers are not generous when understood as discrete acts. But the acts are obligatory only because the individuals chose them in choosing their vocation, and the choice may indeed have stemmed from generous character.

The spirit of generosity may inform obligatory work by drawing on motivation besides duty, motivation supplied by generosity of mind and heart. Generous-mindedness can quicken the work because the recipient is viewed more benignly than warranted. Generous-heartedness can animate our actions through sympathy with those toward whom we have obligations, or in our wish to spare them feeling they are imposing on us.

The natural mingling of generosity of mind and generosity of heart in the servant Gerasim, for example, is expressed in his steady spirit of generosity. In Tolstoy's *The Death of Ivan Ilych*, Gerasim contentedly holds Ivan's legs as if he had nothing in the world better to do. The good nature with which Gerasim performs his servant's duties is fed by his non-judgmental view of Ivan as well as his sympathy for Ivan's suffering. Gerasim performs his task with such goodwill and apparent effortlessness that Ivan can accept his help, and only his help, without resentment.

Taking into account the spirit with which we give enables us to see why even though people must value what they give, the giving need not constitute a sacrifice to them. It might seem plausible to think that the more we value what is given, the more we experience the giving as a loss or sacrifice. Aristotle suggests why this need not be the case in observing that good people delight in noble deeds.[14]

People whose generosity most colors their character, therefore, take pleasure in their giving. Even if generous individuals experience their giving as a loss, the pleasure taken in being generous could offset the pain of deprivation, so that overall they have not really sacrificed.

A more profound generosity, however, is one in which the pleasure in being generous does not merely offset the pain of loss as in an account ledger of credits and debits. Instead, the delight in the outcome of generosity could dissolve any experience of deprivation—not so much an offsetting as a short-circuiting.

The pleasure generous people take in the fruits of their generosity may so enrich them as to prevent any sense of depletion. The Aristotelian account yields the following irony. Because the most virtuous people find their virtuous actions most pleasing, people who do not experience loss might actually be more generous than people who feel their generosity to be a sacrifice.

IV

We saw how that aspect of generosity of spirit, the spirit of generosity, can make generosity compatible with that least generous of acts, doing our duty. But generosity per se, apart from duty, requires that the giving be done in the right spirit, gladly, with an open hand. We should not count as generous people who give reluctantly or grudgingly, no matter how much they give. Individuals who are truly generous do not experience their generosity as a burden, even as the spirit of generosity lifts the onus from fulfilling obligations. Because they pay attention to the good done beneficiaries, generous people enjoy giving.

People who give freely will tend to give much. Aristotle remarks in the most generous people, "a strong tendency to go to ... excess in giving."[15] Excessive giving is worrisome for Aristotle because it can leave generous individuals without the means needed for their own well-being, or for further giving. Giving in the right spirit, easily and unstintingly, is a force for giving too much. On a less wary note, Aristotle explains that generous people are willing, even eager, to take from others in order to give again. They value "material goods not for their own sake but for the sake of giving."[16]

Where Aristotle is chary of the "strong tendency to go to ... excess in giving," Nietzsche views excess as healthy. "You compel all things to come to you and into you, that they may flow back from your fountain as gifts of your love."[17] In addition to replacing Aristotelian prudence with extravagance, Nietzsche transmutes Aristotle's economic orientation into a spiritual one. Nietzsche shifts our attention from giving material goods to giving of ourselves, even as he compares what is given to jewels. "You thirst to become sacrifices and gifts yourselves; and that is why you thirst to heap up all riches in your soul."[18]

With the idea of riches in the soul, we arrive at the final dimension of generosity of spirit: giving virtue or character. Instead of seeking material goods for the sake of giving, Nietzsche's most completely generous individuals seek greatness of character. They want to become rich in virtue so that they may give of their moral bounty. On Nietzsche's view, the ease and magnitude of giving are naturally connected with what is given. The self is freely lavished because it is overfull. Nietzsche's characterization of ideal generosity implies an apotheosis—generosity as expressing a god-like superfluity of being.

This interpretation of paradigmatic generosity may be more Nietzschean than Nietzsche's.[19] A difficulty with interpreting Nietzsche's conception of the bestowing virtue as generosity is that his benefactors may not be properly motivated. Nietzsche's bestowers may be giving to assert a will to power. They could be more concerned with their own effusion than the well-being of the recipients of their gifts. Such motivation would obviously detract from the benevolent ends or goals needed for genuine generosity.

Even if Nietzsche's own view is informed by the centrality of the will to power or self-absorption, however, the insight concerning self-giving does not have to be limited by his larger theory. The joy in self-expression is not necessarily the motive or preoccupation of someone who satisfies Nietzsche's description. The overflowing of energy or fullness of vitality can be the source of self-giving, without being its focus or motive. It could function the way agapic love does as the foundation of generous behavior. My agapic love can be the basis from which I work to build up love in another, rather than that in which I delight.

Like economic or material wealth, the fullness of self is also the means by which we are generous. When we direct it towards another person we need not be reveling in our abundance of vitality any more than when we bestow material goods on someone else we must be enjoying our economic excess. We can be glad that we have so much because we have so much to give.

The fullness of their natures accounts for the unrehearsed, uncalculated giving of individuals who are most completely generous. As Lester Hunt puts it: "Generous behavior is not done because circumstances require it, but because the agent **seeks** [sic] to do such things.... generosity is spontaneous."[20] Spontaneity is compatible with deliberateness and need not be impulsive or thoughtless. The spontaneity signifies a lack of concern for the cost to ourselves, a lack of worry that we may be too giving of ourselves. Superabundance of vitality is the source of the eagerness with which individuals who are exemplary in Nietzschean generosity seek occasions to give. The energy and eagerness do not preclude reflection on how best to give or on what the effects of giving are likely to be.

The concept of giving of character or virtue needs elaboration. Giving our virtue is more than employing it for other people, as when we put our industriousness or resourcefulness at another person's service. Rather, it entails helping other individuals develop the virtue we possess. Virtues of strength when under duress provide illuminating examples. Consider Shakespeare's depiction of how Henry V buoys his vastly outnumbered men before the battle of Agincourt. When the Earl of Westmoreland wishes that some of the men remaining in England were in France at Agincourt, Henry exclaims that he would not want to have his portion of honor diminished by sharing it with even one more man.

Henry concludes by assuring his somewhat daunted, assembled army that at every celebration of their day of battle, St. Crispian's Day, they will be lauded for their valor:

> We few, we happy few, we band of brothers.
> For he today that sheds his blood with me

Shall be my brother....
And gentlemen in England now abed
Shall think themselves accurs'd they were not here,
And hold their manhood cheap while any speaks
That fought with us upon Saint Crispian's Day.[21]

Henry rouses the flagging spirits of his men by sharing with them
his courage, patriotism, and love of honor.

Natural disasters and harsh imprisonment are other dire situations in which individuals of stout character are called upon to
impart their virtue to more fragile cohorts. For instance, individuals with fortitude and optimism may encourage weaker
victims, enabling them to avert despair. The stronger impart their
hopefulness and strength to endure by helping fellow sufferers call
on their own resolve. Rallying other people can go beyond simply
setting an example. It can include instructing individuals in how
to view their present straits or reminding them of how they have
persevered in the past.

We may be able to nurture in other people virtues we possess by
discussing how we deal with our deficiencies. Articulating how
we deal with such defects as lassitude, envy, or resentment, for
example, can guide other people in cultivating the virtues needed
to overcome these defects. For example, we might sketch the stages
we go through in forgiving injuries, such as understanding the
wrong, our emotional response to it, and remedies available to us.
By explaining the forgiving process, including how to meet obstacles along its way, we show other individuals how to develop forgiveness.[22] Because forgiveness exhibits generosity of heart, we can
be generous with our generous-heartedness in a direct, edifying
way.

We can also imbue other people with our virtue in more subtle
ways. Kierkegaard urges that the true office of agapic love is building it up in other people without them realizing what we are
doing.[23] Forgiving individuals who injure us or forgoing opportunities to criticize wrong-doers might open new channels of
thought and feeling in them which foster their capacity to love.
Similarly, by being kind or patient with people who are neither

kind nor patient with us, we may unobtrusively strike a responsive chord. When we are generous with our virtue and not merely by means of it, we further the acquisition or flourishing of the virtue in other people.

Generosity of virtue completes the portrait of generosity of spirit. Giving virtue or character adds a dimension which embraces generous-mindedness, generous-heartedness, and acting with a generous spirit. Character or virtue is a part of personality which completes thought and emotion by organizing them. Giving the virtues of strength we have discussed, such as hopefulness and fortitude, necessarily engages our thoughts and feelings about other people in practical ways. Being generous with our virtues, as well as our thoughts and emotions, is the most complete psychological giving.

Once we recognize that psychological generosity is a necessary supplement to Aristotle's paradigm of material generosity, we appreciate how powerful and far-reaching the virtue is. Generosity can involve sparing people's feelings, giving individuals opportunities and favorable judgments, or enabling people to develop and express their own generosity. Generosity of spirit can also inform the performance of duties, and thereby alleviate their otherwise burdensome aspect. In addition, even material generosity, so apparently different from generosity of spirit, requires an aspect of it, the spirit of generosity. The important place of generosity of spirit in the configuration of this subtle virtue indicates why we should take a more generous view of generosity than has typically been the case.

Notes

1 Jane Austen, *Pride and Prejudice*, ed. Donald Grey (New York: W.W. Norton and Co., 1966), p. 55.

2 Ibid. Elizabeth mentions generosity only in Robert Leonard's 1940 film version of *Pride and Prejudice,* uttering lines written by Aldous Huxley and Jan Murfin. In Austen's text, Elizabeth is said to "honour[ed] him for such feelings."

3 Aristotle, *Nichomachean Ethics,* ed. Martin Ostwald (Indianapolis: Bobbs-Merrill, 1962), Bk. IV, sec. 1, 1119b, p. 83.

4   James Wallace, *Virtues and Vices* (Ithaca, N.Y.: Cornell University Press, 1978), p. 133.

5   Aristotle, op. cit., 1121a, p. 86. At 1120b, Aristotle speaks of generosity being relative to a person's property: "It is quite possible that a man who gives less is more generous, if his gift comes from smaller resources." If material goods did not matter to the person, why would the size of the resources make a difference?

6   Wallace, op. cit., p. 137.

7   Lester Hunt, "Generosity and the Diversity of the Virtues," in *The Virtues,* ed. Kruschwitz and Roberts (Belmont, Calif.: Wadsworth, 1987), pp. 217–28, p. 219.

8   Ibid., pp. 217–19.

9   Here I am dealing with one of several telling observations made by Professor Robin Dillon in response to a shorter version of this paper presented at the Eastern Division of the American Philosophical Association, December, 1995, in New York. I am grateful to her for helping me sharpen my views.

10 Several examples come to mind in which a virtue is compatible with vice or lack of another virtue. We can be courageous but lacking in patience, compassionate although arrogant, or self-controlled and callous. Acting on one virtue may also make it difficult to realize another virtue or to fulfill particular obligations. Compassion for the unfortunate could cause us to neglect ourselves or our friends. Similarly, a passion for the truth, combined with perseverance and industriousness, typical of strenuous scientific inquiry, might discourage family or civic virtues.

11 Wallace, op. cit., p. 132.

12 Martha Nussbaum, "Equity and Mercy," *Philosophy and Public Affairs,* Vol. 22, no. 2 (Spring 1993), pp. 83–125, p. 103.

13 Ibid., p. 108.

14 Aristotle, op. cit., 1120a, p. 84, and 1120b, p. 86.

15 Ibid., 1120b, p. 85.

16 Ibid.

17 Friedrich Nietzsche, *Thus Spoke Zarathustra,* trans. R.J. Hollingdale (Baltimore: Penguin, 1961), Part One, "Of the Bestowing Virtue," p. 100.

18 Ibid.

19 See Lester Hunt's *Nietzsche and the Origin of Virtue,* Nietzsche Studies (New York: Routledge, 1990). I am grateful to Robert C. Roberts for calling this less generous interpretation of Nietzsche's bestowing virtue to my attention.

20 Hunt, op. cit., p. 225.

21 Henry V, Act IV, Scene 3.

22   For a clear, rich examination of the process of forgiving, see Margaret
     Holmgren's "Forgiveness and the Intrinsic Value of Persons," *American
     Philosophical Quarterly,* Vol. 30, no. 4 (Oct. 1993), pp. 341–52.
23   Soren Kierkegaard, *Works of Love,* trans. Howard and Edna Hong
     (New York: Harper and Row, 1962), especially "Love Builds Up" (Part
     Two, Ch. I), pp. 206–7.

2 Gratitude and Justice

Patrick Boleyn-Fitzgerald

More than two decades ago Fred Berger noted the scant attention philosophers had shown the concept of gratitude. It has received more attention since then, but even those who analyze gratitude do not consider it an important concept in ethics. Terrance McConnell, who devoted a whole book to the subject, described gratitude as "on the edge" and only having a "peripheral nature" to moral theory. If we agreed with McConnell, we might wonder why we should look at gratitude at all, but he contends that we can learn much from an investigation into one of morality's side issues.[1]

One reason McConnell and others consider gratitude peripheral to morality is that they believe individuals owe gratitude only in a very restricted set of conditions. If these theorists are right and we are only infrequently called to gratitude, then gratitude does indeed deserve the appellation "on the edge." I will contend, however, that contemporary philosophers give gratitude far too narrow a scope. The problem lies in the questions they try to answer. Philosophers often try to uncover our "debts of gratitude" or figure out when we "owe" gratitude rather than merely asking when we have good moral reasons to be grateful. When we try to discern when we "owe" gratitude we constrain our moral thinking to issues of justice and ignore other relevant moral concerns. To support my view I will analyze two cases where some Buddhists argue for gratitude: gratitude to those who harm you and gratitude to those whom you benefit. In both cases strong moral reasons support gratitude, but neither of these cases fits the contemporary philosophical analysis. The conclusion I draw is that sometimes we should be grateful even when justice does not demand it. Looking at gratitude in this way helps us to see it as one of the most common ways that morality asks us to relate to others.

I Gratitude in contemporary moral theory

Gratitude is an emotion or a set of feelings. One *feels* grateful. This emotion has three components. Gratitude is (1) a warm sense of appreciation for somebody or something, (2) a sense of goodwill towards that individual or thing, and (3) a disposition to act which flows from appreciation and goodwill. Gratitude is not merely an emotion; however, we describe it as a virtue when it contributes to living one's life well. The question of when gratitude is a virtue is controversial, and this is where we will focus most of our attention.

The emotional component of gratitude poses a difficulty that philosophers commonly recognize. Many duties require us to perform particular actions but do not require us to feel any particular way. Gratitude is not like that. One cannot be grateful without feeling grateful. To be grateful for all that my mother has done for me may require actions, such as calling her on her birthday, but it also requires feeling a certain way about her. If, for example, I call my mother on her birthday purely out of a sense of duty, then I am not grateful though I have done all of the *actions* that gratitude may require. I am not grateful to my mother until I appreciate her. Claudia Card noted that this feature of gratitude strikes many oddly. "A duty to be grateful sounds like a joke," she states, pointing out that the obligation involves not only what we do but the spirit in which we do it.[2] This may strike us oddly because, she notes, "according to deontological ethics, I can conscientiously fulfill my obligations even if my heart isn't in it."[3]

The emotional component of gratitude is what differentiates it from the virtue of reciprocity. Many cases of reciprocity are also cases of gratitude. You help me move into my new apartment and I am grateful—I feel appreciation, I have goodwill towards you, and I am disposed to act on my appreciation and goodwill. Consequently, I invite you over to dinner because I think you will enjoy it. Here my gratitude is also reciprocity—my gratitude is also a return for the favor you have done me. Nevertheless, this overlap need not always exist. We can, for example, have reciprocity without gratitude. Suppose again that you help me move into my apartment, but I feel no appreciation towards you. I have just started a new job, and it has captured all of my attention. I realized you did me a great favor, but my worries about my new job fill my mind. Or perhaps the day before my move I attended the funeral of a dear friend and grief overwhelms me. If I invite you to dinner anyway (perhaps because I habitually return favors), then I have reciprocated without being grateful. The emotional state appropriate for gratitude is not present. Anytime we try to reciprocate a benefit, but lack appreciation or goodwill, we have reciprocity without gratitude.[4]

When should we have these feelings of gratitude and express them? When should we be grateful? Contemporary philosophical analyses of gratitude agree on three general points. Philosophers agree that gratitude ought to be a response to a benefit (or perhaps an attempt to provide a significant benefit), a benefit given from an appropriate motivation (usually benevolence), and a benefit that was either wanted or accepted by the beneficiary. These three important areas of agreement are the very areas that I wish to challenge. Before I voice my challenge, however, I will spend the rest of this section fully describing them.

First, gratitude is a response to a favor, a benefit, or an attempt to provide a significant benefit. A.D.M. Walker, for example, argues, "What, first, is the 'proper object' of gratefulness: for what can one be grateful? In a word, gratefulness is a response to favor. That is to say: (I) Gratefulness is a response to what one sees as good; being grateful for what one takes to be unmitigated evil is a logical impossibility."[5] Terrance McConnell offers a similar analysis choosing the term "benefit" rather than "favor". Usually McConnell believes that there must be a benefit provided, but he does make an exception. If someone tries to give another a significant benefit but fails, gratitude may be owed. Gratitude might be owed, for example, when a colleague nominates you for an award even if it turns out that you do not get it. He states, "It must be the case that the person to whom gratitude is owed provided a benefit or through great effort or sacrifice tried to provide a significant benefit."[6] Others presume this condition but do not discuss it directly. Those who endorse the claim that a benefit must be given out of a benevolent motivation, for example, presume that some benefit must be given.

Second, obligations of gratitude are only created when benefactors cause a benefit with an appropriate attitude. Fred Berger, for example, argues that the benefactor must not have been *forced* to grant the benefit. If someone benefits us because he was forced to, we need not be grateful. He imagines, "Suppose someone does something involving a sacrifice on his part which benefits us, but he was forced by threats to do it. In such a case, gratitude is not due; the appropriate response may be to return the gift, if possible, or to make sufficient restitution or replacement of it. The voluntariness with which the benefits are produced for us is thus a factor in determining if gratitude is appropriate when others benefit us."[7] Berger also argues that the benefactor must be aware that he benefited the beneficiary. Berger states, "Where it is clear that such intention was lacking, gratitude is not due." In general, Berger claims that gratitude is a response to *benevolence* and so when a benefactor does not have a benevolent attitude a beneficiary need not be grateful. He states, "Gratitude, then, does not consist in the requital of benefits but in a response to *benevolence;* it is a response to a grant of benefits (or the attempt to benefit us) which was motivated by a desire to help us."[8] Berger's analysis was very influential. More recent papers on gratitude often take his paper as a starting point. Some writers simply endorse his position outright. Nancy Jecker endorsed the position in a paper she wrote on the subject.[9] Card also endorsed it when she stated, "In an illuminating paper on this topic Fred Berger says one's gratitude is a response to another's benevolence, more specifically, to the valuing of oneself presupposed in another's benevolence: gratitude acknowledges and reciprocates that valuing, thereby demonstrating that one does not value others merely as useful for one's own ends."[10] A. John Simmons argues for a similar condition when he discusses gratitude as a possible source of political obligation, but he breaks the point down into three components:

These features concern the benefactor's reasons for granting the benefit. First, his provision of the benefit must be intentional if we are to owe him a debt of gratitude for his performance; a benefit which he gives us unintentionally will not bind us to any repayment. Second, he must have given the benefit voluntarily. A man who benefits me because of the gun at his back does not earn my gratitude, although he may, for instance, be entitled to ask for a return of the benefit (if possible) when the gunman no longer is in control. Third, the benefactor must not have provided the benefit for reasons of self-interest.[11]

McConnell agrees with this general condition and provides a more complete analysis of what kind of intention is necessary. He maintains that the intentional provision of benefit is required only in a weak sense. Jones rescues a drowning man without realizing his identity. Afterward Jones discovers that he has rescued his enemy and reports that he would not have rescued him if he had known who he was at the time. Jones only intended to give his enemy a benefit in a weak sense, but McConnell still thinks that gratitude is owed. Hence, McConnell claims that "the benefit must be granted voluntarily, intentionally (at least in the weak sense), freely, and not for disqualifying reasons."[12]

Third, contemporary theorists argue that beneficiaries must want the benefit, or at least accept it, before they would owe gratitude. Simmons describes the reaction in terms of want. First, "we must *want* the benefit which is granted" and, second, "we must not want the benefit *not* to be provided *by the benefactor*."[13] McConnell agrees that gratitude is due only when the beneficiary responds to a benefit in a particular way, but he believes that Simmons's conditions are too narrow. What if, for example, a wealthy benefactor pays for Bonnie's college tuition, and she accepts the gift not because she wants to go to college but merely because she wants to please her parents. McConnell thinks Bonnie owes her benefactor gratitude even though she didn't want the benefit provided to her. Consequently, McConnell proposes a standard focusing on acceptance rather than want. He states, "3'. The benefit must not be forced (unjustifiably) on the beneficiary against his will. 4'. The beneficiary must accept the benefit (or would accept the benefit if certain impairing conditions were corrected)."[14]

When we stand back and look at contemporary philosophical discussions of gratitude we see that, while there are disputes, the disputes are minor. Philosophers seem to have reached a consensus on the general approach to when we should be grateful. Moreover, this approach to gratitude makes the virtue insignificant. Philosophers generally agree that we ought to be grateful only when very restricted conditions are met. Consequently, gratitude is thought to have a minimal role in our moral life.

II Two anomalous cases

There are many cases where I believe we ought to be grateful that do not fit within the contemporary philosophical analysis of gratitude. Instead of listing every such case and instead of moving directly to the alternative theory that I favor I will take two cases that dramatically conflict with the contemporary analysis. Both cases are found in Buddhist writings, revealing the inspiration for my alternative theory. The cases illustrate a very different way of looking at gratitude. In this section I will describe the cases and some motivation for them. In the next section I will flesh out more systematically the theory that could provide justification for the examples.

A. *Gratitude to those who harm you*

Given the Christian heritage of the West, it does not strike us as strange that we might forgive our enemies. Being grateful to our enemies, on the other hand, sounds absurd. When Jesus was crucified, he asked God to forgive those who crucified him, but he never thanked them. He asked his followers to turn the other cheek, but he never requested that they do so with appreciation for those who slapped them. The idea of practicing gratitude toward one's enemies is not, however, without precedent.[15] Indeed, it is a common ideal within Buddhism. The Dalai Lama often repeats this Buddhist teaching by telling his audiences that he is grateful to the Chinese for giving him the opportunity to practice love for his enemies.[16] In one instance he expressed gratitude for a different but related reason: because the Chinese gave him training in patience and helped his development as a person.

Even our enemies give us the best training in patience. When we reflect on these holy instructions, in a way we should feel grateful to the Chinese. If we were still living in the same old system, I very much doubt that the Dalai Lama could have become so closely acquainted with worldly reality. I used to live in a very sheltered environment, but now that we are in exile there is no stigma attached to facing reality. In our own country, we could pretend that everything was in order because it was shrouded under a cloak of pomp and show. I had to sit on a high throne assuming the attitude of being the Dalai Lama.... It is quite possible that I could have become narrow minded, but because of the Chinese threats and humiliations, I have become a real person. So what happened in Tibet can be seen as a blessing in disguise.[17]

The Dalai Lama's expression of gratitude strikes many as strange, but before we look at possible justifications for his position, we should look at another example so that the details of the Tibetan case do not color our analysis.

Nichiren, a controversial thirteenth-century Japanese Buddhist monk, offers another example. Nichiren gave unyielding criticisms of Japanese religious leaders, governmental support of established religions, and the Japanese religions themselves. Nichiren believed that they had abandoned what he considered the highest Buddhist teaching—the Lotus Sutra. Because of his outspoken manner, the Japanese government twice exiled him and nearly executed him. Nonetheless, Nichiren claimed that he was grateful to the Japanese government and its ruler (during this period in Japanese history the real authority rested neither in the hands of the emperor nor the shogun, but in members of the Hojo family who held the office of regent for the shogun). During his exile to Ito on the Izu Peninsula, Nichiren wrote to a follower, "Those people who slandered me and the ruler [who had me banished] are the very persons to whom I owe the most profound debt of gratitude."[18]

While the ruler had clearly harmed Nichiren through exiling him and attempting to execute him, Nichiren considered these difficulties as essential to his own spiritual progress. He considered the persecution an essential part of a larger picture, a step on his own road to enlightenment. Consequently, he considered the harm the ruler caused as insignificant. He states, "Moreover, in this lifetime, I have been able to take faith in the Lotus Sutra and to encounter a ruler who will enable me to free myself in my present existence from the sufferings of birth and death. Thus how can I dwell on the insignificant harm that he has done me and overlook my debt to him?"[19]

The gratitude expressed by Nichiren and the Dalai Lama clearly does not fit the contemporary philosophical model.[20] First, both Nichiren and the Dalai Lama express gratitude to people who harmed them. While both claim that the very people who harmed them have also benefited them, that benefit is indirect. Both claim spiritual progress: Nichiren could "take faith in the Lotus Sutra," and the Dalai Lama could become "a real person." We should note that neither the Japanese nor the Chinese was the sufficient cause for either of these Buddhists to develop spiritually. The Japanese and the Chinese created conditions, created the opportunity, where a particular kind of spiritual progress was possible. In other words, the benefits accrued by Nichiren and the Dalai Lama were significantly due to their own efforts. Neither was given a direct benefit. If we really wanted to define benefit broadly, we could say that both the Dalai Lama and Nichiren were benefited. This broad sense of benefit, however, is not what the contemporary philosophical analysis typically intends. I will say, therefore, that the Dalai Lama and Nichiren were harmed and given opportunities. Both capitalized on those opportunities by creating benefits out of them.

Second, neither party was benefited intentionally. The Chinese did not try to make the Dalai Lama "a real person," and the Japanese did not try to make Nichiren "the votary of the Lotus Sutra." The Dalai Lama's and Nichiren's expressions of gratitude are clearly not responses to benevolence.

The third criterion, acceptance, is a bit more complicated. While both Nichiren and the Dalai Lama accepted what happened to them in one sense, this sense of acceptance is not the kind envisioned by contemporary moral philosophers. First, the object of acceptance is a benefit in contemporary philosophical analysis, but no benefit is given in these cases. At best we can say opportunities are given. Second, in an important sense both Nichiren and the Dalai Lama did not accept even these opportunities. Neither Nichiren nor the Dalai Lama wanted what happened to them before it happened. Both men do accept the events in retrospect, but neither would choose the persecution if they could. Indeed, if they chose to be persecuted, it would no longer be persecution and would become masochism. An essential part of each of these stories is that hardship was *forced* on these men against their will. In this sense neither accepted even the opportunities that their hardships presented. Instead, they chose to see their hardships as opportunities after they occurred so that they could make the best out of a bad situation or, in the terms of the traditional Buddhist metaphor, "turn poison into medicine."

Thus, in this first case we have two examples of gratitude that do not meet any of the necessary conditions proposed by contemporary philosophers. These two examples are clearly anomalous to the contemporary analysis.

B. *Gratitude to someone whom you benefit*

A second anomalous case for contemporary accounts of gratitude is the case of benefactors who feel grateful to those they benefit. This again is a Buddhist theme, but it is also common in non-Buddhist writings. Individuals who perform volunteer work or community service sometimes speak of the benefits they gain from the service and express gratitude to those who present them with the opportunity to serve. This often occurs with volunteers, but sometimes it also occurs with individuals who are members of service professions. One example of the latter case can be found in a recent article in the *Journal of the American Medical Association* by Dr. David Hilfiker: "I am beginning to realize that we in medicine need the poor to bring us back to our roots as a servant profession. Medicine drifts understandably yet ominously toward the technical and the economically lucrative, and we find it difficult to resist. Perhaps we *need* the poor at this very moment to bring us back to ourselves. The nature of the healer's work is to be with the wounded in their suffering. Can the poor in their very vulnerability show us how?"[21] Hilfiker expresses feelings of gratitude for the poor, but it is not because of any beneficent actions that the poor take on behalf of doctors. Instead the poor create an opportunity for members of the medical profession to define their working lives around helping the vulnerable rather than getting lost in technical details or money making. Without the poor to serve, the profession would lose itself and move away from its professional ideal.

Buddhists often advocate a similar attitude toward those that one serves. Here the reason for a debt of gratitude toward those in need comes from the importance of compassion. Having compassion is thought to be essential for one's happiness. Jack Kornfield explains, "There's a tremendous sorrow for a human being who doesn't find a way to give. One of the worst of human sufferings is not to find a way to love, or a place to work and give of your heart and your being."[22] Ram Dass and Paul Gorman explain the Buddhist view of compassion in terms of self-discovery: "Caring for one another, we sometimes glimpse an essential quality of our being. We may be sitting alone, lost in self-doubt or self-pity, when the phone rings with a call from a friend who's *really* depressed. Instinctively, we come out of ourselves, just to be there with her and say a few reassuring words. When we're done, and a little comfort's been shared, we put down the phone and feel a little more at home with ourselves. We're reminded of who we really are and what we have to offer one another."[23] Because compassion is thought to be immensely beneficial to those who feel it, it is considered appropriate to feel grateful to those who cause one's compassion. There can be no rescuer without someone to rescue; there can be no benefactor without a beneficiary. If giving to those in need enriches one's life, then one owes a debt of gratitude to those who needed the gift. Consequently, Buddhism enshrines a debt of gratitude to all living beings. Nichiren comments, "One who studies the teachings of Buddhism must not fail to repay the four debts of gratitude. According to the *Shinjikan* Sutra, the first of the four debts is that owed to all living beings. Were it not for them, one would find it impossible to make the vow to save innumerable living beings."[24]

Here again the expressions of gratitude need not fit *any* of the conditions found in the contemporary philosophical model. First, beneficiaries need not give benefactors any benefits. A benefactor may benefit from a beneficiary trying to return the favor he received or a benefactor may get emotional benefits from a beneficiary expressing gratitude, but neither of these benefits always occurs. Beneficiaries often do nothing to try to help their benefactors. If one is grateful for the opportunity to give in these cases, then one is grateful to someone who does not *give* benefits. Hilfiker's suggestion to the medical community is an example of this. He does not argue that poor patients perform actions that benefit doctors. Indeed the lack of an ability to give doctors the typical benefit they receive for their services—money—is the very reason Hilfiker sees serving the poor as important. The plight of poor patients gives the medical profession an opportunity—an opportunity to return the medical profession to a servant profession. Like our previous case of gratitude to those who harm you, gratitude to those whom you benefit is gratitude for opportunities (which if not taken are merely harms or burdens) rather than gratitude for benefits.

Second, the benefits derived from giving need not be intended by those who receive. It is unlikely that a poor person will receive aid merely because it might help the giver develop compassion. Even less likely is the case of a person becoming poor, or in need of other assistance, merely because it might help some self-absorbed individual rise to a higher moral or spiritual plane. Those who receive aid rarely do so out of beneficent intentions. This kind of gratitude is not a response to beneficence.

Third, it is again hard to talk of a benefactor accepting the benefits of giving. No one is intending to give her anything, and all that she receives is an opportunity for a benefit (that if not developed is merely a burden) rather than an actual benefit. Any kind of acceptance that we could attribute to this kind of gratitude would not be the kind suggested by the contemporary philosophical analysis. Being grateful to those whom one aids is like being grateful to those who harm you, an anomaly for the contemporary philosophical analysis of gratitude. It is anomalous because none of the three conditions thought necessary for gratitude need be present.

III Possible justifications for gratitude

We could respond to these two anomalous cases in three general ways: (1) we might criticize those who feel grateful because we think they ought not be grateful; (2) we might praise the grateful for their gratitude; or (3) we might neither criticize nor praise the grateful, maintaining that their gratitude is neither favored nor disfavored by moral reasons. If we take option (1) and we criticize the grateful, then the two cases that I presented pose no problems for the contemporary philosophical analysis. The same is true if we take option (3), and we conclude that morality neither favors nor disfavors these cases of gratitude. Since the contemporary philosophical analysis tries to identify only those cases where gratitude is owed, these cases—where people feel gratitude even though they do not owe it—are no problem. These cases are only a problem if we think that morality favors gratitude in the two cases. If morality favors gratitude and the contemporary philosophical analysis can give no account of this, then the contemporary philosophical analysis is incomplete. I support (2). I think morality favors the expressions of gratitude in the cases I have described.

A. Six possible justifications

Before arguing that gratitude is justified in the two anomalous cases, it will be helpful to categorize the kinds of moral reasons we might have for gratitude at any time. There are at least six distinct types of moral reasons one might have for gratitude. Usually we will have more than one moral reason for gratitude, so we could use a single example to illustrate many or all of them. Still, even when there is overlap, one reason may dominate or be more important than another. I am not sure that this list is exhaustive, but the most important point may be that there is a list at all, that there are many possible moral reasons for gratitude. As I will argue in the next section, moral philosophers (probably reflecting commonsense morality) often seem to assume that only one kind of moral reason is relevant for gratitude—reasons of justice. This assumption, however, is not justified.

We can begin with the most common type of moral reason cited in favor of gratitude—justice. In these cases we have *juridical* reasons for gratitude. The recipients of gratitude "deserve" it, "merit" it, are "entitled" to it, or ingratitude may be somehow "unfair." Those who ought to be grateful "owe" gratitude or have a "debt of gratitude." Suppose George stops to jump my car one cold winter morning, and I give him a perfunctory "thank you." The next morning I see George in the same predicament—now he is in need of a jump—but instead of stopping I drive on, aspiring to get first pick of the free donuts that await me at my office. Some would say that I owe George a jump or that he deserves my help, or that he is entitled to my help or that I treat him unfairly if I do not help. If any of these reasons is correct then I have a juridical reason to be grateful. My ingratitude would be a case of injustice.

Gratitude might also be called for because it will prevent a harm or burden. In these cases we have *nonmaleficent* reasons for gratitude. When my father tells me "don't forget your mother's birthday or you will break her heart," he is giving me a nonmaleficent reason for a particular expression of gratitude. Unless I express gratitude to my mother by recognizing her birthday, I do her harm or cause her distress. If, however, my father tells me, "You could bring your mother a lot of joy if you could show your appreciation," then my father points to a different moral reason for gratitude. Here my gratitude will benefit my mother. In these cases we have *beneficent* reasons for gratitude.

Gratitude might be useful to promote or preserve a special relationship such as a relationship with a friend or a lover. Since the ethic of care emphasizes these kinds of relationships, we can say that in these cases we have *caring* reasons for gratitude. Suppose I come home, and my friend has made me dinner. Of course, I have many moral reasons to be grateful, including the ones discussed above. My gratitude may prevent my friend's distress (nonmaleficent) or cause my friend joy (beneficent), but my gratitude may also be essential for preserving the friendship. Most people do not enjoy being friendly with the ungrateful. If I am not grateful to my friend and show no appreciation or show appreciation only out of a sense of duty, then my friend may not want to remain my friend. So ingratitude may be cause for severing or weakening the friendship. If I treasure the relationship then I have a good reason to be grateful, and if I consider the relationship morally important (because of its intrinsic value, its instrumental value in shaping my character, or for another reason), then I have a good moral reason to be grateful.

Gratitude might be useful for promoting or preserving communal relationships. In these cases we have *civic* reasons for gratitude. Cases like this often arise when we look at norms of gratitude. What might be a moral justification for the norm of being grateful to someone who holds the door open for you? We might try to explain it in terms of beneficence (it reinforces a practice that brings joy) or nonmaleficence (it protects against hurt feelings), but a better explanation is probably communal. The practice of being grateful to strangers who hold doors open produces a small communal feeling, a slight feeling of solidarity or connectedness. When we take care to prevent a door from coming between us the act brings us together both literally and figuratively. This is a better explanation than a juridical one. It sounds very strange to say that I owe something to Joe for holding the door open, or that Joe is entitled to something because he held the door open, or that I treat Joe unfairly if I am not grateful for his holding the door open. But this does not mean that the practice of holding doors open is irrelevant to morality, it only means that the practice of holding doors open is irrelevant to justice. Gratitude, then, has the potential of reinforcing communal ties, and some norms of gratitude may find their primary justification in this very feature.

Finally, gratitude also may aid in the development of virtues or help prevent the formation of vices. In these cases we have *perfectionist* reasons for gratitude. Gratitude may be especially important as an antidote to feelings of anger and resentment and thus to the formation of an angry or resentful character. Suppose that I have a friend who has given me many benefits, but just last week harmed me significantly. Although we have discussed last week's incident, and he has apologized and done what he could to make things better, I am unable to forget it. Whenever I see him, I feel my fists and jaw clench, my blood pressure rise, and my mind returns again and again to the wrong that he did me. In the presence of my friend I become an angry and resentful person. If I reflect on my mental life, I may wish I were not so resentful, and I may realize that my character would improve if I could overcome my resentment. Gratitude is a potential antidote to these unwanted emotions. If I focus on the benefits that my friend has given me, and if I can focus on those benefits with appreciation, then I will find it difficult to feel angry, at least for a moment. Gently returning my attention to the broader perspective where the presence of my friend is a benefit competes with my mind's tendency to focus on the incident of harm. Cultivating gratitude (by focusing my attention on the wider perspective where I receive benefit), therefore, reduces anger and resentment. The more that I do this the more grateful and the less angry my character becomes.

B. The case for gratitude to those who harm you

I have described six different kinds of moral reasons that one may have to be grateful. Now what should we say of our two anomalous cases? What moral reasons might favor feeling grateful to those who harm you? The primary reason cited by both Nichiren and the Dalai Lama is perfectionist. According to the Dalai Lama, for example, the purpose of Buddhist practice is to combat disturbing emotions: "It is important to remember that all the Buddha taught was meant to help sentient beings and guide them on their spiritual path. His philosophical teachings were not just abstract speculation but part of the processes and techniques for combating disturbing emotions."[25]

From the perspective of someone who is working to eliminate their own disturbing emotions, incidents where people harm you can be an important opportunity. Those who irritate us the most give us the opportunity to develop our patience and extend the boundaries of our compassion. Hence, it is the very antagonistic attitude, the absence of beneficence in the "enemy"—a general term in Buddhism used to refer to any individual with whom one has a conflict—that enables the individual to develop virtue. The Dalai Lama states, "It is sometimes the case that beings with actively hostile intentions can help us to the highest realizations. Enemies are very important, because it is only in relation to them that we can develop patience. Only they give us the opportunity to test our patience. Not your spiritual master, your friends, or your relatives give you such a great opportunity. The enemy's antagonism would normally arouse your anger, but by changing your attitude you can transform it into an opportunity to test and practice patience."[26] When we deal with an "enemy" we can focus on the harm that they have done us and become angry. Alternatively, we can focus on the opportunity that the "enemy" gives us and develop gratitude and compassion. The Dalai Lama argues that it would be better to focus on the opportunity that our "enemy" gives us. "We need to appreciate that the kindness of sentient beings is not confined to when they have been our parents or friends; it extends to when they have been our enemies as well. This is something to be pondered deeply. It will serve as a great inspiration for cultivating compassion. When you recollect the special kindness of sentient beings in this way, your wish to repay them will be much stronger."[27]

I have quoted extensively from the Dalai Lama because I began with the example of his gratitude toward the Chinese, and because I think his writings give the reader a good sense of how gratitude to those who harm us may be useful. However, the Dalai Lama's teaching is not unique in this respect. It is a central tenet of Buddhism. In Buddhist thought, anger is one of our most destructive emotions (classified as one of the "three poisons" of the mind) and consequently calls out for our attention. Because anger is so powerful we will probably have to use many methods to deal with it if we are to bring it under our control, but the cultivation of gratitude is one important way. Gratitude can be an antidote to a mental state that causes suffering in ourselves and those around us. Putting this argument more formally might be helpful:

1. We have good moral reasons to overcome our anger or hatred.
2. Sometimes cultivating gratitude will be the most effective way to overcome anger or hatred.
3. Therefore, in some cases of anger or hatred we have good moral reasons to cultivate gratitude.

The support for premise 1 has thus far been cast in perfectionist terms—cultivating gratitude is an antidote to the vice of anger. Additional support can be crafted from nonperfectionist moral reasons. Again the Dalai Lama's gratitude toward the Chinese illustrates this. The Dalai Lama is not merely concerned about his own character and the characters of those who listen to him. He is moved by a desire to create peace in Tibet and China, and he believes that responding to the Chinese occupation with gratitude would be more effective than anger. By cultivating gratitude he and others can refrain from action motivated by resentment and thus refrain from committing or supporting violent acts. Anger threatens peace and gratitude is an antidote for anger. Consequently, this one case of gratitude might be justified in many different ways. It might be justified in civic terms because the Dalai Lama wants to create communal ties between Tibetans and Chinese, in nonmaleficent terms because he wants to prevent the harm that may come from Chinese/Tibetan hostilities, in beneficent terms because he wants to create the benefits of peace, in caring terms because he thinks he may have a better relationship with his students if he dispels his own anger or in perfectionist terms because he thinks that his own gratitude will make him a better person.

Support for premise 2 must be contextual. Sometimes the suggestion of cultivating gratitude to those who harm you may be unhelpful. The very idea may seem psychologically impossible or undesirable, and suggestions to the contrary may only create psychological resistance. Even if cultivating gratitude would help a resentful person, it may not help to tell her to cultivate gratitude. Furthermore, gratitude's value in each case lies in its effectiveness as a psychological strategy, and we have no reason to believe that the gratitude strategy is equally effective in all cases. Sometimes approaching one's anger in a different way may be better. So premise 2 does not and should not read, "Gratitude is always the best way to counteract anger" and the conclusion does not and should not read, "All individuals should try to cultivate gratitude for those who harm them." It would, I believe, be a better world if we were all grateful to those who harmed us, but sometimes trying to cultivate gratitude may do more harm than good. So premise 2 does not speak to everyone in every situation. It does, however, speak to some people in some situations, and perhaps it speaks to everyone in at least some situations. When one notices anger arising or resentment festering, and if cultivating gratitude is the most effective way to counteract these feelings, then one has good moral reasons for gratitude.

C. The case for gratitude to those you benefit

We can now turn to the justification for being grateful to those whom you benefit. Those who claim this kind of gratitude rarely give intricate justifications, but we should consider three. First, gratitude to beneficiaries is sometimes justified by referring to the importance of compassion. This is the justification that Nichiren gives when he cites the bodhisattva's debt of gratitude to all living beings. Without those individuals in need there would be no way to become a bodhisattva—an individual who vows to liberate innumerable living beings from suffering. Since the bodhisattva is a *perfectionist* ideal in Buddhism, we may describe this reason in perfectionist terms.

We might describe a similar sentiment in *juridical* terms. If not caring for others inevitably leads to suffering, as Jack Kornfield maintains, then the individual who becomes the object of one's caring has done one a great service. "If it weren't for you," the benefactor might say to the beneficiary, "I would be miserably self-absorbed." The reasoning here is juridical. The beneficiary does the benefactor a great service, though it was probably not intentional, and gratitude is due.

A third possible justification focuses on preventing harm. Consider a common criticism of charitable giving. Some say charitable giving disempowers or otherwise psychologically harms beneficiaries. Rousseau, for instance, worries that if one individual always receives help and is never allowed to give it then he is likely to feel powerless. Kant claims that helping out a poor man "involves a dependence of his welfare upon my generosity, which humiliates him."[28] If giving has this consequence, or creates a similarly unhealthy relationship between benefactor and beneficiary, then it poses a difficult problem for a genuinely beneficent benefactor. If one truly wishes another well, how can one provide material support without also degrading the very individual one desires to help? Card notes that this may convince benefactors that they do not want their beneficiaries to feel indebted: "Sensitive benefactors may want their beneficiaries *not* to feel indebted to them, for it alters their relationship."[29] But how are benefactors to do this as they provide material support?

Must one refrain from giving to prevent such an unhealthy interpersonal dynamic? One might conclude that nonmaleficence, the desire not to harm, argues against giving (except in such dire cases where the material benefits of the aid outweigh the psychological harm).

Such a strong conclusion is unwarranted, however, because the problems associated with giving do not always occur. Rather, the problems associated with giving depend on both the attitudes of the beneficiary and of the benefactor. Consider the effects of the attitudes of a benefactor with a simple thought experiment. Suppose that you collect stamps, and you strongly want to acquire rare stamps when you see them. Also suppose that someone else has a stamp that you want, and they will give it to you but have no interest in letting you buy it. Now imagine the different reactions you might have for each of the following individuals giving you the stamp you want: a longtime friend whom you have often helped; an associate whom you have always felt is trying to prove that he is better than you; a Jehovah's Witness who has just knocked at your door to tell you about the true path to salvation; an associate who always resents giving but typically does give out of a sense of duty; a lover; a family member. The obvious implication of this thought experiment is that the value you place on getting your desired stamp may vary widely with who your benefactor might be. What may the benefactor want or expect in return? Is that something you want to give? The effect of receiving a gift, even when it is the same material object in each case, varies when the benefactor is someone who wants to see you happy, someone who wants you to join their religion, or someone who wants to see you in a position subservient to them. The general point, then, is that the attitude of the benefactor can significantly affect the well-being of the beneficiary. Consequently, the ethics of giving cannot stop at the material object given but must extend to the attitude with which it is given.

One attitude that may harm is a feeling of superiority. If the benefactor looks at his beneficiary as something pitiful or thinks of himself as better than the beneficiary, then acceptance of a material gift may come at the price of self-respect. So, if you are about to offer help to another and you realize that you are likely to feel superior to your beneficiary, or if you are in the midst of helping another, and you come to notice feelings of superiority, or if you realize that the person you are about to help could easily believe that you want to help in order to feel superior, and you don't want to harm or challenge another's self-respect—what should you do? On one occasion Kant suggested that a benefactor should "carry out his beneficence completely in secret." But it is unclear that this is really a solution. The beneficiary is still likely to feel pitiful, perhaps even more so since the benefactor had to hide his activities. The very secrecy seems to reinforce the idea that the recipient should feel pitiful or deeply indebted to receiving this aid. Perhaps for these very reasons Kant prefers a different approach. He states, "The benefactor must express himself as being obligated or honored by the other's acceptance, treating the duty merely as a debt he owes."[30] It is only if a benefactor cannot do this that he should resort to giving in secrecy. The idea here seems to be that the benefactor should try to transform the giving relationship into something that does not degrade recipients.[31] Gratitude in giving offers an analogous approach. What if we truly valued the opportunity to help another individual because we considered it essential for our own happiness? When we see an instance where we know we really can be of help, what if we felt thankful for the chance to rise out of our self-absorption or simply thankful for the chance to do something worthwhile? Kornfield's description of Buddhist psychology seems to suggest such a sentiment. If one of the worst human sufferings is not finding a way to love then the benefactor may get as much, if not more, out of giving than the beneficiary receives. Consequently a feeling of gratitude transforms an act of giving into a trade—"I will support you materially and in the process you will help me rise above my self-centeredness" (or, " ... and you will help me do something worthwhile," or simply, " ... you will help me love"). This trade means that no debts linger after material aid is given. No inferior position is required of the beneficiary. Charity does not wound.

This is not the only way to counter the asymmetries of the gift relationship. Often it may be more important to create opportunities where a beneficiary can pay back aid in kind or feel that the aid is part of a larger system of mutual aid to which she could later make contributions. But this may be difficult or impossible to achieve. Sometimes the opportunity to pay a benefactor back may be impossible or unlikely, and the beneficiary may be unable to contribute to any system of mutual aid. Imagine a hospice volunteer who continually gives services to strangers who are terminally ill. If this volunteer wants to help those whom she serves then she clearly would not want to leave them with feelings that they owed her something for her help. It would be cruel to create feelings of unpaid debts in people who are about to die. In these and other cases gratitude in giving may be invaluable in preventing psychological harms that may come about from receiving.

IV Ought versus owe

Contemporary philosophical analyses of gratitude are too narrow. They give gratitude too limited a place in our moral life and argue for the cultivation of gratitude on too few occasions. The two anomalous cases that I chose were designed to be the most dramatic demonstration of my claim. In these cases we have good moral reasons for gratitude, but the contemporary philosophical analysis has no means to account for them. If I am right about these extreme cases, then there should be many more that are less dramatic. The reasons why the contemporary philosophical analysis fails also seem to suggest this conclusion. The contemporary philosophical analysis fails because it only entertains juridical reasons for gratitude and ignores others. This assumption is rarely articulated but is typically apparent in the limited range of moral terms that philosophers use to discuss the morality of gratitude. This seems especially clear in one passage in Card's article. She states, "It should be noted, however, that gratitude need not be deserved to be in order. Gratitude is not always *to* someone, although it is *for* something. I may be grateful *that* the weather 'cooperated' with plans for the picnic, or *that* the highway patrol officer was distracted as I sped by, without being grateful to anyone for either event.... My interest, however, like Berger's, is in deserved gratitude."[32] Notice the move that Card makes here. She doesn't want to discuss cases of gratitude that seem irrelevant to morality,[33] but instead of merely excluding gratitude that is morally irrelevant she narrows the discussion to a particular kind of moral reason—desert. Card is not alone in making this move. She attributes the same position to Berger, and others use similar moral language. Jecker asks which persons merit gratitude, and McConnell tries to answer the question of when gratitude is owed.[34] This common move sets the terms of the debate by limiting the kinds of moral reasons we might have to be grateful. The question asked is not, "When do we have good moral reasons to be grateful?" but, instead, "When do we have the specific moral reasons of desert, merit, or debt?"

In one sense it is understandable why Card and others might frame the issues in this way. The limitations reflect common moral intuitions or at least common moral language. Terms like "desert", "merit", and' "debt" are commonly used to discuss cases of gratitude and ingratitude. If we were interested in merely uncovering the modern moral intuitions regarding gratitude, then it might seem plausible to limit our discussion in the way philosophers have.

In another sense, however, this limitation seems quite mysterious. What moral justification is there to believe that gratitude is only supported by juridical reasons? Why should we only be worried about ingratitude that is unjust? When reflecting on whether to cultivate gratitude, this limitation is clearly arbitrary and artificial. A moral agent ought to be concerned with all relevant moral reasons, not just whether gratitude is deserved, merited, or owed. If gratitude is not owed but can nonetheless cause great benefit or prevent great harm or repair communal ties, then the agent has a good moral reason to be grateful. The question of whether gratitude is owed is simply not the whole story. So if the contemporary philosophical discussion of gratitude accurately reflects common moral beliefs about when we should be grateful, then those beliefs are wrong....

V Conclusion

It is not surprising that contemporary philosophers have considered gratitude to be one of morality's side issues. By focusing on

when gratitude is owed they have focused on a practically unimportant question. Instead philosophers should ask the broader
question of when do we have good moral reasons to be grateful.
This broader question is far from a side issue. Many moral reasons
may argue for gratitude and consequently morality may ask for
our gratitude quite often. Gratitude is not a side issue, then, in the
sense that it is a common moral demand. And gratitude is not
a side issue in another sense. Gratitude, unlike duty, has an emotional component. Since morality commonly demands gratitude,
it commonly demands that we cultivate specific emotions. By
looking at gratitude we see the poverty of an approach to ethics
that focuses too heavily on action. Morality makes serious
demands about the character of our mental life. By analyzing gratitude we are reminded of the importance of the work that we must
do to shape our internal life in beneficial ways. Finally, gratitude is
not a side issue in the sense that the consequences of gratitude can
be significant. Gratitude offers a way to avoid many sources of
suffering in ourselves and in others. It offers a way to avoid psychological patterns that can harm us physically and psychologically, destroy our most important relationships, and lead to
actions that harm others. In all of these ways gratitude is at the
center of ethics, not the fringe.

Notes

* I would like to thank Lawrence Becker, Philip Bennett, Miriam Bowling, Claudia Card, David Schmitz, Kit Wellman, members of the Louisiana State University Philosophy Club, and several anonymous editors and ref-erees from *Ethics*. Their comments and concerns considerably improved the quality of this article. I am grateful to all of these individuals because of their goodwill. Given the thesis of this article, however, I would be remiss if I only mentioned those who have been beneficent to me. I would also like to thank everyone I have ever hated (they are far too numerous to list) and everyone who has ever granted me the opportunity to give. I could never have written this article without them.

1 Terrance McConnell, *Gratitude* (Philadelphia, Pa.: Temple University Press, 1993), p. 12.

2 Claudia Card, "Gratitude and Obligation," *American Philosophical Quarterly* 25 (1988): 115–27, p. 117.

3 Ibid., p. 117.

4 See Lawrence C. Becker, *Reciprocity* (New York, NY: Routledge & Kegan Paul, 1986), p. 105.

5 A.D.M. Walker, "Gratefulness and Gratitude," *Proceedings of the Aristotelian Society* (1981): 39–55, p. 48.

6 McConnell, p. 44.

7 Fred R. Berger, "Gratitude," *Ethics* 85 (1975): 298–309, p. 299.

8 Ibid., p. 299.

9 Nancy S. Jecker, "Are Filial Duties Unfounded?" *American Philosophical Quarterly* 26 (1989): 73–80, p. 74.

10 Card, p. 117.

11 A. John Simmons, *Moral Principles and Political Obligations* (Princeton, NJ: Princeton University Press, 1979), pp. 171–72. See also P.F. Strawson, "Freedom and Resentment," in *Studies in the Philosophy of Thought and Action,* ed., P.F. Strawson (Oxford: Oxford University Press, 1968), pp. 75–6.

12 McConnell, p. 44.

13 Simmons, pp. 177, 178.

14 McConnell, p. 44.

15 Nietzsche seems to suggest an analogous position. He states, "But if you have an enemy, do not requite him evil with good, for that would put him to shame. Rather prove that he did you some good" *(The Portable Nietzsche,* trans. Walter Kaufman [New York: Viking, 1968], p. 180).

16 Malcolm David Eckel, "Gratitude to an Empty Savior: A Study of the Concept of Gratitude in Mahayana Buddhist Philosophy," *History of Religions* 25 (1985): 57–75, p. 59.

17 His Holiness the Dalai Lama, *Awakening the Mind, Lightening the Heart: Core Teachings of Tibetan Buddhism,* ed., Donald S. Lopez, Jr. (San Francisco, Calif.: Harper Collins, 1995), p. 38.

18 Nichiren Daishonin, *The Major Writings of Nichiren Daishonin,* Vol. 5 (Tokyo: Nichiren Shoshu International Center, 1988), p. 8; brackets in quoted translation.

19 Ibid., p. 9.

20 Similar examples can be found in other spiritual traditions. The Sufi poet Rumi writes about a priest who prays for thieves and muggers, "because they have done me such generous favors. Every time I turn back toward the things they want I run into them. They beat me and leave me in the road, and I understand again, that what they want is not what I want. Those that make you return, for whatever reason, to the spirit, be grateful to them. Worry about the others who give you delicious comfort that keeps you from prayer" (quoted in Jack Kornfield, *A Path with Heart:*

A *Guide through the Perils and Promises of Spiritual Life* [New York: Bantam Books, 1993], p. 74). In the Christian tradition the Christian Desert Fathers use a parable that relates a similar sentiment. A student is told by his master to give money to anyone who insults him. After three years of this practice he is told to go to Alexandria and truly learn wisdom. When he gets to the gates of Alexandria he meets a wise man who insults everyone who enters. After the wise man insults the student, the student bursts out laughing. The wise man asks him why he laughs and the student says, "For years I have been paying for this kind of thing, and now you give it to me for free!" The wise man tells the student to enter the city, "It's all yours" (ibid., p. 64).

21 David Hilfiker, "Unconscious on a Corner," *Journal of the American Medical Association* 258 (1987): 3155–6, p. 3156.

22 Jack Kornfield, *Roots of Buddhist Psychology,* quoted in Frederic Brussat and Mary Ann Brussat, *Spiritual Literacy: Reading the Sacred in Everyday Life* (New York: Scribner's, 1996), p. 327.

23 Ram Dass and Paul Gorman, *How Can I Help? Stories and Reflections on Service* (New York: Knopf, 1985), p. 7.

24 Nichiren, p. 8.

25 Dalai Lama, p. 17.

26 Ibid., p. 108.

27 Ibid.

28 Immanuel Kant, *Metaphysical Principles of Virtue,* in *Ethical Philosophy,* trans. James W. Ellington (Indianapolis, Ind.: Hackett, 1983), pp. 112–13.

29 Card, p. 117.

30 Kant, p. 118.

31 For a discussion of gratitude in Kant's writings, see Jean P. Rumsey, "Re-Visions of Agency in Kant's Moral Theory," in *Feminist Interpretations of Immanuel Kant,* ed., Robin May Schott (University Park, Pa.: Pennsylvania State University Press, 1997), pp. 125–44.

32 Card, p. 117.

33 It is questionable, however, that these cases are morally irrelevant. The case of being grateful for good weather may be entirely appropriate for a deep ecologist who excludes nothing from the moral sphere. Others may think that developing gratitude to things or processes is a virtuous character trait that holds in check a tendency to exploit the environment.

34 Jecker, p. 73; McConnell, p. 13.

3 Humility

Nancy E. Snow

Despite the resurgence of interest in the virtues, humility remains neglected by contemporary philosophers. Yet several insights are to be gained from thinking about humility. Humility is a complex virtue with more than one variety. Analyzing humility shows its role in the moral psychology of agents, why it is worth having, and how it relates to other virtues. In section one, I examine a sample of statements that attest to the diversity of situations in which we experience humility. In section two, I develop two alternative senses of humility that emerge from the discussion. The aim of section three is to argue towards a unifying conception of humility broad enough to apply to both senses. In section four, I answer the question, "Why be humble?"

I Explaining our experiences of humility and being humbled

Conceptions of humility should explain our experiences of being humbled, and analyses of these experiences should inform our conceptions of humility. Ordinary language attests to a variety of contexts in which the concepts of humility and being humbled are meaningfully and appropriately used in speaking about personal behavior or experiences. Consider this sample of statements:

(1) Though she is successful as a cellist, she is humble about it.
(2) Linus wants to be a humble little country doctor.
(3) Hercule Poirot is not humble about his talents as a detective.
(4) I humbly ask your forgiveness.

(5) Being upset in the match was a humbling experience for the tennis player.

(6) Einstein was humbled by the scientific complexity of the universe.

(7) I was humbled before the grandeur of the Rockies.

I assume that we make sense when we use these and similar statements, and that an adequate account of humility should be able to give convincing explanations of the meanings of "humility" and "being humbled" in several of these contexts.

In a recent book on humility, Norvin Richards argues that humility is "an inclination to keep one's accomplishments, traits, and so on in unexaggerated perspective, even if stimulated to exaggerate."[1] He claims that humility is not exaggerating your importance.[2] He refers to it as a form of self-understanding that consists in keeping yourself and your accomplishments in perspective and results in a disinclination to exaggerate.[3]

Richards' conception seems able to explain what we mean by humility in examples 1–3. Perhaps what we mean when we say that the cellist is humble about her success is that she doesn't exaggerate her prowess, that she keeps a level head about her accomplishments. Maybe Linus wants to be a humble little country doctor because he does not overestimate his abilities and realizes that a lowly station in life suits him. And, as Agatha Christie fans know, Poirot is the opposite of Linus and the cellist. He is right about his value as a sleuth but is immodest. He claims, for example, that he is the greatest detective in the world. His attitude lacks humility.

A Poirot episode reveals a point that clarifies the internal, cognitive dimensions of humility. In *The A.B.C. Murders*, the detective is baffled.[4] He resorts to an unorthodox step: turning to friends and relatives of the victims for help in solving the case. Here Poirot is humbled by his inability to solve the case without aid. His humility in accepting help consists not just in resisting the tendency to exaggerate his value, but is occasioned by, and is a manifestation of, the awareness of his limits.

Identifying the knowledge of deficiency or limits as the key cognitive element of humility enables us to explain more fully why

Linus wants to be a humble little country doctor and no more. He doesn't exaggerate, and this is a part of humility, but perhaps he doesn't exaggerate because he knows his limits. The same might be said of the cellist. The knowledge of deficiency curbs the tendency to exaggerate and rightly motivates humility.

Consider example 4. Sometimes we need to ask forgiveness because we have exaggerated our merits and erred as a consequence, or because we lack the self-knowledge that could prevent us from exaggerating. But on many occasions, overestimation of merits or lack of self-knowledge are not the causes of error.

An analysis truer to the facts of our experience partially parallels that given of Poirot's humbling experience in *The A.B.C. Murders*. Before Poirot could accept help, he had to admit deficiency. Similarly, to humbly and sincerely ask forgiveness requires that we admit having erred, which often involves acknowledging deeper personal failings. Frequently, these faults have nothing to do with the tendency to overestimate merits. I might have innocently forgotten my spouse's birthday, for example, and so failed to give him or her a gift. This kind of failing is not necessarily due to my overestimating my value relative to my spouse's. If his or her feelings are hurt, I should ask forgiveness, even if I initially regard the oversight as negligible. But before I can sincerely ask forgiveness I must own up to my error and be sorry for it, which can require swallowing some pride. Central to the role of humility is the acknowledgement of error or personal deficiency and its negative impact on others. Humility in this and similar contexts is not essentially connected with resisting the tendency to overestimate merits or with having the self-knowledge to prevent this.

In examples 5 and 6 we could say that being defeated in the match or encountering the scientific complexities of the universe show the player and Einstein that they have wrongly exaggerated their abilities, and thus, that they lacked the self-knowledge that could have prevented overestimation. They are humbled by being made aware of the error of their exaggeration and of the flawed self-estimate on which it was based. In example 7 it is conceivable that experiencing the grandeur of the Rockies might make someone aware that he or she has wrongly overestimated merits because of faulty self-understanding, but more explanation is needed of how and why a person would arrive at this awareness by visiting the Rockies.

Further explanation is available. In each case the person is made aware of the error of overestimating abilities by being confronted with previously overlooked limits. The confrontation with limitations, whether through defeat in the match, inability to fully comprehend scientific complexities, or exposure to the greatness of nature in comparison with which self and personal concerns appear small, is humbling. The awareness of having wrongly exaggerated your merits is a consequence of the encounter.

People can have humbling experiences even though they don't exaggerate their merits and know enough not to. We can be humbled without being guilty of this error of self-appraisal. Even those who do not exaggerate, thanks to sound self-knowledge, are capable of having experiences, which remind them of deficiencies of which they're already aware or which acquaint them with hitherto unnoticed flaws. The humbling experience in these cases is occasioned by the knowledge of deficiency.

Consider example 5. Even tennis players who do not overestimate their merits are susceptible to defeat by better players. Meeting their match highlights respects in which they are inferior by comparison with their opponent. The confrontation with deficiencies in the pursuit of desired goals occasions humility.

Regarding example 6, we might say that Einstein's inability to fully master the scientific complexities of the universe makes him aware of his intellectual limits. Because he is made aware that his limitations frustrate his pursuit of a desired goal, his failure to achieve scientific comprehension is a humbling experience. The analysis thus far parallels that given of Poirot and partially parallels the tennis player's defeat at the hands of an opponent. However, the tennis player's knowledge of deficiency is gained by comparing and contrasting her abilities with the superior merits of another player. This differs from Einstein and Poirot, who become aware of their limits not by comparing and contrasting themselves with someone more successful in their field, but by their inability to do something they value. Both are stumped. Common to all three cases is the experience of defeat or frustration in pursuing valued goals, which highlights the knowledge of deficiency and thereby occasions humility.

Reading Einstein's memoirs and letters suggests a different interpretation of example 6, for you get the sense of a person who, in encountering the mysteries of the universe, confronts more than his intellectual limitations.[5] In admitting his intellectual limits, he acknowledges the finitude of the human condition. He has an inkling of a larger, more complex reality in contrast with which the limitations of human beings become all too apparent. The confrontation with his human finitude, brought about by an awareness of a more complex reality, is a humbling experience. He says:

everyone who is seriously involved in the pursuit of science becomes convinced that a spirit is manifest in the laws of the Universe—a spirit vastly superior to that of man, and one in the face of which we with our modest powers must feel humble.[6]

The contrast between the smallness of human powers and the greatness of the spirit at work in the universe brings home the limitations of the human condition, thereby occasioning humility.

Example 7 can be understood along similar lines. Here personal failings are not accented by defeat or frustration in pursuing desired goals. Humility is occasioned by a recognition of the insignificance of your concerns, and perhaps also of the limits of the human condition in general, which is brought about by contrasting your smallness with the majesty of the Rockies.[7]

II Two senses of humility

Two distinct senses of humility emerge from this discussion. The first sense, involved in the explanation of examples 1–5 and the first interpretation of number 6, can be called "narrow humility," since it is humility about specific personal traits perceived as deficiencies. The second sense, used in the second interpretation of examples 6 and 7, can be called "existential humility," since it goes beyond humility about specific personal characteristics to include an aspect of the human condition in general, human finitude.

Narrow humility is occasioned by an acknowledgment of personal weaknesses. This acknowledgement can be prompted by an experience that highlights personal failings, such as defeat, frustration, or error. It is a way in which we're brought low and forced to swallow our pride. However, no necessary connection exists between becoming aware of our defects and being humbled. We might be made aware of our deficiencies yet not care, regard them as trivial, persistently ignore them, or even deny that the traits in question are defects. To be humbled, we must acknowledge and care about our flaws. We must take them seriously and, whether mildly or deeply, be disturbed by having them. Thus, being humbled consists of a cognitive and an affective component. To be humbled in the narrow sense is to be appropriately pained by, or to feel sorrow or dejection because of, the awareness of personal deficiencies.[8]

Being humbled in the narrow sense is often painful because our defects can be so personal. To be humbled is to be made aware or reminded of respects in which I, as a person, have failed or am inadequate. Narrow humility is compatible with a variety of attitudes toward our flaws. We can be humbled by a failing, deeply regret it, wish we didn't have it, and do everything possible to be rid of it. Or we can regret yet accept the flaw, and do the best we can to control it and minimize its negative effects.

Proper humility requires that our affective reaction be appropriately commensurate with the seriousness of the failing. Just as not being deeply humbled by the awareness of a serious deficiency would be a failure of proper humility, so too would being overly humbled by a minor flaw. In a different way in each case, the failure of humility can be traced to a flawed sense of self-worth.

Not being properly humbled by the knowledge of a serious failing betrays inflated self-worth. The attitude shown by hotel magnate Leona Helmsley's remark that "only the little people pay taxes," and displayed in her persistent evasion of tax payments is a case in point. She evidently thought herself above paying taxes, regarded taxes as a burden to be shouldered by others, and was not disturbed by the fact that, by not paying her fair share, she was unfairly shunting tax costs onto others. However else it can be characterized, her attitude lacked humility.

Being overly humbled by minor deficiencies also reveals a faulty sense of self-worth, though of a different kind: a deep-seated sense of personal inadequacy and insecurity that causes you to magnify even trivial errors. This insecurity is compatible with neurotic self-absorption or obsession with yourself, especially with failings.

A different analysis can be given of existential humility.[9] As the Einstein example shows, existential humility can be occasioned by narrow humility. An awareness of limitations prompted by an experience of personal failure or inability can give rise to more extensive reflections about the nature of the human condition. Human limitations in general are then thrown into relief by contrast with a more complex and valuable reality that in some way extends beyond limitations imposed by the human situation. The awareness of human limitations in general, not just the knowledge of specific personal flaws, is humbling. Example 7 shows that an experience of failure, defeat, or frustration is not a necessary prerequisite for either narrow or existential humility. In that case, humility is not occasioned by the awareness of a personal defect emphasized by an experience of failure or frustration. Instead, your personhood, and humanity in general, appear small before the greatness of nature.

As with narrow humility, being humbled in the existential sense has an affective as well as a cognitive dimension. To be humbled in the existential sense is to be made aware of the limitations of the human condition. This can be painful if the reflections that lead to this awareness are prompted by a recognition of personal inadequacies. But existential humility can assuage the negative emotions that often accompany the knowledge of personal flaws by reminding us that limitations are part and parcel of the human condition, not the exclusive bane of individuals.

Affectivity can enter into being humbled in the existential sense in other ways. The general cognizance of human limitations gained by encountering a larger, more complex reality can evoke emotions other than solace, such as awe, pride, admiration, or even despair. You might be soothed by knowing that your flaws are not unique, but part of a common humanity. But you might also feel (1) awe before the complexity of the universe or the grandeur of nature, (2) pride or admiration before a complex work of art that, despite human limitations, is nonetheless a human achievement, or (3) despair at the insignificance of your endeavors or of human strivings in general. All of these reactions are compatible with being humbled in the existential sense. A feature common to such humbling experiences is an appreciation of the value of the reality that extends beyond your circumstances or transcends limitations imposed by the human condition. Even despair at human insignificance—an extreme reaction—can be coupled with this appreciation.

Differences in the ontological status of the reality extending beyond the self raise questions for my analysis of existential humility. In experiencing the complexities of the universe or the grandeur of nature, we encounter realities extending beyond the self that are not human products. Even our knowledge of these things is limited by our human abilities. We can readily understand how encountering these realities would underscore our human limitations. But what about an encounter with great music or art, which do not transcend human reality in the same way as nature?

Both pride and humility before human achievements can be explained as follows. Great music and art are the products of human efforts, so our sense of common humanity allows us rightly to take pride in them. Yet we recognize qualities in them that partially transcend the limitations of the human condition by significantly rising above the level of effort or achievement that we ordinarily see in our daily affairs. The greatness of the achievement in comparison with the smallness of more ordinary efforts can call to mind the limitations of the human condition and thereby occasion existential humility.

Proper existential humility requires that your affective reaction to the cognizance of human limitations occasioned by encountering some valuable reality extending beyond the self be appropriately commensurate with the seriousness of that knowledge. Consequently, we can think of someone either underreacting or overreacting, and thus, not being sufficiently humbled or being overly humbled in the existential sense. Consistently failing to be humbled by contacts with some valuable reality extending beyond the self is prima facie evidence of a failure to appropriately value things that have value independently of their relation to yourself or to the group with which you identify.[10] To be underly humbled is prima facie evidence of a narrow absorption that is not necessarily a neurotic or obsessive preoccupation with self, but is sufficient to blind you to other values. Consider, for example, the business executive who, vacationing in the Rockies, remains preoccupied with work and oblivious to their beauty, or the undergraduate who contemptuously dismisses the value of philosophy or literature because these studies do not advance immediate career pursuits. These attitudes can plausibly result from an overly narrow, self-absorbed perspective that allows for giving yourself and your concerns too much value in the grand scheme of things. To think too much of yourself and too little of values extending beyond the self is to lack proper humility.

Not every failure to appropriately appreciate a valuable reality extending beyond the self is a failure of humility. Some failures of appropriate valuation are due to insensitivity, lack of knowledge, or narrow-mindedness. This can be true even of consistent failures of appreciation and does not undermine the point that some of these failures also manifest a lack of proper humility. If an insensitive or ignorant individual is adequately apprised of the value and complexity of nature, science, or great art, yet persists in not appropriately appreciating their significance, this is prima facie evidence for the belief that his or her lack of proper valuation is due to a lack of proper humility, that is, to an undervaluation of that which extends beyond the self, and an overvaluation of self and personal concerns by comparison.

Another less common kind of failure of proper existential humility is being overly humbled. This is due not so much to the overvaluation of things of value extending beyond the self, as to the undervaluation of yourself and, in extreme cases, of humanity in general.

III Toward a unifying conception of humility

Both senses of humility explain different experiences of being humbled, but can they explain the character of a humble person? Existential humility is able to do this. A person who is humbled by a grasp of the limitations of the human condition would likely see himself or herself as limited by his or her humanity. A humble person would be cognizant of human finitude.

What about narrow humility? Being humble about traits is not necessarily to be a humble person, since we easily overlook our failings and compartmentalize disparate aspects of our lives. In the same person, humility about flaws can easily coexist with arrogance about merits. But arrogance about merits disqualifies you from being considered a humble person.

A proponent of narrow humility could respond that no one's abilities are unlimited. Only the most unreflective among us are unaware of respects in which their talents are circumscribed. Even an undefeated tennis player should have sufficient knowledge of his or her game to know that some plays are just lucky or due more to an opponent's weaknesses than to his or her strengths. Consequently, narrow humility, too, can explain the character of a humble person. A humble person is aware of and takes seriously deficiencies, even in areas of strength. On this view, we all have sufficient reason to be humble.

Someone who has an experience of being humbled in either the narrow or the existential sense will not necessarily become a humble person. To be a humble person is to recognize your limitations, to take them seriously, and thereby to foster a realism in attitudes and behavior regarding self and others. Humility can be defined as the disposition to allow the awareness of and concern about your limitations to have a realistic influence on your attitudes and behavior. At the heart of this realism is a perspective gained through accurate appraisal of your limitations and their implications for your circumstances, attitudes, and behavior.

This realism has many manifestations.[11] Sometimes it results in a lowering of self-estimate. For example, humility counters the tendency to exaggerate merits and other symptoms of improper pride by fostering the attitude that we are limited. Insofar as all human beings are imperfect, we are no better than they. Humility can also force us to realize that others are better than we in some respects, and thereby enable us to give due recognition to their talents and abilities, as well as to ask their help when we need it. Sometimes real-

istically appraising our flaws facilitates our ability to compassionately or sympathetically identify with others' foibles, and forgive
them when appropriate. The realism fostered by humility helps us
know when we have wronged others and should ask forgiveness.

IV Why be humble?

The question "Why be humble?" can be broken down into two
further questions. Should we be humble because humility is intrinsically valuable, or because of the desirable effects of humility? The
answer is, "Both."

The argument for the intrinsic value of humility starts from the
premise that we generally value knowledge apart from its effects:
knowledge is an intrinsic good. Self-knowledge is also generally
regarded as intrinsically good, something to be valued apart from
its effects. This attitude is reflected in the view that you are better
off knowing the truth about yourself than not, even though the
knowledge is painful. But knowledge of limitations is proper to
humility. Consequently, humility is a form of self-knowledge and
thereby is intrinsically valuable.

This argument can be bolstered with an argument by analogy.
We generally regard self-respect, proper pride, justified self-
esteem, and warranted self-confidence as intrinsically valuable.
This is because all are forms of knowing and valuing the self that
we think it good to have, even if we never get the chance to benefit
from the consequences of having them. We should value humility,
knowing and being concerned about limitations, as another analogous, and analogously valuable, form of self-knowledge and self-
concern, even though we might never benefit from the results of
our humble disposition or actions.

We can also argue for humility on grounds of its beneficial
effects. They include fostering desirable traits, such as compassion,
the propensity to be forgiving, and the ability to ask forgiveness
when appropriate, and checking vices, including improper pride,
boastfulness, vanity, arrogance, and conceit. Insofar as humility
facilitates the development of other virtuous dispositions and
curbs the development of vices, it is a trait worth having.

Some philosophers, such as Spinoza, Hume, and Nietzsche, consider humility a negative, debilitating trait that contributes to the disempowerment of the agent.[12] We might think that humility and humbling experiences could have negative effects on an agent's self-conception and dispositions. Amélie O. Rorty argues that virtues and traits can oppose one another by being exercised in actions whose outcomes frustrate or undermine one another's intention, direction, or satisfaction, as well as by inhibiting one another's development.[13] Both humbling experiences and the exercise of humility in actions might be thought to undermine or frustrate the exercise in actions of positive traits, such as self-respect, self-confidence, proper pride, self-esteem, and autonomy, as well as inhibit their development, and in so doing, have pervasively negative effects on an agent's self-conception and capabilities for effective action.

We can identify four distinct cases: (1) the effects of humbling experiences on the exercise in actions of positive traits other than humility; (2) the effects of humbling experiences on the development of positive traits other than humility; (3) the effects of the exercise of humility in actions on the exercise in actions of other positive traits; and (4) the effects of the exercise of humility in actions on the development of other positive traits.

We can readily see how (1) humbling experiences might deter the exercise in actions of self-respect, self-confidence, self-esteem, and so on, and (2) impede the development of these positive traits. Humbling experiences can be discouraging. They are frequently occasions on which we fall short of our goals and the expectations that we base on our self-conceptions. They can make us skeptical of our talents and abilities and afraid to exercise autonomy for fear of failing again. Repeated failures and discouragement can undermine self-confidence and self-esteem, and, under some social conditions, say, of oppression, can threaten self-respect, which is fundamental to a positive self-conception and personal well-being.[14]

Cases 3 and 4 might seem more benign, since the exercise of humility in actions is usually not fraught with failure or discouragement, and, provided that standard conditions are met, is an exercise of autonomy. However, exercising humility could be thought to frustrate the exercise of self-respect, self-confidence, and so on, and hinder their development by reinforcing a conception of self as limited, as unable to successfully perform or pursue ends. To exercise humility is continually to remind yourself that you are limited, and consequently, that you should not expect too much. Interpreted as such, exercising humility is disempowering, insofar as it places a self-imposed psychological curb on the desires and ambitions of the agent. By contrast, self-respect, self-confidence, self-esteem, and actions exercising autonomy do not reflect negative self-conceptions and empower the agent by sending positive, supportive messages about the agent's abilities and ambitions.

Consider cases 1 and 3. In a personality in which the development of positive traits is not in question, the discouraging effects of humbling experiences and the subtler messages about self and expectations conveyed through exercising humility in actions do not necessarily or permanently erode self-respect, self-confidence, self-esteem, or psychological support for the agent's ambitions. This is because in the psychology of the agent self-respect and the other positive traits are already firm, well-developed parts of the agent's psychological make-up. This is not to deny that in a fully formed, well-balanced personality humbling experiences can be discouraging. But discouragement is less likely to be debilitating in personalities in which other positive traits are fully formed and firmly entrenched than in personalities in which such traits are more tenuous.

This is due to the ability of other positive traits to keep reasonably in check the negative and potentially damaging psychological effects of humbling experiences, as well as the effects of the possible reinforcement through actions of a conception of self as limited.[15] Positive traits can do this by supplying a sense of merits and strengths that logically and psychologically counterbalances the awareness of and concern about deficiencies. Positive traits provide a context of self-understanding and self-assessment within which flaws appear to be neither less nor more serious than they actually are. The counterbalances furnished by these traits can check the effects of humbling experiences and of the exercise of excessive humility and thereby can prevent humility from degenerating into self-deprecation or self-contempt. Both of these negative attitudes often involve affective overreactions to flaws, as well as false beliefs about their seriousness.

Harder cases include those such as 2 and 4, in which humbling experiences and the exercise of humility in actions affect the development of positive traits in personalities not yet fully formed or in need of greater balance or adjustment. Here the danger is greater that their development will be obstructed by the discouraging effects of humbling experiences and the possible reinforcement through actions of a conception of self as limited. Especially in children, a good deal of encouragement from sources outside the agent—parents, other family members, teachers—is needed to offset the potentially negative effects of humbling experiences and the exercise of humility in actions.

Conditions of oppression, too, present problems for my account of humility, because moral exhortations, including calls to humility, can be used by oppressors to inculcate false consciousness, disesteem, and lack of self-respect and ambition in members of the oppressed group. The oppressed must be wary of any advice from oppressors, and of any putatively moral claim that permits oppression. However, we cannot argue from the fact that exhortations to humility may be tools of oppression to the conclusion that the oppressed should shun humility, just as we cannot argue from the fact that more general admonitions to moral behavior may be similarly misused to the conclusion that the oppressed should eschew morality in general. The intrinsic value of humility gives oppressed people reason to be humble, just as the intrinsic value of morality gives them reason to be moral in general. These reasons are independent of any advantages that the manipulation of humility or morality might afford oppressors, or disadvantages that it might cause for the oppressed. However, the efforts of oppressed people to benefit from the effects of humbling experiences and humility are made harder by hostile social conditions. Accordingly, greater value accrues to the role of other positive traits and encouragement from sympathetic external sources in keeping reasonably in check the potentially negative psychological effects of humbling experiences and of the exercise of humility in actions.

A more positive side to all of this deserves mention. For those whose personalities are fully formed and well-balanced, for those whose personality formation is incomplete or needs adjusting, and even for those who are oppressed, humbling experiences and the exercise of humility in actions are parts of the educative process of personal growth, maturation, and ongoing development. We learn our limits through humbling experiences. Despite the discouragement that these occasions sometimes bring, humbling experiences contribute valuable information to our stock of self-knowledge. After failing and being humbled, we know better. The next time we act, we know enough to succeed, or to avoid failure. Success builds self-respect, self-confidence, self-esteem, proper pride, and autonomy. Thus, in a commonplace way that contributes to personal growth and development, the self-knowledge supplied by humbling experiences is empowering and supports the formation of other positive traits. This can be especially valuable in overcoming oppression.

Exercising humility in actions can have similarly positive, empowering effects. Exercising humility need not reinforce a conception of self as limited, and even when it does, this does not necessarily curb personal ambition. Consider a student who is advised to become a paralegal instead of pursuing a career in law. If, based on accurate self-knowledge, the student declines the advice and opts for a career in law, he or she would display humility by not being offended by the advice, taking it in the spirit in which it was intended, and not showing wounded pride or vanity. None of these reactions necessarily reinforce a conception of self as limited, yet all display proper humility. On the other hand, suppose the student rightly decides to follow the advice and to become a paralegal, thereby acknowledging deficiencies that would have prevented him or her from achieving a career as a lawyer. This would be to exercise humility, provided the student has the proper attitude. Exercising humility here would be a strategy to attain success despite the acknowledgement of limits. Exercising humility in actions in this sense builds self-respect, self-confidence, self-esteem, increased autonomy, and so on, as do successes achieved in these circumstances. Consequently, the exercise of humility in actions, when viewed as a strategy for success despite the awareness of limitations, is empowering and supports the development of other positive traits. For this and the other reasons mentioned, humility ought to be regarded as a virtue worth having.

Notes

1 Norvin Richards, *Humility* (Philadelphia: Temple University Press, 1992), p. 8.
2 Ibid., pp. 41–3; 102–3.
3 Ibid., p. 188.
4 See Agatha Christie, *The A.B.C. Murders* (New York: Dodd, Mead, and Co., 1962), pp. 117–19; 122–4.
5 See *Albert Einstein: The Human Side: New Glimpses from His Archives,* selected and ed. Helen Dukas and Banesh Hoffman (Princeton: Princeton University Press, 1979), p. 33; and Einstein, *The World as I See It,* trans. Alan Harris (New York: Philosophical Library, 1949), pp. 28–9.
6 Dukas and Hoffman, *Albert Einstein: The Human Side,* p. 33.
7 See Thomas E. Hill, Jr., "Ideals of Human Excellence and Preserving Natural Environments," in *Autonomy and Self-Respect* (Cambridge, England: Cambridge University Press, 1991), p. 112.
8 See Thomas Aquinas, *Summa Theologica* II–II, trans. the Fathers of the English Dominican Province (New York: Benziger Brothers, 1947), Q. 161, "Of Humility"; Bernard of Clairvaux, *The Steps of Humility,* trans. with introduction and notes by George Bosworth Burch (Cambridge, Mass.: Harvard University Press, 1950); Baruch Spinoza, *The Ethics and Selected Letters,* trans. Samuel Shirley, ed. and introduced by Seymour Feldman (Indianapolis, Ind.: Hackett, 1982), pp. 184–5; and David Hume, *A Treatise of Human Nature,* 2nd edn with text revised and notes by P.H. Nidditch (Oxford: Clarendon Press, 1978), p. 277.
9 This analysis fits many conceptions of humility, both theistic and non-theistic. See Aquinas, *Summa Theologica* II–II, Q. 161; Bernard of Clairvaux, *The Steps of Humility;* Immanuel Kant, *The Doctrine of Virtue: Part II of The Metaphysics of Morals,* trans. Mary J. Gregor (Philadelphia: University of Pennsylvania Press, 1964), pp. 100, 101; Spinoza, *Ethics,* pp. 184–5; Iris Murdoch, *The Sovereignty of Good* (London: Ark Paperbacks, 1985), pp. 89–90, 95, 103–4; Thomas Nagel, *The View from Nowhere* (Oxford: Oxford University Press, 1986), pp. 222–3; and Hill, "Ideals," pp. 112–13.

10 See Hill, "Ideals," p. 112.

11 See Richards, *Humility,* chs 3 and 4.

12 See Hume, *Treatise,* pp. 277; 598–9; also Annette C. Baier, *A Progress of Sentiments: Reflections on Hume's Treatise* (Cambridge, Mass.: Harvard University Press, 1991), pp. 206–7; Friedrich Nietzsche, *Beyond Good and Evil: Prelude to a Philosophy of the Future,* trans. by Walter Kaufmann (New York: Vintage Books, 1966), pp. 204–5; and Spinoza, *Ethics,* p. 185.

13 See Amélie O. Rorty, "Virtues and Their Vicissitudes," *Midwest Studies in Philosophy,* 13 (Notre Dame, Ind.: University of Notre Dame Press, 1988), p. 143.

14 See John Rawls, *A Theory of Justice* (Cambridge, Mass.: Harvard University Press, 1971), p. 440, on self-respect as a primary good.

15 Here I presuppose a check and balance conception of the virtues. See Rorty, "Virtues," pp. 142–3.

4 The Practice of Pride

Tara Smith

I Introduction

Pride has been denounced as one of the seven deadly sins and praised as the crown of the virtues.[1] Perhaps because of the difficulty of navigating between these appraisals, pride has not been paid very much attention by ethicists. Moreover, pride is so familiar as a feeling that the suggestion that it could be a virtue may seem misplaced.

Considering the prevalent conception of a virtue as, at least in part, a disposition to act in a certain way has led me to wonder about what the correlative actions of the virtue of pride might be.[2] Investigating the *practice* of pride can help us to appreciate pride's significant moral value.

Pride has not only been underappreciated, but often maligned. Admonitions to swallow one's pride and the folk wisdom that "foolish pride" is an obstacle to be overcome are far more famil-iar than praise or encouragement of pride. The evangelist Billy Graham has implored people to "smash pride, step on it, crush it, mash it, break it...."[3] At best, pride tends to win occasional, grudging acceptance as an afterthought; limited doses will be tol-erated as long as they are kept in check. Humility, seen as pride's antithesis, enjoys a far warmer welcome among mainstream attitudes.

It has not always been so. Aristotle unapologetically applauded pride, and the ancient Greeks more generally did not treat humility as a virtue.[4] Religious doctrine, however, has offered a stream of hostility towards pride. "Pride goes before destruction," we read in the Book of Proverbs. In the New Testament, we are warned that "whoever exalts himself will be humbled, but he who humbles himself will be exalted." Augustine scorned pride as "an appetite for inordinate exaltation" and "the beginning of all sin," the source of Adam and Eve's fall. Aquinas extolled humility, which "expels pride." The shared theme is that humility reflects recognition of God as the source of all the goodness that we experience. Pride reflects a misplaced assumption of responsibility for what is actually the beneficence of God.[5]

Obviously, a definitive defense of any specific virtue stands on substantial premises concerning the foundations of all moral evaluations. That is far beyond the scope of a single essay. Still, I should briefly indicate my pivotal assumptions.

Essentially, I am working from the thesis that morality is teleological in that it is aimed at the goal of individual human flourishing. By "flourishing" I mean, roughly, the happy, healthy condition of leading and experiencing one's life as well as possible. Flourishing is living well in the twin senses of acting as one should and enjoying the results of such action. (I shall refer to "flourishing," "happiness," and "well-being" interchangeably.)[6] All the virtues are grounded in their contribution to that aim, and they are distinguished by the particular types of decisions for which they provide guidance. Justice, for instance, governs questions of how to judge and treat other people; honesty concerns one's portrayal of beliefs both to others and oneself. Virtuous action does not guarantee one's flourishing, since that may be affected by other things beyond one's control, but virtuous action *is* the course prerequisite for flourishing. The authenticity of any proposed virtue depends wholly on its relationship to that end. I am also assuming that what furthers and what hinders an individual's flourishing is a matter of objective fact. While there may be considerable variety in the particular activities and goods that serve different people's happiness, at a broader level we can identify types of actions, reflected in principles and virtues, that will tend to promote anyone's happiness. Mine is thus a realist, practical, and egoistic conception of morality. Without launching a direct defense of this entire framework, I should be able to indicate why a renewed appreciation of pride would be salutary.

My aim is to defend pride on the grounds of its practical value. Since much hostility toward pride is rooted in misconceptions, correcting these should go a long way to defrosting its usually chilly reception. Thus, challenging entrenched attitudes will occupy a considerable portion of the essay. In particular, though, explaining how pride functions as a *virtue*, a disposition to certain sorts of action, should reveal its beneficial effects. Recovering the idea of the practice of pride will indicate its distinct value.

The discussion will proceed in three stages. First, I shall clarify what pride consists of; second, I shall identify the payoffs of pride; finally, I shall briefly speculate on possible sources of hostility towards pride.[7]

II What pride is and is not

A survey of historical treatments reveals that evaluations of pride are more readily available than statements of exactly what pride is. Nonetheless, a few authors have offered descriptions.

Aristotle held that "the man is thought to be proud who thinks himself worthy of great things, being worthy of them." "The truly proud man must be good"—indeed, he must be good in the highest degree. While this account centers on the proud man's warranted high self-regard, Aristotle also attributes comparatively superficial traits, such as a slow step and a deep voice, to the proud man.[8]

David Hume devoted extensive discussion to pride in Book Two of his *Treatise of Human Nature*. After announcing that it is impossible to give an adequate definition of pride, Hume proceeds to provide an astute analysis of the *feeling* of pride, culminating in the claim that pride is "that agreeable impression, which arises in the mind, when the view either of our virtue, beauty, riches or power makes us satisfied with ourselves." In proceeding to this conclusion, Hume identifies several salient features of this feeling (e.g., that it is pleasurable, yet distinct from joy). Hume contends that "a due degree of pride, which makes us sensible of our own merit," can be useful, affording "confidence and assurance."[9]

Hume's friend Adam Smith, on the other hand, presents a more negative assessment. Though Smith distinguished pride from vanity, he still saw pride as typically reflecting an inflated opinion of one's own merits, and in some respects portrays it as worse than vanity.[10] Baruch Spinoza, earlier, had similarly viewed pride as based on a distorted self-image. "Pride should be defined as the pleasure arising from false belief, in that a man thinks himself above others," Spinoza wrote. "Pride is the pleasure arising from a man's thinking too highly of himself." Consequently, "the proud man loves the company of parasites or flatterers, and hates the company of those of noble spirit."[11]

If we discard the unwarranted assumption that a high opinion of oneself is necessarily unjustified, we can describe the feeling of pride largely as Hume did. Pride is a kind of attitude concerning the self. To be proud is to be pleased with oneself in some respect. Pride differs from joy in that the sources of pride are things for which the proud person is responsible or to which she bears some especially close association. One can be proud of one's accomplishment or victory, for instance, or of one's child or teammate. This possessive element is important; you can only take pride in what is, in some sense, yours.[12]

Generically, pride seems a positive self-evaluation, based on the belief that the source of this evaluation is itself worthwhile. Yet ordinary images of pride often convey more than self-approval. Consider a few examples.

The celebrated refusal of Rosa Parks, a black woman living in the Jim Crow South, to obey a driver's orders to move to the back of the bus reflected pride insofar as she would not allow other people's views of her status to determine her own evaluation of it. Nor would she conform to the conduct that the views of others dictated. In the play and film *The Great White Hope* (based on a true story),[13] the hero's pride shines through his refusal to throw a boxing match in order to extricate himself from legal and financial crisis. A victim of an unjust law, Jack Jefferson had been thrust into an increasingly desperate position. Having adopted definite standards of how the game should be played, however, Jefferson was too dedicated to those standards to fold.

One needn't look to history or drama to find pride in action. The student who sets high standards for the quality of work she will turn in, struggling to maintain those standards rather than settling for the quickest route to an acceptable grade, is often driven by pride. Similarly, the athlete who does not relax his efforts when trailing in an obviously losing cause is often propelled by pride in his performance. The poor person who will not beg for charity but instead seeks work may be exhibiting pride insofar as he is upholding a conviction about the propriety of earning what one receives. He will not betray that conviction for other apparent gains.

Bearing such cases in mind, we can narrow in on a more accurate conception of the virtue, as opposed to the feeling, of pride.

Richard Taylor has embraced an essentially Aristotelian portrait; Taylor characterizes pride as "justified love for oneself," a summation of the other virtues. The proud person is not arrogant or overbearing, since pride is not a matter of appearances or manner. It reflects a more deeply rooted personal excellence. The proud person is his own in the truest sense, by winning his own approbation. *Self*-evaluation is what counts. The good opinion that a proud person seeks is his own.[14]

The most revealing account that I know of for understanding pride as a virtue is from Ayn Rand. Rand characterizes pride as moral ambitiousness.[15] To be proud is to set high moral standards and to strive to become ever-better in attaining them—i.e., more alert to all of their demands and more consistent in fulfilling them.

Rand's reasoning is straightforward. In skeletal form: living requires a person's belief in his own value. A fundamental conviction of one's worth is essential to one's acting in ways that will achieve one's happiness. The only means of sustaining that belief is through one's ongoing, practiced commitment to proper standards. This is what moral ambitiousness demands.

The striking advance of this account over traditional images of pride is in its forward direction, its attention to the future.[16] Pride is not simply a backward gaze or savoring of past glories; it is not merely a feeling of satisfaction with one's accomplishments, justified as such feelings may be. As a virtue, pride must include an inclination to act in a particular way. Rand captures the nature of that action: the energetic, ambitious application of one's moral code.

Since moral ambition might arise from less than ideal motives (e.g., guilt, compulsion, a thirst to impress other people), perhaps we should add that this policy must be adopted for morally proper ends. Moreover, the virtue of pride requires that the code being practiced itself be morally correct. The proud racist or sexist may experience the *feeling* of pride thanks to his ambitious allegiance to his warped beliefs, but he does not thereby manifest the virtue of pride. It is important to recognize that the obstacle to praising such people is not their pride, but their first-order values. While the feeling of being pleased with oneself may arise for all sorts of reasons, admirable and not so admirable, the virtue of pride occurs only as an outgrowth of authentically moral practice. The feeling of pride must be harnessed to morally right belief and action in order to reflect the virtue of pride.[17]

This is also why I think that a person cannot be proud of her humility. If humility is the opposite of pride, then pride in one's humility would amount to pride in a vice. While that feeling might arise, it would not be virtuous. If humility were a virtue, it would instruct a person to root out any stirrings of pride. Thus, to the extent that a person was proud, he would not be humble. The two traits cannot peacefully coexist *as virtues*.[18]

All of this suggests that pride, as a virtue, is the disposition to practice proper and demanding moral standards. Pride is the commitment to achieve one's moral excellence.

Let us try to corroborate this account by considering this virtue in practice. A proud person takes her values seriously. She has adopted definite ideas of right action and comports herself accordingly. The examples already noted reflected the idea that one should practice one's principles not only where it is safe (e.g., on a bus filled with like-minded people) or when it is safe (when the stakes are minimal or success is likely). A proud person's commitment to her code is too firmly entrenched to wobble before the vagaries of circumstance.

When a business boasts that it is "serving you with pride," it is pronouncing its devotion to high standards, attempting to distinguish itself from competitors who take less care in their work. When we refer to a person's taking pride in her work, her house, her children, or her appearance, we mean that firm standards govern her activities in those domains. When a person possesses the *moral* virtue of pride, however, the domain of firm standards is much wider: it is the realm of morality itself.

Correspondingly, there are certain things that a proud person will not do. Certain actions are beneath her, such that she would not contemplate them as viable options. She would not accept favors, for instance, that violate legitimate rules. One of the *Oxford English Dictionary's* definitions identifies this aspect of pride: "a consciousness or feeling of what is befitting or due to oneself or one's position, which prevents a person from doing what he considers to be beneath him or unworthy of him."[19] This nicely captures the link between the attitude of pride and certain standards of conduct.

In conflict with others, a proud person would not back down *for no good reason.* (I will say more on stubbornness a bit later.) In presenting herself to others, a proud person is not likely to boast, as that would suggest the need for others' esteem. As Taylor emphasized, a truly proud person is more concerned with her self-evaluation than with the opinions of anyone else. Rostand's Cyrano de Bergerac eloquently recognizes that a boaster is parasitic on others' positive impressions when he asserts: "I am too proud to be a parasite."[20]

What we usually overlook is that there are also certain sorts of things that the proud person will do. Foremost, a proud person will be careful in the adoption of her moral code, making considered decisions about its constituent values and virtues. One would have no reason to take morality seriously, as the proud person does, if one were not committed to its contents. To be so committed, though, requires careful deliberation in the adoption of that code. Further, as we have indicated, the proud person will assiduously abide by this code, following its guidance through thick and thin.

"Ambition" signifies the dedicated and tenacious pursuit of challenging goals. Pride is the adoption of this policy toward morality itself. A proud person has clearly-identified values and makes high demands of herself. She will thus be alert to the moral ramifications of decisions that crop up in her daily life, poised to act on her principles. Moreover, the proud person will not coast or vegetate. She will not resign herself to flaws in her character, but will work to overcome particular weaknesses.[21] She cares about herself in the healthy sense of making the most of her life—by doing the best, in her actions. This is why she would not waste her energies on actions that betray her principles. If she did stray, she would not blithely excuse the lapse, but would inspect it to understand why she faltered and to learn from the episode so as to avoid similar lapses in the future. It would thus be a mistake to conceive of the proud person as analogous to the blind patriot, abiding by the policy "me, right or wrong." Contrary to stereotypes, a proud person will admit fault on appropriate occasions, out of fidelity to the same principles that guide all her actions. While a proud person can admit fault, she would not be complacent about her faults and would not accept them as immutable.

So described, one might detect a resemblance between pride and integrity. If integrity is the commitment to cultivate an integrated moral character and abide by one's moral principles on all relevant occasions, then both integrity and pride concern the application of other virtues. Actions often manifest several virtues, and pride and integrity do tend to overlap.[22]

Whereas integrity consists of allegiance to one's moral code across every area of one's life, however, pride forges forward, introducing an upward-striving dimension. The proud person has "integrity-plus," as ambition propels her to strengthen her virtuous dispositions and attain higher levels of moral excellence. We might envision integrity as lateral, primarily concerned with resisting temptations and maintaining moral standards, and pride as vertical, steadily driving one to higher elevations. The proud person aims not simply to adhere to her standards more consistently, but pushes the standards themselves to higher thresholds.[23] Moreover, pride may inspire a person's integrity. The admirable sense of self-importance, taking one's character seriously, that is pivotal to pride may help explain why a person would strive to maintain her integrity.

A. Humility

Since pride is commonly contrasted with humility, it may be instructive to glimpse at this alternative "virtue."[24] Humility primarily concerns two things: a person's aspirations and a person's presentation of herself to others. Typically, the humble person does not want very much. She is content with a minimal standard of living, or job, or romance, and satisfies herself with relatively low-level needs and aims. Humility also refers to the way that a person projects her abilities and accomplishments. The humble person does not seek to spotlight her success or try to publicize her achievements; she may even be uncomfortable with praise or attention and may typically deflect credit to others.

These presentation and aspiration dimensions are probably related. If a person believes the belittling self-image that she projects, she will not view herself as worthy of much, so it will seem appropriate that she trim her aspirations and make do with the minimum.

Accounts of exactly what constitutes humility vary. Norvin Richards describes humility as "an inclination to keep one's accomplishments, traits, and so on in unexaggerated perspective." Nancy Snow defines humility as "the disposition to allow the awareness of and concern about your limitations to have a realistic influence on your attitudes and behavior." She adds that "humility is occasioned by a recognition of the insignificance of your concerns." According to Aquinas, "humility conveys praiseworthy self-abasement." He approvingly cites various religious authorities who elaborate on humility as "acknowledging oneself contemptible."[25]

Humility's appeal, I think, relies primarily on its contrast with the vain, pompous show-off who is not content with her own self-estimate, but broadcasts her feats to make sure that everyone else is aware of them, as well. Alongside that alternative, something *is* attractive about a humble person. I am no more a fan of arrogance or vanity than are most people. Yet people's reactions to pride and humility undeniably vary, and this may be a tip-off that our assessments in this area are often a matter of taste. Much of what we react to about the humble or proud person (at least in initial, visceral responses) are stylistic differences in personality rather than issues of character and moral virtue. Aristotle's and Taylor's claims about the carriage, voice, and conversation topics of the proud may contribute to this emphasis on superficial personality issues.

As long as we bear in mind that a person's self-estimate or genuine worth and her manner of expressing it are different things, however, we should be able to see that pride is often the wrong target of ridicule. One can loathe ostentatiousness and parading self-congratulation without condemning pride. Indeed, such displays usually bespeak the wish to be seen by others in a certain light and thus reveal a misplaced priority on the opinion of others. In other words, such displays involve counterfeit pride. Note, further, as we saw earlier, that objections to pride are sometimes based on its source, the reason for which a person is proud. If one disagrees with a proud person's assessment of the value of some of her actions, one's objection is not to pride per se, but to that person's values or judgment.

B. Misconceptions

Before turning to the practical case for pride, we should clear away a few further misconceptions.

Conventional ideas about pride are riddled with false alternatives. To think that a person must be either a boaster or self-effacing does not accurately convey the range of possibilities. A realistic, high self-estimate is compatible with a low-key demeanor. Similarly, to think that a realistic self-appraisal (as Snow and Richards claim humility demands) precludes the possibility of pride is to pose another false alternative: between being truthful about oneself and thinking well of oneself. This assumes that the only realistic self-appraisals are low ones.

Another frequent mistake is the equation of pride with stubbornness. In popular imagery, a proud person will not consider the possibility that she is mistaken or being unreasonable. Yet if a person adopts this stance, pride is not the problem. Self-honesty is. A person should never think that her position is correct simply because it is her position. But that is an elementary error, Stupidity 101. That sort of obstinance reflects utter dishonesty about one's fallibility. If honesty were among a proud person's principles, she would not permit herself to indulge in such blatant self-deception.

Yet a further misconception concerns the basis of pride. Many people assume that pride depends on comparisons with other and/or the esteem of others. Hume repeatedly remarked that comparisons fuel pride; its impact is negligible unless "seconded by the opinions and sentiments of others." Robert C. Roberts emphasizes that at least certain forms of pride are a function of assessments of a person's status vis-à-vis others. Aaron Ben Zeev claims that pride conveys a negative evaluation of other people.[26] This social/comparative conception of pride probably contributes to its unpopularity. For it converts pride into a menace.

Generally, humble people—who present themselves in an unassuming, self-deprecating light—are not threatening. By contrast, a proud person often is threatening *if* the basis for one's self-regard is comparison with others. If you believe that the proper barometer of your worth is others' worth, and that the better other people are, or the more highly they appear to think of themselves, the less likely they are to be impressed by you, then every proud person is perceived as a threat to your self-esteem. Pride becomes a game of me versus you; who's "better" determines who's "good" and who's entitled to think well of herself. Since the company of the humble is more comforting, to many, this comparative conception of pride fans antagonism toward it. For it fosters the reading of another person's pride as a sign of one's own inferiority.

On this, however, Taylor was right to stress the proud person's self-evaluation as pivotal. Recall Taylor's claim that the proud person seeks her own favorable assessment. A person can hold herself to high standards and reach an honest assessment of how well she is following them without assigning relative positions to others. How well one individual is living up to her moral principles simply does not rely on how well others are living up to theirs. We can *all* be morally ambitious.[27]

We should thus be able to detect the related error in supposing, as people often do, that pride is necessarily a virtue restricted to a select class of superior people. In fact, pride is attainable by everyone; the only qualification is practiced moral ambition, honestly doing one's best. Whatever a given individual's level of understanding and ability, she can be as ambitious as she can be. To the extent that she is, she will be rightfully proud.[28]

Our tendency to think of pride primarily as a feeling may also stoke confusion. Feelings, notoriously, are not always well-founded. Unwarranted feeling good about oneself is so widespread that "self-satisfied" has come to carry predominantly negative connotations. Complacency, certainly, is not what I am endorsing. If the allegedly proud person's position is that she has exerted all the effort that she's going to, that is neither constructive nor admirable. When a person is justified in being satisfied with her performance in some area, however, it is perfectly fine to feel that. (Indeed, it may be destructive not to, as I will discuss in the next section.)

The crucial point is that the virtue of pride can only be reached through certain routes. Pride must be earned. A proud person is morally conscientious, and thus practices all the other virtues of her moral code. The justified feeling of pride is made possible by that course of virtuous action.

In full, healthy blossom, then, pride is both a practiced drive to be moral and a respect for oneself, as a result. Pride is not only a matter of self-evaluation, but of conducting one's action in a particular manner. It demands setting and holding oneself to high standards. To the extent that part of pride is "feeling good about oneself," that feeling arises for a good reason: one's morally admirable action.

III The payoffs of pride

We are now in position to ask: What good is pride, in terms of its practical ramifications? How does pride contribute to a person's flourishing?

As a virtue concerned with the practice of other virtues, pride's general benefit is straightforward. Pride heightens and fortifies one's commitment to other moral virtues.

Aristotle's famous pronouncement that pride is the crown which is not found without other virtues was accompanied by a further claim that is often overlooked: that pride makes the other virtues greater.[29] Rand's account, emphasizing pride as directing one's conduct, illuminates how this occurs. Recognizing pride as something beyond satisfaction with past accomplishments reveals pride's work as a spur, driving a person to be ever more virtuous, to continually sharpen her moral skills. Pall Ardal agrees that pride is invigorating, potentially stimulating praiseworthy actions.[30] Pride serves as an engine of morality, you might say, propelling a person's moral growth. (And the more a person stretches herself in exercising her principles, in all likelihood, the stronger grows the conviction that certain behavior is beneath her.)

Heightened sensitivity to moral issues, in turn, translates into a greater number of occasions of morally guided action. Thus, pride brings an ever-readier recognition of occasions on which morality is relevant and virtuous action is possible. Because pride requires practicing other virtues, it will strengthen a person's disposition to virtuous action, steadily eroding the internal obstacles. Habit-strengthening occurs with all the virtues, of course. My point is that insofar as pride consists of practicing other virtues, it will fortify all of them.

Correspondingly, since pride requires practicing one's moral code, pride will deliver the more particular benefits of the code's specific prescriptions. Pride could deliver the rewards of honesty, for instance: truthfulness as the basis for one's decisions and actions. It could deliver the rewards of justice: objective evaluations of other people as one's basis for dealing with them, rather than evaluations based on arbitrary preferences or prejudices.

In addition to all of these benefits, pride also provides a more distinctive reward in its impact on a person's psyche. Pride nourishes self-esteem. Insofar as a positive view of oneself is necessary to live—to the will to live, and to one's sense of worthiness to live—this is its most significant payoff. Pride offers tremendous psychological benefits.[31]

A person needs to value herself in order to take any code seriously and believe it important that *she* abide by it. If a person did not value herself, what reason would she have to adhere to any particular regimen? She needs a minimum of self-regard to consider her actions sufficiently significant to matter. A morality aimed at individual happiness particularly requires a belief in one's worthiness of happiness. Pride addresses this need. For the higher one's goals and the more consistent one's practiced dedication to them, the greater one's sense of efficacy will grow, the stronger one's self-confidence, the more secure one's self-esteem. Pride encourages moral action, which, in turn, nourishes belief in one's goodness; this belief reinforces one's commitment to strengthening that moral character. The practice of pride thus enables a person honestly to think of herself as fit to live, able to act as she should and to achieve all the rewards of so doing.[32]

One might suspect that this explanation of pride's benefits carries an untenable implication.[33] If high self-regard is necessary for proper, pride-producing actions, one must already be proud in order to take such actions. Yet if that is the case, such actions are not necessary for achieving that attitude. Put more forcefully: if pride is a spur to moral excellence, then if it is justified, it is not necessary (since the justly proud person is already excellent); but if pride is needed, it cannot be justified (since its need bespeaks absence of the excellence that would justify it).

The defect in this objection is that it is not true to experience. It rests on a misleadingly static portrait of moral character. The excellence that justifies pride is not a one-time-only acquisition which, once achieved, naturally remains and permanently marks one's character. We are always works-in-progress whose excellence may be strengthening or deteriorating along different dimensions. I am not psychologist enough to posit exactly how the mechanisms of self-satisfaction and the drive for moral improvement interact, but ample anecdotal evidence testifies that people frequently see themselves as neither fully good, fully bad, nor fully finished products. We grow; we try to grow for the better, in specific respects. And we frequently experience the uneasy realization that grounds for satisfaction with our performance in the past (say, two years ago) will not suffice today. The pleasure of recognizing one's achievements wears thin, over time. All of which supports the view that pride can serve as both spur and reward in the way I have described.

Pride helps a person to build self-esteem, which results from proud action; that self-esteem, in turn, nourishes higher standards and thus encourages still further proud action. A mutually reinforcing dynamic develops between virtuous action and consequent self-esteem, escalating the levels of each.

One might object that the proud person I have described sounds like a tired person, this moral conscientiousness depleting her energy for much else. Yet this seems more a comment on the scope of morality than on the nature of pride. If morality is aimed at the promotion of individual flourishing, then whatever bears a significant impact on that objective falls within its compass. Morality is not reserved to one neatly confined compartment of life. Since all sorts of actions may affect a person's happiness, morality is a full-time job from which no domains can be declared exempt. Like any virtue, pride requires genuine effort. As a virtue that demands the practice of other virtues, pride's workload is simply especially noticeable. Bear in mind, too, that the more one practices pride, the less "fatiguing" it will be.[34]

This broad scope of morality also helps to address another possible question.[35] While one might applaud a person's pride in certain professional, athletic, or culinary accomplishments, such pride's morality may seem mysterious. Can't such pride be admirable without being morally virtuous?

Yes. Nothing in my account entails that all admirable pride is necessarily moral. Nonetheless, insofar as pride in such areas reflects the commitment to do well in one's pursuits and to care well for one's values, such pride can contribute to the person's flourishing. If it does, this would be the basis for its moral status.

Others might raise a different objection: all this attention to one's moral character amounts to unseemly preening. The proud person seems overly concerned with the appearance of her character and inadequately concerned with the nature of her actions. Bernard Williams has explored the similar possibility that concern with one's integrity may be subject to "reflexive deformation." Williams sees a possessive attitude toward one's own virtue as a kind of self-indulgence.[36]

This objection is also misplaced, however. It would be fair to dismiss cultivation of pride as preening only if one assumed that the stakes were artificial. The serious commitment to morality that pride represents would be pointless only if morality were pointless, or if its benefits were unnecessary. Without addressing the basic function of morality, I hope to have indicated why the value of self-esteem cannot be lightly dismissed. Even Williams acknowledges: "It may well be that the route to acquiring and sustaining the first-order virtuous motivations requires a kind of self-esteem which may involve to some degree and in some form second-order motivations."[37]

Cynicism toward calls for self-esteem is understandable, given the industry of pseudo-self-esteem that has mushroomed in recent years. I am not proposing that whatever makes a person feel better about herself is beneficial or praiseworthy. Self-congratulation for no good reason is not virtue. While the danger of self-deception or a distorted absorption in the appearance of one's character is genuine, so is the danger of neglecting pride and failing to cultivate the value—the ambitious dedication to morality—that it nourishes. My proposal is not that the proud person should be concerned with her character *instead* of with morality. Rather, she should be concerned with herself *as* a moral agent.

The virtue of pride builds and bespeaks healthy love of self. To equate cultivation of pride with preening either denies that such building of self-esteem is possible, or denies that it is beneficial. In my view, the proud person is concerned not with the appearance of her character, either to others or to herself, but with the actual substance of her actions. She strives to be a good, and ever-better, person.

A. In the absence of pride

Another way to appreciate pride's value is to reflect on the repercussions of its absence. Consider the effects of swallowing pride. The advice, to "swallow one's pride" usually tells a person to compromise, make a concession. What is the practical value of such a course?

One might argue that this is based on the recognition that you can't always have your way and you are not always right. Correspondingly, you will be more successful in dealing with others if you face up to this.

Fair enough. But what follows from these observations? What do they show about the propriety of swallowing pride?

Presumably, one should make concessions only in certain circumstances. When one's goals are unrealistic (given time or personnel constraints, for instance), or when one is making unjustified demands, it is appropriate to back down. This implies that we should be honest and reasonable in our demands, however, not that concession is per se desirable. Sometimes it is, sometimes it isn't. The propriety of giving in depends on several factors, such as what is at stake, what you are surrendering, and for what reasons. It is not admirable to compromise when you are right and doing so violates your justified standards. That would relinquish the practical benefits that are served by allegiance to those standards.

While it may be perfectly appropriate to retreat in certain circumstances, when it is, doing so is not a surrender of pride. Rather, it is an admission of honest error, or sometimes, of prior stubbornness or stupidity. But why equate those with pride?

Pride can actually be the source of such reversals. Since a proud person takes her moral principles seriously, if she realizes that she has made a mistake in applying them to a particular case, her conscientiousness will prompt her to change her position. Rather than dissembling to project an image of infallibility, the proud person would forthrightly correct her mistake.

Altering one's position in such circumstances should not be confused with conceding some inherent defect or unworthiness in oneself or one's aims. It is not, in other words, a reflection of humility. And it is important to realize the danger in supposing that it is. Misrepresenting an appropriate change of position as an instance of humility perpetuates the idea that retreat is good in its own right, that one should deny oneself for no particular reason, and that *that* is the salient choice that one faces: to maintain one's convictions or to abandon them. This policy completely ignores the substance of those convictions. It neglects the most relevant question, namely, whose demands are justified in a given case? The recommendation of compromise or humility actually downgrades the importance of such issues by implying that their content is of no significance. All that matters is giving in.

In sum, to swallow your pride is to turn your back on your moral code. That could be appropriate only if one had discovered serious defects in the code itself. Yet if that were the case, one would not be abandoning pride, but following its counsel to correct one's code.

B. The effects of humility

To appreciate fully the value of pride, we should also consider the fallout of its usual adversary, humility. What does one gain from being humble?

Aquinas held that humility suppresses hope and confidence in oneself. It makes man submissive to divine grace. Snow contends that humility fosters compassion, the propensity to forgive and to ask forgiveness, and inhibits vices such as boastfulness, vanity, arrogance, and conceit. Richards agrees that a benefit of humility is its conduciveness to forgiveness.[38]

If these are meant as alternatives that exclude pride, they again misrepresent it. For one does not need to be humble in order to have compassion or forgive. One simply needs to be honest in sizing up another person.

Nor does pride preclude asking for forgiveness. In appropriate circumstances, a proud person would not accept less of herself. Because she takes morality seriously, she will acutely regret errant action. Once she recognized that she had committed a breach, she would face up to it. If she regretted wronging a friend, for instance, she would want the friend to know that she does not consider her behavior acceptable, that the offending action was not indicative of what she wants her character to be or of her opinion of what her friend deserves. Joan Didion has put the point nicely: "[P]eople with self-respect have the courage of their mistakes."[39]

It is no dilution of pride to acknowledge a lapse. It would be, though, to engage in denial or cover-up. For that would add at least two breaches to the original sin: it would be unjust in not giving the friend the apology that she deserves, and it would be dishonest with the friend and with oneself about one's actual beliefs. Such a course elevates a flattering self-image over sincere concern for one's character and code. Pride does not sanction such a course.

More broadly, recall Snow's claim that humility is occasioned by a recognition of our insignificance. What is the likely effect of this?

It would seem to encourage a schizophrenic self-image: I am no good, I must try to be good; I am not worthy of concern, I must act as if my actions matter. At the same time, if I am good, acting as I should, I may not feel satisfaction from that. Since we are insignificant, of what import are any of our actions? What basis for satisfaction could they provide?

This outlook is likely to cripple one's morale. By puncturing one's commitment to any purpose, it will deflate one's energy, enthusiasm, and appetite for action.

Consider the person who constantly brushes off others' compliments or dismisses signs of her effectiveness at work. Practicing humility, she tends not to take credit or view any success as a reflection of her effort or skill. What results will this bring?

For starters, it denies the person one type of satisfaction from her work. Certainly it is enjoyable to receive a compliment or hear signs of one's success. Others' praise should not be one's reason for engaging in an activity, but presumably the person did what she did because she wanted to be effective. If she deprives herself of recognition that she is succeeding, she is bypassing a pleasurable byproduct.

Moreover, she is forgoing fuel that can help sustain her in times of difficulty, doubt, or fatigue. When others' praise is warranted, it is useful information. It indicates that one's efforts are having their desired effect. If something is worth doing, it is done for a reason, so that reason (achieving the objective) matters. We need to know how we are doing in order to know what sorts of adjustments in our efforts we should make.

Further, acknowledging success nourishes self-esteem, which fuels further efforts necessary for further success. Denial of evidence of success, not "taking" it, out of humility, can slowly but surely erode one's ambition and foster an attitude of indifference: why bother?

This psychological toll is likely to exact a material toll, inhibiting one's action. Aristotle recognized that the unduly humble will be "unduly retiring" and "stand back even from noble actions and undertakings, deeming themselves unworthy." More recently,

Daniel Statman has worried that a humble person, concluding that he is less deserving than he actually is, "might be willing to give up things that he should, by no means, give up."[40]

The praise of humility urges people to aim low.[41] Encouraging humility applauds a person when she recognizes limits, steering us to, decidedly *un*ambitious paths. Naturally it is good for people to be realistic in their self-appraisals. Yet humility carries a further edge. It celebrates limits.

The implication is that our limitations reflect a truer picture of the world. The significance attached to that "realization" is counsel to rein in your dreams, lower your sights, and be satisfied with less. This policy works directly against the prescriptions of pride.

Notice that compassion and forgiveness, often cited as humility's benefits, are reactions to human frailty. They are ways of responding, to a person's misfortunes or her sins. As such, they play to human weaknesses, rather than encouraging the kinds of strength needed to flourish. And compassion and forgiveness are typically urged not for the sake of improving those weaknesses; we are simply encouraged to accept them.

Why would this be good? Mightn't have the effect of encouraging weaknesses? Certainly wanton forgiveness can send the wrong message about the acceptability of certain behavior, withholding the negative repercussions that should sometimes result from it. My point is not that compassion and forgiveness are always inappropriate, but simply that they are not unqualified goods and do not always carry constructive effects.[42]

The general point is that humility advises a conspicuously unambitious course. It prescribes resignation to limits and acceptance of others' weaknesses rather than active devotion to one's moral code and continual strengthening of one's character. Far from the proud person's being complacent, *this* is where the dangers of complacency lurk.

To the extent that humility counsels realistic assessment of one's merits and ability, this is undoubtedly beneficial. Accurate self-appraisal is the best position from which to make reasonable decisions about what to seek and how to act. These benefits result from honesty, however, rather than from anything peculiar to humility. (The same holds of compassion and forgiveness. They are appropriate only when warranted by honest evaluation.) We have discovered no advantages to be gained through humility other than those offered by honesty. Only if what one really means to encourage is minimizing one's merits and wants, rather than simply refraining from exaggerating them, will one have reason to carve humility as a distinct virtue.

IV Sources of opposition to pride

At this stage, a reader might suspect that arguments about the propriety of pride can be reduced to terminology. A little fiddling with the definitions of pride and humility, and we will be left with little of philosophical significance. Because I believe that differing attitudes toward pride actually stand on deeper, substantial premises, it may be useful before concluding, to suggest a few possible sources of opposition to pride. Future investigation of these is likely to inform a more definitive resolution of pride's status as a virtue.

One flank of opposition may be premised on a particular evaluation of human nature. Some people believe that man is base and that we should comport ourselves accordingly. The explanation for this might be religious (we are so far inferior to god) or naturalistic (we are not so superior to other animals). Obviously these are not mutually exclusive and do not exhaust the possibilities. A dim view of human nature might stem from a thesis about our efficacy, attributing all human success to divine generosity or genetic inheritance. The point is, on certain views, a person should never be pleased with herself; humility is our naturally appropriate posture. If one accepts that human beings are inherently weak or base, then pride is necessarily unjustified.

Others might resist the individualism of pride. It is not only inflated self-regard that worries some people; they are wary of self-regard itself. Any favorable opinion of oneself strikes them as excessive.

Pride is undeniably a self-oriented virtue. A fundamental valuing of oneself serves as its bedrock. Pride is self-focused both in its instruction—advising a person to act on her considered principles—and in its welcomed effects, advising a person to take satisfaction from her virtuous action. As such, pride does not sit well with altruism, which is still widely equated with morality.

Humility is far more congenial to altruism. The belief that a person should deflate her own importance and curtail her desires paves the way for sacrifice to others. To the extent that humility mitigates love of self, it weakens a potential obstacle to one's making altruistic offerings.

Pride's position vis-à-vis individualism and altruism is also reflected in an anomaly in dominant attitudes toward pride. People tend to look far more kindly on social pride. When pride is taken in some group association or collective enterprise (e.g., ethnic pride, national pride, company pride, gay pride) or when pride is presented as advantageous to others (e.g., at Ford Motors or in the Marine Corps), many stand ready to applaud. The proud craftsman offers a good product to his customers; the proud clerk provides quality service. Altruism can permit pride as long as it is valuable to others. Pride that is not so other-directed, however, confronts icy scepticism.

Finally, the description of pride as moral ambitiousness is also bound to encounter resistance, as the term "ambition" is widely heard as a dirty word. Many are suspicious of ambition per se, regardless of what one is ambitious for. Without waiting to hear its target, they assume that ambition must be directed toward sinister purposes.

This attitude may stem from a conception of morality as severed from "real-world," practical concerns. Since ambition is typically attached to things of this world, some assume that the ambitious person is out for nonmoral, if not downright immoral, ends. What needs to be challenged is that conception of morality. For immediate purposes, suffice it to note the obvious error in passing a blanket condemnation of ambition rather than, more carefully, of particular exercises of it. Morality is something that *should* be pursued with vigor and high ideals; *moral* ambition seems a most admirable trait.

V Conclusion

Pride has been underappreciated because it has been widely mis-represented. Common opinion focuses on the feeling of pride severed from its source, the actions that can legitimate that feeling. People frequently suppose that pride is simply high self-regard, and further assume that such regard is unwarranted.

In fact, the virtue of pride is not simply a state of self-satisfaction. A proud person's high self-esteem is the effect of her virtuous activity. Caricatures of the proud person as boasting, haughty, or condescending frame nonessential personality variables rather than the core of the character trait. A proud character is built and defined by certain kinds of action. The proud person strives to meet high moral standards. Her pride establishes definite boundaries around what she allows and demands of herself.

The practice of pride thus cultivates self-esteem. Self-esteem is not the direct object of pride; its direct object is moral action. But the significant effect of such action is the sense of one's worth that is essential for a genuine commitment to a moral code and necessary for genuine flourishing.

Pride encourages the practice and strengthening of other virtues. The proud person takes morality seriously. Why this is valuable depends on the nature and function of morality, a subject beyond the scope of this essay. If I am right that the proud person's high self-regard must be earned through moral action, however, then a proud person should be admired—and pride should reclaim its status as a virtue.

Notes

Thanks to the editor and all the contributors for useful questions and comments on an earlier draft; to John Paulus, Steve Rogers, and Ann Ciccolella for thoughtful discussions of these issues; to Cooper Henson for his research assistance; and to the University of Texas Research Institute for a grant funding that assistance.

1 Aquinas' discussion of the deadly sins is probably the best known, though the classification goes at least as far back as St. Gregory the Great in the sixth century. *Encyclopedia Britannica* (Chicago: Encyclopedia

Britannica, Inc., 1975), p. 232. On pride as the crown of the virtues, see Aristotle, *Nicomachean Ethics*, trans. W.D. Ross, in *Introduction to Aristotle*, ed. Richard McKeon (New York: The Modern Library, 1947), 1124a1, p. 384.

2 For this characterization of virtue, see, for instance, Julia Annas, *The Morality of Happiness* (New York: Oxford University Press, 1993), p. 9.

3 William F.R. Graham, "Learn the Lesson of the Worm," *A Treasury of Great American Speeches*, selected by Charles Hurd, ed. Andrew Bauer (New York: Hawthorn, 1970), p. 339.

4 Daniel Statman, "Modesty, Pride, and Realistic Self-Assessment," *Philosophical Quarterly*, Vol. 42, no. 169, (October 1992), p. 432. Aaron Ben Zeev reports that the Greeks had no word for the concept of modesty; see Aaron Ben Zeev, "The Virtue of Modesty," *American Philosophical Quarterly*, Vol. 30 (July 1993), p. 239.

5 Proverbs 16:18; Luke 18:9–14; Augustine, *City of God* (Garden City, NY: Doubleday, 1958), pp. 308–10; St. Thomas Aquinas, *Summa Theologica*, trans. Fathers of the English Dominican Province (London: Burn Oates and Washbourne Ltd., 1932), p. 226.

6 For some elaboration of flourishing's character, see my *Moral Rights and Political Freedom* (Lanham, MD: Rowman and Littlefield, 1995), chs 2 and 3. I am working on an extended defense of this teleological conception of morality in a book on the foundation of values.

7 Since we cannot completely sever the nature of pride from the practice of pride and its attendant benefits, elements of the discussion in Section II will sometimes blend into the subject of Section III, and vice versa.

8 Aristotle, *Nicomachean Ethics*, 1123b1, 1123b30, 1125a13, pp. 383, 384, 387. (My pronouns will vary in gender with different examples and for consistency with different authors.)

9 David Hume, *A Treatise of Human Nature* (Oxford: Clarendon Press, 1978); pp. 277, 297, 292, 596–7. See also ibid., pp. 315–16, 323, 598–600.

10 Adam Smith, *The Theory of Moral Sentiments* (Oxford: Clarendon Press, 1976), pp. 247–61.

11 Baruch Spinoza, *The Ethics and Selected Letters*, ed., Seymour Feldman (Indianapolis: Hackett, 1982), p. 186.

12 Since my focus is on the virtue of pride, I shall not take up various possible questions about the perimeters of the feeling of pride, such as whether the source of pride must cross some threshold of significance or difficulty, or whether one can be proud of things for which one is not responsible (e.g., inherited physical features or ethnic ancestry).

13 The playwright was Howard Sackler, and the story was based on the life of Jack Johnson (renamed Jack Jefferson in the play). James Earl Jones won

acclaim for his portrait of Jefferson in both the Broadway production and the film.

14 Nonetheless, like Aristotle, Taylor describes certain marks of pride that seem overly particular, claiming, for example, that a proud person will not be garrulous and does not discuss the weather; see Richard Taylor, *Ethics, Faith, and Reason* (Englewood Wood Cliffs, NJ: Prentice-Hall, 1985), pp. 99–105.

15 Ayn Rand, "The Objectivist Ethics," in *The Virtue of Selfishness* (New York: New American Library, 1964), p. 27. See also Leonard Peikoff, *Objectivism: The Philosophy of Ayn Rand* (New York: Dutton, 1991), pp. 303–10.

16 Robert Mayhew first called this contrast to my attention.

17 I thank Michael Slote and L.W. Sumner for pressing me to make these clarifications.

18 Benjamin Franklin contemplated this scenario: "[P]erhaps no one of our natural passions is so hard to subdue as pride. Disguise it, struggle with it, beat it down, stifle it, mortify it as much as one pleases, it is still alive.... [E]ven if I could conceive I had completely overcome it, I should probably be proud of my humility." *The Autobiography of Benjamin Franklin* (New York: Collier Books, 1962), p. 90. Thanks to David Solomon for suggesting that I consider this possibility.

19 *Oxford English Dictionary* (New York: Oxford University Press, 1971).

20 Edmond Rostand, *Cyrano de Bergerac,* trans. Brian Hooker (New York: Bantam Books, 1979), p. 176.

21 Rand, "The Objectivist Ethics," p. 27.

22 Rosa Parks is often cited for her courage, which I consider to be a type of integrity.

23 Standards are pushed in the sense that, over time, a person may gradually recognize more of the sorts of actions that are appropriately governed by a particular moral principle, thus expanding her appreciation of the scope of that principle's demands. Conversation with John Paulus helped me to clarify aspects of this difference.

24 Pall S. Ardal claims that the Christian idea of humility prevents us from seeing the propriety of pride; see Ardal, "Hume and Davidson on Pride," *Hume Studies,* Vol. 15, no. 2 (November 1989), pp. 390–1. Aquinas saw pride and humility as definite antagonists.

25 Norvin Richards, *Humility* (Philadelphia: Temple University Press, 1992), p. 8; Nancy E. Snow, "Humility," *Journal of Value Inquiry,* Vol. 29 (1995), pp. 210, 206; Aquinas, *Summa Theologica,* pp. 217, 228–31.

26 Hume, *Treatise of Human Nature,* pp. 292, 315–16, 323; Robert C. Roberts, "What Is Wrong with Wicked Feelings?" *American Philosophical*

Quarterly, Vol. 28 (January 1991), pp. 15–16; Ben Zeev, "The Virtue of Modesty," p. 244.

For good discussions of Hume's view of pride, see Pauline Chazan, "Pride, Virtue, and Self-Hood: A Reconstruction of Hume," *Canadian Journal of Philosophy,* Vol. 22, no. 1 (March 1992), pp. 45–64; and Amélie O. Rorty, "'Pride Produces the Idea of Self': Hume on Moral Agency," *Australasian Journal of Philosophy,* Vol. 68 (September 1990), pp. 255–69.

27 One might suspect that I am too quickly dismissing the relevance of comparisons. Can't I feel proud if I beat the tennis opponent who usually beats me? Maybe. If I won because I played unusually well, I can be proud, but in that case the pride stems from my own better-than-usual performance. If, however, I won because of my opponent's uncharacteristic bevy of double faults and unforced errors or his slack coordination due to the flu, pride in my victory would be unfounded. It is no accomplishment (and no ground for pride) to consistently beat inferior players. Even losing efforts in which one plays unusually well, however, can be grounds for pride. So again, pride is not a function of one's position vis-à-vis others, but vis-à-vis one's own capacities and standards. (Thanks to George Sher for prodding me to consider this sort of case.)

28 Thus, we can see the answers to some of the questions raised in note 12. There is no independent level of difficulty or significance that an action must pass in order to serve as a legitimate source of pride. To determine whether one possesses the virtue of pride, the salient question is whether a person is ambitiously pursuing moral excellence. As for inherited traits that are often the source of "ethnic pride": these are not based on a person's acting in any particular way. The fact that a person might take some pleasure in the accomplishments of her ancestors says nothing about the strengths of her character. Any attempt to reap self-esteem from others' accomplishments is obviously ill-fated.

29 Aristotle, *Nicomachean Ethics,* 1124a1–3, p. 384.

30 Ardal, "Hume and Davidson on Pride," p. 393.

31 See Rand, "The Objectivist Ethics," pp. 27–9, and Peikoff, *Objectivism,* for good discussions of this.

32 I am treating self-esteem as an appraisal and the practice of the virtue of pride as the means of earning that appraisal. For a psychological analysis of the role of competence and efficacy in boosting self-esteem, see Robert W. White, "The Urge Towards Competence," *American Journal of Occupational Therapy,* Vol. 25 (1971), pp. 271–4.

33 John Kekes prompted me to consider reservations along these lines.

34 Julia Annas is among recent authors who have recognized this broader scope for moral concern. See her discussion of the Greek view of ethics as

concerned with one's life as a whole, in Annas, *The Morality of Happiness*, pp. 39–45.

No doubt, the nature of the moral code that one is practicing will also influence its impact on one's life. And note the irony in shifting from common complaints that pride is base to protests that it is too demanding.

35　Thanks to John Cooper and John Kekes for prompting this clarification.

36　Bernard Williams, "Utilitarianism and Moral Self-Indulgence," in his *Moral Luck* (New York: Cambridge University Press, 1981), pp. 40, 49. Williams considers this to be a particular pitfall of utilitarianism.

37　Ibid., p. 46.

38　Aquinas, *Summa Theologica*, pp. 220, 224, 226; Snow, "Humility," pp. 210–11; Richards, *Humility*, pp. 15–17, 39–43. I shall leave aside Aquinas' projections of the effects of pride, since they stem from such a fundamentally different metaphysics.

39　Joan Didion, "On Self-Respect," in *Vice and Virtue in Everyday Life*, ed. Christina Sommers and Fred Sommers (New York: Harcourt Brace Jovanovich, 1989), p. 655.

40　Aristotle, *Nicomachean Ethics*, 1125a16–28, p. 387; Statman, "Modesty, Pride, and Realistic Self-Assessment," p. 424.

41　Consider the Latin root, "humilis," meaning low. To be humbled is to be brought low in some respect; to humiliate is to debase a person's stature.

42　For clarification of when forgiveness is and is not justified, see my "Tolerance and Forgiveness: Virtues or Vices?" *Journal of Applied Philosophy*, Vol. 14, no. 1 (1997). Jeffrie Murphy has challenged popular assumptions about forgiveness in Jeffrie G. Murphy and Jean Hampton, *Forgiveness and Mercy* (New York: Cambridge University Press, 1988).

5 The Cognitive Structure of Compassion

Martha C. Nussbaum

Philoctetes was a good man and a good soldier. When he was on his way to fight with the Greeks in the Trojan War, he had a terrible misfortune. By sheer accident he trespassed on a sacred precinct on the island of Lemnos. As punishment he was bitten in the foot by the serpent that guarded the shrine. His foot began to ooze with foul-smelling pus, and the pain made him cry out curses that spoiled the other soldiers' religious observances. They therefore left him alone on the island, a lame man with no resources but his bow and arrows, no friends but the animals that were also his food.[1]

Ten years later they come back to bring him back: for they have learned that they cannot win the war without his bow. The leaders of the expedition think of Philoctetes as simply a tool of their purposes. They plan to trick him into returning, with no sympathy for his plight. The chorus of common soldiers, however, has a different response. Even before they see the man, they imagine vividly what it is like to be him, and they enter a protest against the callousness of the commanders:

For my part, I have compassion for him. (*oiktirô nin egôge*)
Think how
with no human company or care,
no sight of a friendly face,
wretched, always alone,
he wastes away with that savage affliction,
with no way of meeting his daily needs.
How, how in the word, does the poor man survive? (169–76)

117

As the chorus imagine a man they do not know, they stand in for the imaginative activity of the audience, for whom the entire tragic drama is a similar exercise of imagination and compassionate emotion.

The drama strongly suggests that this emotion is linked with beneficent action, as the chorus, having seen Philoctetes with compassion, begin to question the plot against the suffering man, imploring their young leader to grant his wish and send him home. Their speech of urging begins with the words, "Have compassion on him, lord" ("*oiktir', anax,*" 507). Philoctetes himself relies on this connection when he asks for aid: just before pleading to be sent home, he says:

Save me, have compassion for me (*eleêson*),[2] seeing that all mortal life lies open to risk and terrible affliction:[3] good things can happen, but the opposite can also happen. The person who is outside of suffering ought to look out for terrible affliction, and when someone's life is going well, then above all he should watch out, lest he be ruined unawares. (501–6)

The connection determines the shape of the plot: for it is when the young commander Neoptolemus feels for the first time the tug of compassion, witnessing an attack of Philoctetes' pain, that he repudiates his own deceitful conduct and returns the stolen bow to its rightful owner. Philoctetes, blinded by pain, asks, "Where are you, my child?" (805)—and Neoptolemus replies, "I have long been in pain (*algô palai*), grieving for your suffering" (806). He gives his location in the world by naming his emotions. The distress by which he locates himself is ethical distress: when Philoctetes refers to the discomfort his affliction causes others, Neoptolemus says, "Everything is discomfort, when someone leaves his own character and does what is not fitting" (902–4). And at last, when it is time to sail with the stolen bow, he says, "terrible compassion (*deinos oiktos*) for this man has fallen upon me"—comparing his emotion to the sudden afflictions mentioned by Philoctetes, which fall upon mortals unawares. The affliction of compassion prompts a decision to treat Philoctetes justly and humanely.

Philoctetes' story displays the structure of compassion, drawing attention to the elements of its cognitive structure that are stressed in standard theoretical accounts. It is useful to begin with the fine analysis given by Aristotle in the *Rhetoric,* which has guided the subsequent philosophical tradition. Aristotle's analysis is continuous with less systematic earlier treatments in Homer, the tragic poets, and Plato; it is taken over, in most respects, by defenders of compassion such as Rousseau, Schopenhauer, and Adam Smith, and by opponents of the emotion such as the Greek and Roman Stoics, Spinoza, Kant, and Nietzsche.[4] Finally, the very same elements are stressed in many contemporary psychological accounts and in Candace Clark's analysis of current American beliefs. As I follow Aristotle's account, I shall also assess it in the light of the subsequent tradition, and criticize it in view of my own developing argument.[5]

Compassion, Aristotle argues, is a painful emotion directed at another person's misfortune or suffering (*Rhet.* 1385b13 ff.). It has three cognitive elements. It seems to be Aristotle's view that each of these is necessary for the emotion, and that they are jointly sufficient. Apparently he thinks that the pain itself is caused reliably by the beliefs: he calls it "pain at ... the misfortune one believes to have befallen another," and gives the aspiring orator advice about how to induce or remove it, by inducing or removing the beliefs. Later we will have to ask (both on Aristotle's behalf and on our own) whether the pain is a necessary element of the definition, over and above the cognitive elements. For now, however, we may begin with the fact the cognitive elements are, at the least, among the constituent parts of the definition: the pain of pity is distinguished from the pain of grief, or fear, only by the type of cognition it involves.

The first cognitive requirement of compassion is a belief or appraisal[6] that the suffering is serious rather than trivial. The second is the belief that the person does not deserve the suffering. The third is the belief that the possibilities of the person who experiences the emotion are similar to those of the sufferer. (I shall later argue that this third element is not strictly necessary, and that another as yet unspecified element is.) Let us examine each Aristotelian element in turn.

Take seriousness first. Compassion, like other major emotions, is concerned with value: it involves the recognition that the situation matters for the flourishing of the person in question. Intuitively we see this quite clearly. We do not go around pitying someone who has lost a trivial item, such as a toothbrush or a paper clip, or even an important item that is readily replaceable. In fact, internal to our emotional response itself is the judgment that what is at issue is indeed serious—has "size," as Aristotle puts it (1386a6–7).

What misfortunes are taken to have "size"? Once again, not too surprisingly, there is remarkable unanimity about core instances across time and place. The occasions for compassion enumerated by Aristotle are also the ones on which tragic plots, ancient and modern, most commonly focus: death, bodily assault or ill-treatment, old age, illness, lack of food, lack of friends, separation from friends, physical weakness, disfigurement, immobility, reversals of expectations, absence of good prospects (86a6–13). Candace Clark's study of appeals to compassion in America[7] includes the same elements— adding some variants specific to contemporary life:

When I looked at what had triggered sympathy, I discovered dozens of plights. The inventory encompasses all of those enumerated in blues lyrics (e.g., poverty, a partner's infidelity, death of loved ones). It includes illness (including "functional" or behavioral illnesses such as alcoholism and drug use), physical or mental disabilities or deformities, injury, and pain. The respondents also mentioned war trauma, sexual abuse, physical abuse, crime victimization, disaster victimization (e.g., by earthquakes, hurricanes, or air-plane crashes), homelessness, infertility, divorce (or loss of "partner"), dis-crimination (e.g., in jobs or housing), political victimization (e.g., liberties abridged by tyrannical government), role strain (e.g., single parenthood), unwanted pregnancy, physical unattractiveness, car accidents, car trouble, house trouble (e.g., leaky roof), insensitive parents, ungrateful children, social ostracism, loss in competition (e.g., sports or job), depression, fear, public humiliation, accidental embarrassment, fatigue, bad judgment, ruined vacations, boredom, and discomfort (e.g., enduring heat, cold, or traffic jams).[8]

Apart from the fact that (as Clark stresses) Americans today tend to include more relatively mild predicaments in the list of "plights" than they did formerly, the list she presents is remark-ably similar to Aristotle's—and to Rousseau's, and to Smith's. Even though her list includes more items, she insists that this is because they are seen as having "size," not because "size" is not considered important:

> For a person to be considered unlucky, his or her plight must fit prevailing standards of direness—that is, it should be considered sufficiently harmful, dangerous, discrediting, or painful.... Moreover, the plight must be bad and unlucky for those with the person's particular set of gender, age, social class, and other characteristics. (82)

One interesting difference between Aristotle's list and the "plights" enumerated as dire by Clark's subjects is that various forms of political injustice and oppression play a more central role for Americans than they do in Aristotle's account. But even this is not a general historical/cultural difference. For in omitting this occasion for emotion Aristotle has neglected central cases of Greek tragic compassion, where slavery and loss of citizenship are pivotal; even in Philoctetes' case, the fact that he had suffered undeserved political injustice is as important as are his isolation and his pain.

We may conclude that societies (and individuals) vary to some degree in what they take to be a serious plight; they vary, too, in the level of damage required before something is taken to be a serious plight.[9] Moreover, changes in the shape of life construct new predicaments: obviously enough, car and airplane crashes were not on Aristotle's list. Nonetheless, the central disasters to which human life is prone are remarkably constant; constant as well is the fact that people take these disasters to be central.

An important question now arises: from whose point of view does the person who has compassion make the assessment of "size"? Consider the following two examples. Q, a Roman aristocrat, discovers that his shipment of peacock's tongues from Africa has been interrupted. Feeling that his dinner party that evening will be a total disaster in consequence, he weeps bitter tears, and implores his friend Seneca to pity him. Seneca laughs. R, a woman in a rural village in India, is severely undernourished, and unable to get more than a first-grade education. She does not think her lot a bad one, since she has no idea what it is to feel healthy, and no idea of the benefits and pleasures of education. So thoroughly has she internalized her culture's views of what is right for women that she believes that she is living a good and flourishing life, as a woman ought to live one. Hearing of her story and others like hers, workers in the province's rural development agency[10] feel deeply moved, and think that something must be done.

What these examples bring out is that people's judgments about what is happening to them can go wrong in many ways. Suffering and deprivation are usually not ennobling or educative; they more often brutalize or corrupt perception. In particular, they often produce adaptive responses that deny the importance of the suffering; this is especially likely to be so when the deprivation is connected to oppression and hierarchy, and taught as proper through religious and cultural practices.[11] On the other hand, people can become deeply attached to things that on reflection we may think either trivial or bad for them; their suffering at the loss of these things may be real enough, even though the onlooker is not disposed to share in it. Compassion takes up the onlooker's point of view, making the best judgment the onlooker can make about what is really happening to the person, even when that may differ from the judgment of the person herself.

Adam Smith makes this point powerfully, using as his example a person who has altogether lost the use of reason. This, he argues, is "of all the calamities to which the condition of mortality exposes mankind ... by far the most dreadful." It will be an object of compassion to anyone who has "the least spark of humanity." But the person affected does not judge that his condition is bad—that, indeed, is a large part of what is so terrible about it:

But the poor wretch ... laughs and sings perhaps, and is altogether insensible of his own misery. The anguish which humanity feels, therefore, at the sight of such an object, cannot be the reflection of any sentiment of the sufferer. The compassion of the spectator must arise altogether from the consideration of what he himself would feel if he was reduced to the same unhappy situation, and, what perhaps is impossible, was at the same time able to regard it with his present reason and judgment.[12]

In short: implicit in the emotion itself is a conception of human flourishing and the major predicaments of human life, the best one the onlooker is able to form.

This is another way of putting our familiar point that the object of compassion is an intentional object—interpreted within the emotion as he or she is seen by the person whose emotion it is.[13] Therefore, as with any emotion, it may also happen that the person who has the emotion is wrong about what is going on, and the suffering person is right. Many judgments about the suffering of others are skewed by inattention, or bad social teaching, or by some false theory of human life. Seneca does not have compassion for Q, and here he is probably correct. As a Stoic, however, he would also refuse compassion to R, because he would judge that hunger and lack of education are not very important. Most of us will think him wrong, and to the extent that we do, we will be more likely to have compassion for R. Compassion, or its absence, depends upon the judgments about flourishing the spectator forms; and these will be only as reliable as is the spectator's general moral outlook.

The judgments of the sufferer are not altogether irrelevant to pity, where these differ from the personal judgments of the pitier: for the onlooker may judge that the sufferer is right to accord importance to a certain sort of loss, even though she herself does not do so. For example, a wind player whose lip becomes even slightly injured may judge the suffering to be of tremendous size, and I may have compassion for him on that account, even though I myself would find a similar injury trivial. But this is because, at a more general level, I validate the judgment of the sufferer: for I agree with him that it is a terrible thing to be deprived of one's career and one's mode of expression, whatever it is, and I see his injury as such a deprivation. My compassion revolves around the thought that it would be right for anyone suffering a loss of that sort to be very upset. On the other hand, the wind player will be right to laugh at me if I complain a great deal about a minor injury to my own lip: for the very thing that would mean loss of career to him means no such thing to me, and it is this general description that validates the judgment of "size." Human beings have different ways of specifying the content of the major constituents of human flourishing: but unless the onlooker can bring the suffering back to one of these major components, as she conceives of things, she will not have the emotion.

Sometimes the relationship between onlooker and sufferer may militate against an independent judgment of "size." Often love takes up the viewpoint of the loved person, refusing to judge a calamity in a way different from the way in which the beloved has appraised it. Other circumstances, too, may suggest evaluative deferral. For example, if I know that a group in my society has suffered greatly in ways that I, a privileged person, have a hard time understanding, I may choose to take the estimate of misfortune offered me by qualified members of that group. But even in such cases I am, in effect, making a judgment of my own: namely, the judgment that the other person's estimate of "size" is the one I shall go by.

Now I turn to *fault*. Insofar as we believe that a person has come to grief through his or her own fault, we will blame and reproach, rather than having compassion. Insofar as we do feel compassion, it is either because we believe the person to be without blame for her plight or because, though there is an element of fault, we believe that her suffering is out of proportion to the fault. Compassion then addresses itself to the nonblameworthy increment. This comes out very clearly both in Aristotle's account and in the poetic material on which he bases it. *Eleos,* he insists, sees its object as "undeserving (*anaxios*)" of the suffering.[14] Such undeserved suffering appeals to our sense of *injustice* (1386b14–15). He adds that for this reason the emotion is more likely to be felt towards people who are seen as in general good (1386b6–8): for then we will be more likely to believe that they do not deserve the bad things that befall them.[15] But it is not inconsistent with his account to have compassion for people for things they do out of their own bad character or culpable negligence—so long as one can either see the suffering as out of all proportion to the fault *or* view the bad character or negligence as itself the product of forces to some extent excusably beyond the person's control.

This point about desert is strongly emphasized in Homeric and tragic appeals for compassion. When the suffering is plainly not the person's fault, as in Philoctetes' case, the appeal for compassion need not be preceded by argument. But where there is a possible disagreement about culpability, the appeal to pity comes closely linked with the assertion of one's innocence. Throughout the *Oedipus at Colonus*, Oedipus insists on the unwilling nature of his crimes—in order to hold the emotions of the characters (and of the audience). Similarly, Cadmus, at the end of Euripides' *Bacchae*, joins to his admission of wrongdoing a claim that the god, by inflicting "unmeasurable sorrow, unbearable to witness" (1244) has exceeded the just penalty.[16] Only this justifies, it seems, his claim to compassion from the other characters (1324); the audience is being asked to share those judgments and that emotion.[17]

A significant further step is taken in Sophocles' *Trachiniai*. Hyllus insists that the tragic predicament of Heracles was caused by the negligence *(agnômosunê)* of the gods. This being the case, it is appropriate for the human actors to have compassion for his plight—it is "an object of compassion for us *(oiktra men hemin)*." But it would not be appropriate for the gods to have compassion, since it was their fault: instead the events are "an object of shame for them *(aischra d'ekeinois)*." So compassion requires blameless- ness not only on the part of its object, but also on the part of the onlooker. It would be simply hypocritical to weep over a plight that you yourself have caused. In other words, the onlooker has to see the disaster as falling on the person from outside, so to speak; and she will be unable to do this if she believes either that the person has caused it or that she herself has caused it.[18]

These ideas are developed in a fascinating way in Clark's study of contemporary American attitudes. Her subjects all feel sympa- thy only for plights caused by "bad luck" or "victimization by forces beyond a person's control" (p. 84). And "[a] plight is *unlucky* when it is *not* the result of a person's willfulness, malfea- sance, negligence, risk taking, or in some way 'bringing it on him or herself' " (p. 84). Such assessments, of course, are profoundly influenced by prevailing social attitudes. Clark finds that Americans are not very tolerant of ambiguity: they tend to place events "either in the realm of inevitability, chance, fate, and luck or in the realm of intentionality, responsibility, and blame" (p. 100). In order for emotion to occur, they need to be able to conceive of the event as something that simply strikes someone, as if from outside: they use terms such as "befalls," "besieges," "ails," "struck," "hit her like a ton of bricks." Where it appears that agency makes some difference, they are unwilling to see any admixture of external bad luck. Thus Clark finds that Americans are on the whole less ready than Europeans to judge that poverty is bad luck, given the prevalence of the belief that initiative and hard work are important factors in determining economic success. Similarly, Americans have been slow to judge that sexual assault is a "plight," even if it is clearly a wrongful act against the woman, because they retain attitudes suggesting that the woman "brought it on herself"—by walking alone in a dangerous place, for example. On the other hand, alcoholism and drug abuse are surprisingly likely—and more likely than in previous generations—to be seen as things that "fall on" the person through no fault of her own.[19]

This cognitive element of the emotion is, then, highly malleable. The rhetoric of "sympathy entrepreneurs" such as politicians and journalists can make a considerable difference to public emotion. Sociologist Michele Landis has argued, for example, that Roosevelt was a brilliant rhetorician of compassion during the New Deal, when he got Americans to think of economic disaster as something that strikes people from outside through no fault of their own, like a flood or a dust storm. Even the term "the Depression" was a masterstroke, with its links to hurricanes ("a tropical depression") and ensuing flash flooding.

We often have compassion for people whose "plights" are in large part of their own creation. A parent, for example, may feel compassion for the mess an adolescent child has gotten into, and yet think that it is the child's own fault. Still, when we have such thoughts, we are, I believe, making a two-stage judgment. In one way, it is the child's own fault; and yet the condition of adolescence, which is not her fault, brings with it a certain blindness and a liability to certain types of error. For these sorts of errors, culpable though in one way they are, we also have compassion; we would not in the same way feel compassion for errors that do not seem to be a part of the predicament of adolescence. Thus, we are likely to feel compassion for a teenager who has been arrested for drunk driving, but not for one who has tortured and killed a dog.

The latter does not seem to be a part of any kind of "bad fate," even the bad fate of being sixteen.

Compassion requires, then, a notion of responsibility and blame. It also requires, as we can now see, the belief that there are serious bad things that may happen to people through no fault of their own, or beyond their fault. In having compassion for another, the compassionate person accepts, then, a certain picture of the world, a picture according to which the valuable things are not always safely under a person's own control, but can in some ways be damaged by fortune. As we shall see in Chapter 7, this picture of the world is profoundly controversial. Nobody can deny that the usual occasions for compassion occur: that children die, that cities are defeated, that political freedoms are lost, that age and disease disrupt functioning. But how important, really, *are* these things? To what extent are important human goals really at the mercy of fortune?

Let us now turn to the third requirement of compassion, as Aristotle and the poetic tradition understand it. (My account will depart from Aristotle at this point.) This is a judgment of *similar possibilities*: compassion concerns those misfortunes "which the person himself might expect to suffer, either himself or one of his loved ones" (1385b14–15). Thus, Aristotle adds, it will be felt only by those with some experience and understanding of suffering (1385b24 ff.); and one will not have compassion if one thinks that one is above suffering and has everything (1385b21–22, b31). This fact is repeatedly stressed in poetic appeals to compassion: thus Philoctetes reminds his visitors that they, too, may encounter uncontrollable pain. To Achilles, who is slow to identify his lot with that of ordinary mortals, Homer's Priam points out the vulnerability he shares with them through the old age of a beloved father (*Iliad* 24). In the *Odyssey*, Antinoos' belief in his own immunity from reversal (the state of mind that Aristotle perceptively calls a "hubristic disposition") apparently suffices for his refusal of compassion to Odysseus, disguised as a beggar.

This element in compassion is the focus of the marvelous discussion of that emotion in Rousseau's *Émile*. Drawing his account from the classical tradition, Rousseau takes as his epigraph Dido's statement from the *Aeneid,* "Not inexperienced in suffering, I learn how to bring aid to the wretched." He argues, agreeing with Aristotle, that an awareness of one's own weakness and vulnerability is a necessary condition for *pitié;* without this, we will have an arrogant harshness:

Why are kings without pity for their subjects? Because they count on never being human beings. Why are the rich so hard toward the poor? It is because they have no fear of being poor. Why does a noble have such contempt for a peasant? It is because he never will be a peasant.... Each may be tomorrow what the one whom he helps is today.... Do not, therefore, accustom your pupil to regard the sufferings of the unfortunate and the labors of the poor from the height of his glory; and do not hope to teach him to pity them if he considers them alien to him. Make him understand well that the fate of these unhappy people can be his, that all their ills are there in the ground beneath his feet, that countless unforeseen and inevitable events can plunge him into them from one moment to the next. Teach him to count on neither birth nor health nor riches. Show him all the vicissitudes of fortune.[20]

Both Rousseau and Aristotle insist, then, that compassion requires acknowledgment that one has possibilities and vulnerabilities similar to those of the sufferer. One makes sense of the suffering by recognizing that one might oneself encounter such a reversal; one estimates its meaning in part by thinking what it would mean to encounter that oneself; and one sees oneself, in the process, as one to whom such things might in fact happen. This is why compassion is so closely linked to fear, both in the poetic tradition and in Aristotle's account.[21]

As I observed earlier, this judgment of similar possibility requires a demarcation: which creatures am I to count as sharing possibilities with me, and which not? If it really is true that I will have compassion only to the extent that I see the possibilities of others as similar, this means that the emotion will depend on my ability to see similarities between myself and others. Aristotle insists that the similarity should be not to my own possibilities alone, but to those of my loved ones as well—a plausible addition, given that this is a prominent way in which we make sense to ourselves of disasters befalling people of different age, for example, or different gender.

Here we arrive at another place where social and familial teachings play a powerful role, and errors may easily occur. The beings who are likely to be seen as similar to myself or to my loved ones will probably be those who share a way of life, those whom society has marked as similar. Rousseau argues that acquaintance with the usual vicissitudes of fortune will make it impossible for Émile (who does not inhabit a diseased society) to exclude the poor, or members of the lower classes, since he will know that people lose money and status all the time, and their political entitlements. But he also tells us that in his own society many people sever themselves in thought from the possibilities of the lower classes: nobles and kings therefore lack compassion for those beneath them. In a similar way, in our own society, juries often have a hard time sympathizing with the life story of a criminal defendant who is very different from them in class and background; they have even more difficulty if they are provided, at the same time, with a "victim impact" statement from people who are more similar to them.[22] All kinds of social barriers—of class, religion, ethnicity, gender, sexual orientation—prove recalcitrant to the imagination, and this recalcitrance impedes emotion.

Finally, the species boundary usually proves difficult to cross in emotion, since the possibilities of another creature for good or ill are opaque to us. Spinoza takes this difference in emotional nature to justify indifference to the suffering of animals.[23] Most major theorists of compassion also draw the species boundary firmly, focusing on human ills alone. Rousseau, by contrast to many, feels that Émile will naturally judge the lot of small animals as similar to his own, and will learn compassion best if he begins by focusing on their sufferings.

Why are similar possibilities important? Is the judgment of similarity on a par with the judgments of seriousness and of fault—that is to say, is it a necessary constituent part of the emotion, a part of its very definition? Or is it only a helpful epistemological device, a way of getting clear about the significance of the suffering for the life of the person who has it? The point made by Aristotle and Rousseau seems to be that the pain of another will be an object of my concern, a part of my sense of my own well-being, only if I acknowledge some sort of community between myself and the other, understanding what it might be for me to face such pain. Without that sense of commonness, both Aristotle and Rousseau claim, I will react with sublime indifference or mere intellectual curiosity, like an obtuse alien from another world; and I will not care what I do to augment or relieve the suffering. Spinoza supports this, when he links his denial that humans and animals have a "similar nature" with the judgment that it is all right to cause animals pain. What should we make of this claim?

One can see that a certain sort of stranger cannot help being indifferent and unconcerned: for if he or she has no experiential sense of the importance of these matters, it will be hard even to grasp that suffering *is* suffering, and hard not to be clumsy or callous in dealing with it in consequence. But need this be so? Is this just a point about the limitations of understanding? Could we imagine a divine or perfect being feeling compassion for the sufferings of mortals without an awareness of sharing the same possibilities and vulnerabilities? Frequently, in the classical tradition, the gods are depicted as obtuse and lacking in compassion; this lack is connected to their lack of vulnerability. To a being who cannot feel more than temporary or trivial discomfort, the appalling suffering of a Heracles will be hard to see correctly.[24] But gods (and godlike humans) sometimes do have compassion: Zeus weeps for the death of Sarpedon; the Christian god feels ceaseless compassion for the errors and sufferings of mortals; the Buddhist who has successfully escaped from personal vulnerability and pain experiences compassion for the sufferings of those still fettered. Such cases are tricky to estimate: for usually in one or another way they do after all fulfill Aristotle's requirement that the person acknowledge similar vulnerability, "either himself or one of his loved ones." In pitying Sarpedon, Zeus pities his own son, for whom he also grieves; this personal vulnerability gives him a basis for more general pity of those dead in the war. The Christian god is vulnerable in a similar way, suffering agony and death both in his own person and in the person of his son. The boddhisatva has experienced the ills that he pities, even if by now he no longer expects to do so. Furthermore, the attachment to the concerns of the suffering person is itself a form of vulnerability: so a god, in allowing himself to be so attached, renders himself to a degree needy and non-self-sufficient, and thus similar to mortals. Religious conceptions such as those of Epicureanism, Stoicism, and Platonism, which imagine the godlike condition as strictly self-sufficient, also deny compassion to the godlike.

Must this be? What is really at issue here, it would seem, is the eudaimonistic character of the emotions, as I have defined them. I have argued that in order for grief to be present, the dead person must be seen, and valued, as an important part of the mourner's own life, her scheme of goals and projects. Similarly, in order for compassion to be present, the person must consider the suffering of another as a significant part of his or her own scheme of goals and ends. She must take that person's ill as affecting her own flourishing. In effect, she must make herself vulnerable in the person of another. It is that *eudaimonistic judgment,* not the judgment of similar possibilities, that seems to be a necessary constituent of compassion. For that judgment to occur, it is not strictly necessary that she focus on the other person's relation to herself. A truly omniscient deity ought to know the significance of human suffering without thinking of its own risks or bad prospects, and a truly loving deity will be intensely concerned for the ills befalling mortals without having to think of more personal loss or risk. (For such a deity, all humans are already children or loved ones, part of its scheme of goals and ends.) But human beings have difficulty attaching others to themselves except through thoughts about what is already of concern to them. Imagining one's own similar possibilities aids the extension of one's own eudaimonistic imagination.

The recognition of one's own related vulnerability is, then, an important and frequently an indispensable epistemological requirement for compassion in human beings—the thing that makes the difference between viewing hungry peasants as beings whose sufferings matter and viewing them as distant objects whose experiences have nothing to do with one's own life. Such a judgment is psychologically powerful in moving other people into one's own circle of concern. Even when we feel compassion for animals, whom we know to be very different from ourselves, it is on the basis of our common vulnerability to pain, hunger, and other types of suffering that we feel the emotion. Even when we feel compassion for precisely those aspects of an animal's suffering that are unlike our own—for example, their lack of legal rights, their lack of power to shape the laws that affect their lives, or (in some cases) their lack of understanding of what is happening to them—it is most often on the basis of a sense of shared vulnerability to pain that we extend our sympathy. We think, how horrible it would be to suffer pain in that way, and without hope of changing it.

This fact explains why so frequently those who wish to withhold compassion and to teach others to do so portray the sufferers as altogether dissimilar in kind and in possibility. In *The Destruction of the European Jews,* Raoul Hilberg shows how pervasively Nazi talk of Jews, in connection with their murder, portrayed them as nonhuman: either as beings of a remote animal kind, such as insects or vermin, or as inanimate objects, "cargo" to be transported. (Later we shall see how disgust aids that project, bounding off the sufferers from their tormentors.) When by surprise an individual sufferer was encountered in a manner that made similarity unavoidably clear, one frequently saw what philosopher Jonathan Glover, reflecting on a wide range of cases of genocide and evil, calls a "breakthrough," in which the seriousness of the suffering was acknowledged and pity led to shame and confusion.[25] Sometimes the catalyst of a breakthrough is simple physical proximity. Sometimes it is the reminder of a similar type of family life.[26] Sometimes it may even be sexual desire. A remarkable moment of that kind is shown in the film *Schindler's List,* when the Nazi camp commandant confronts the beautiful Jewish housemaid. As she stands in her basement room trembling in her slip, he grasps her chin, stares violently into her eyes, and asks, in some strange agony of conscience, "Is this the face of a rat?"[27]

In short, the judgment of similar possibility is part of a construct that bridges the gap between the child's existing goals and the eudaimonistic judgment that others (even distant others) are an important part of one's own scheme of goals and projects, important as ends in their own right. Equipped with her general conception of human flourishing, the spectator looks at a world in which people suffer hunger, disability, disease, slavery, through no fault of their own. She believes that goods such as food, health, citizenship, freedom, do matter. And yet she acknowledges, as well, that it is uncertain whether she herself will remain among the safe and privileged ones to whom such goods are stably guaranteed. She acknowledges that the lot of the beggar might be (or become) her own. This leads her to turn her thoughts outward, asking about society's general arrangement for the allocation of goods and resources. Given the uncertainty of life,[28] she will be inclined, other things being equal, to want a society in which the lot of the worst off—of the poor, of people defeated in war, of women, of servants—is as good as it can be. Self-interest itself, via thought about shared vulnerabilities, promotes the selection of principles that raise society's floor.

It is through this set of ideas that compassion is standardly connected, in the tradition, to generous giving. Once again, generous giving could take place without the prudential thoughts of similarity, if the person already cared intensely about the good of the recipients. But the prudential thoughts do frequently assist in this process, as we shall see shortly (section IV of Chapter 6 of *Upheavals of Thought*).

Compassion, then, has three cognitive elements: the judgment of *size* (a serious bad event has befallen someone); the judgment of *nondesert* (this person did not bring the suffering on himself or herself); and the *eudaimonistic judgment* (this person, or creature, is a significant element in my scheme of goals and projects, an end whose good is to be promoted). The Aristotelian *judgment of similar possibilities* is an epistemological aid to forming the *eudaimonistic judgment*—*not* necessary, but usually very important.

Finally, let us recall that, like all emotions directed at living beings, compassion frequently either contains or is closely linked to a non-eudaimonistic element of *wonder* (see Chapter 1, section V of Chapter 6 of *Upheavals of Thought*). In viewing Philoctetes with compassion, as worthy of concern and help, I also consider him as a human being, and I see that humanity itself with an emotion that is likely to be, at least in part, non-eudaimonistic; but the non-eudaimonistic element of wonder strongly reinforces or motivates my eudaimonistic concern. Similarly, when I see with compassion the beating of an animal, a wonder at the complex living thing itself is likely to be mixed with my compassion, and to support it. (Thus we rarely have compassion for the deaths of creatures, such as mosquitos and slugs, toward whom we do not have wonder.) Wonder's role varies in different cases of compassion, and it is always hard to say whether we ought to see it as a part of the emotion itself, or as a different emotion closely associated with it. (I am inclined to the latter view.) But I think that wonder does often play a very important role in marking the world for our concern, and thence in directing our attention to the sufferings of its members. It shapes, in that way, our conception of *eudaimonia*.

What is the relationship of the cognitive elements to the emotion itself? It is natural to ask at this point whether one could not have all of the judgments without having the painful emotion. One might grant the necessity of these judgments without granting that they are sufficient for having the full emotion[29]—still less, that the emotion itself is a certain sort of acknowledgment of their truth. I see a stranger in the street. Someone tells me that this woman has just learned of the death of her only child, who was run over by a drunken driver. I have no reason not to believe what I have been told. So: I believe that this woman has suffered an extremely terrible loss, through no fault of her own. I know well that I myself might suffer a similar loss. Now I might at this point feel compassion for the woman; but then again, I might not. As Adam Smith says, giving a similar example, the fact that she is a stranger might make it difficult for me to picture her suffering; or I might simply be too busy and distracted to focus on what I have been told.[30] Doesn't this show that I can, after all, have all of the judgments without the emotion?

Notice, however, that the person does not in fact have all of the cognitive elements of compassion, as I have defined it: for she lacks the *eudaimonistic judgment*. She does not see the woman as an important part of her own scheme of goals and projects. Often the judgment of similar possibilities will suffice to value the person as a part of one's circle of concern; but in this case that common psychological connection has not been made, probably because the person is a stranger; or the person might be distanced from the self in some other way. Furthermore, in this case it is not entirely clear that she even thinks the suffering a serious bad thing; she may know that for the woman it is bad, but it is not clear that she has affirmed its serious badness from her own viewpoint. A sadistic torturer knows that his victim's suffering is bad from the victim's point of view, but from his own point of view it is a good thing. In our example, the woman's suffering is probably not seen as either good or bad—because the eudaimonistic judgment is lacking. Here we see how closely the judgment of size and the eudaimonistic judgment are related. If the judgment of size relies on the onlooker's point of view, it will fail if the onlooker is just not very concerned with the fate of the suffering person one way or another.

Another way in which compassion may fail is connected with immaturity: one may have the judgments on authority, and yet not understand their true significance. Rousseau describes an Émile who has suffered himself, and who has it on good authority that others suffer too. He sees gestures indicative of suffering, and his teacher assures him that they mean in the case of others what they would in his own. But, Rousseau claims, he does not really believe or judge that this is so, until he has become able to imagine their suffering vividly to himself—at which point he will also suffer the pain of *pitié*. "To see it without feeling it," he writes, "is not to know it."[31] By this he means something very precise: that the suffering of others has not become a part of Emile's cognitive repertory in such a way that it will influence his conduct, provide him with motives and expectations, and so forth. He is merely paying it lip service, until he can perform the thought experiment that is, in Rousseau's view, sufficient for being disturbed.

To cast doubt on my claim that the three cognitive requirements are sufficient for the emotion, we need, then, a different kind of example, one where it is clear that the judgment of size is not just parroted but comprehended, and where it is clear that the eudaimonistic judgment has been made. So let us imagine that my own child, an important part of my scheme of goals and ends, has just suffered a serious loss. I know that it is serious, and I know that it was not her fault. Is it possible for me to have all these judgments and yet to fail to have compassion for her plight? Only, I would say, in a case similar to my case of delayed mourning in Chapter 1, where I simply haven't yet taken in what has happened. I may be able to say the words, but their significance has not sunk in. This means, however, that the belief itself has not become a part of my cognitive repertory, in such a way that it will affect the pattern of my other beliefs and my actions. In other words, the example does not show that some noncognitive element, such as an ache or a pain, is required in addition to the three judgments.

But what about the case of an omniscient and invulnerable god—or even a boddhisatva, who has succeeded in severing himself from personal vulnerability to pain? Couldn't such a being have all the judgments involved in compassion without having the upheaval of the painful emotion itself? What this question reveals is that I have arrived at my result only because I have not seen compassion as strictly entailing a judgment of similar possibilities. For Aristotle, such beings would not have compassion; according to my account they do. In my account, unlike his, compassion does not entail personal vulnerability, although the recognition of personal vulnerability is extremely important, psychologically, in getting imperfect humans to have compassion for another person's plight. This means, too, that compassion is not linked to personal fear in my account, as it is in Aristotle's: one may have compassion for another without having anything at all to fear for oneself— although, again, in imperfect humans this link will usually prove psychologically valuable, in promoting concern.

One might then object that what the nonfearful and nonvulnerable person has is not the painful emotion itself, but just some distanced version of it, and that my three judgments are sufficient for, and constitute, that distanced attitude—let us call it humane concern. They are not, perhaps, sufficient for the upheaval of compassion itself. Now there may be some cases where we do want to say that a self-sufficient being has humane concern and not compassion: the Stoic sage is like this, and perhaps, in some interpretations, the boddhisatva as well. But the sage really does not share my three judgments, because he denies that the vicissitudes of fortune have "size." Marcus Aurelius gives us a good image: we are to think of the sufferings of others as like the sufferings of a child who has lost a toy—they are real enough, and worthy of our concern, but only in the way that we'd console a child, not because we ourselves think that the loss of a toy is really a large matter. If, instead, we imagine a self-sufficient being who really does care deeply about the vicissitudes of fortune, and who really does think that they are a big thing—the Christian and Jewish images of God, for example—then I think we do want to say that the three judgments are sufficient—not merely for humane concern, but for the upheaval of the emotion itself. Such a being, though not vulnerable to upset personally, has become vulnerable to upset in the person of another. That is how such a being differs from the Stoic sage.

If the cognitive elements are both sufficient for compassion and constituent parts of it, we still need to ask, as always, whether there are other necessary elements as well. Here again, the response will have to be, what might those other elements be? I shall assume that in Chapter 1 we have ruled out the possibility of a general type/type correlation between a given emotion and a specific physiological state, and that we have also cast a great deal of doubt on the claim that feelings of a determinate kind always arise in the case of any given emotion, as constituent parts of it. But that possibility needs to be considered here once again, in the following way. Aristotle mentions pain in his definition: compassion is a particular type of pain. And it seems natural to describe the experience this way. Indeed, the pain seems crucial to compassion's motivational role. But what is this pain? Is it something over and above the thought that something very bad is happening and that it matters for one's scheme of goals and projects? On the one hand, we are strongly inclined to say yes, it is something more. It is a disturbance, a tug at the heartstrings. But that doesn't quite solve our problem, because we know by now that thoughts are some of the most disturbing things there are.

First of all, we must ask whether the pain is being imagined as just a fluttering or a spasm, only contingently or causally linked to the thoughts, or whether it is itself so closely linked to the thoughts that we might call it the affective dimension of the thought, a pain "at the thought of" the bad thing, as Aristotle puts it. If it is the former, a knot in the stomach or a lump in the throat, then, here as elsewhere, it seems implausible to require that any particular such pain be present in order to ascribe compassion to someone. People are extremely variable in the modes in which they experience their emotions physically, and even phenomenologically. Even if every compassionate person has *some* pain or other, it would surely be arbitrary and wrong to require any particular type of such pain. And the possibility of non-conscious compassion makes us still more skeptical: for surely it is possible to have compassion and not be aware of it—if one is not reflecting on one's own emotions, or if one has been led to suppose that real men don't have such soft sentiments. Then one could well have and be motivated by the thoughts, without being in any noticeable phenomenological state.

If, however, by "pain" we mean something more organic to the thoughts, that is, if the very character of this pain cannot be described without ascribing to it the intentionality embodied in the thought, then it is not clear after all that it is a separate element. At the very least it looks as if a pain of that sort—Aristotle's "pain at" the thought of someone's suffering—is reliably caused by the thought, and does not have much, if any, causal independence. Once we begin to think harder about how to define such a pain, moreover, it appears that it does not have much conceptual independence either: not any old throbbing or tugging will do, but only the sort that is "about" or "at" the misfortune. It is mental pain directed towards the victim that we want, not some obtuse physical spasm; but what is this mental pain, if not a way of seeing the victim's distress with concern, as a terrible thing? Perhaps we could call it the affective character of the thoughts: but the notion of "affect" is notoriously slippery and vague, and it is unclear whether we have really succeeded in defining a truly separate element.[32] In short: if we do discover a separate element in the notion of pain, to the extent that it is separate from the cognitive material it also seems to be too various to be a necessary element in the definition. To the extent that it is closely tied to, or even an element in, the cognitive material, we probably haven't succeeded in introducing a separate element. Certainly, when we are trying to ascertain whether Émile has learned compassion or not, we are satisfied by the evidence of a certain sort of imagination and thought, a certain way of viewing the distress of others. We don't inquire whether in addition he has a throbbing or an aching. This suggests that we really do not think that pain in that sense is a further necessary element.

Notes

1   I narrate Sophocles' version of the story. In the lost versions by Aeschylus and Euripides, we know that the island was inhabited.

2   I have not been able to find a significant difference between *eleos* and *oiktos*; their interchangeable use in the play seems governed more by poetic considerations than by considerations of sense.

3   In the Greek, *deina pathein*. The repetition of *deina* below does not explicitly include *pathein*, but I have translated both as "terrible affliction" to indicate the repetition.

4   I discuss Aristotle's account in M. Nussbaum, *The Fragility of Goodness: Luck and Ethics in Greek Tragedy and Philosophy* (Cambridge: Cambridge University Press, 2nd edition with new preface, 2001), Interlude 2, and also in M. Nussbaum, "Tragedy and Self Sufficiency: Plato and Aristotle on Fear and Pity," in A. Rorty, ed., *Essays on Aristotle's Poetics* (Princeton: Princeton University Press, 1992), pp. 261–90, Nietzsche's in M. Nussbaum, "Pity and Mercy: Nietzsche's Stoicism," in R. Schacht, ed., *Nietzsche: Genealogy, Morality* (Berkeley and Los Angeles: University of California Press, 1993), pp. 139–67. See also the very perceptive analysis of both Aristotelian and tragic pity in S. Halliwell, *Aristotle's Poetics* (Chapel Hill: University of North Carolina Press, 1986).

5   Although Aristotle's Greek term *eleos,* is usually rendered "pity," I shall continue to translate it as "compassion," as seems more appropriate to the nuances of the two English terms.

6   Aristotle uses the participle of the verb "appear"; in M. Nussbaum, *The Therapy of Desire: Theory and Practice in Hellenistic Ethics* (Princeton: Princeton University Press, 1994), Chapter 3, I argue that this does not entail that he is thinking of *phantasia* as contrasted with judgment or belief. In fact, he regularly uses belief-words interchangeably with appearance-words.

7   This part of her account focuses on both interview data and the annual listing by the *New York Times* of its "Neediest Cases," whose descriptions

of "debilitating plights" involving "death, mental and physical illness, disability, poverty ... loneliness" show that our sense of tragedy is not discontinuous with that expected from the audience of the *Philoctetes*.

8   C. Clark, *Misery and Company: Sympathy in Everyday Life* (Chicago: The University of Chicago Press, 1997), p. 83.

9   Here Clark's use of the term "sympathy" may be significant: it is hard to imagine that her subjects would have described themselves as having "compassion" for people caught in traffic.

10 For these and similar cases, see M. Chen, *A Quiet Revolution: Women in Transition in Rural Bangladesh* (Cambridge, MA: Schenkman, 1983), Chen's paper in M. Nussbaum and J. Glover, eds, *Women, Culture, and Development* (Oxford: Clarendon Press, 1995), and M. Nussbaum, *Women and Human Development: The Capabilities Approach* (Cambridge: Cambridge University Press, 2000).

11 See Nussbaum, *Women and Human Development*, Chapter 2, with references to the literature on this question.

12 A. Smith, *The Theory of Moral Sentiments* (Oxford: Clarendon Press, 1976), p. 12, from which the two previous citations are drawn as well. Smith goes on to talk of a mother's pity for the suffering of her infant, as yet unable to understand the difficulties of its situation, and of our pity for the dead. Contrast J.-J. Rousseau, *Émile*, trans. A. Bloom (New York: Basic Books, 1979), who holds that "the pity one has for another's misfortune is measured not by the quantity of that misfortune but by the sentiment which one attributes to those who suffer it" (p. 225). L. Blum, "Compassion" in A.O. Rorty, ed., *Explaining Emotions* (Berkeley and Los Angeles: University of California Press, 1980), p. 510, follows the Rousseau position, where what he calls "compassion" is concerned; he distinguishes "pity" from "compassion," arguing that the former involves a degree of distance and condescension to the sufferer. This may be right about some current nuances of usage, but not about the history of their philosophical use; nor would it be right to suppose that approaching the predicament of another with one's own best judgment, rather than the sufferer's, need involve condescension. I would say that there is condescension in suspending one's own reflection, and true compassion in trying to get things right.

13 Aristotle registers this point by insisting that compassion, like other major emotions, relies on the "appearances" and beliefs of the person whose emotion it is.

14 *Rhetoric* 1385b14, b34–86a1, 1386b7, b10, b12, b13; *Poetics* 1453a4, 5.

15 He adds that if one believes that people in general are pretty bad, one will rarely have compassion, for one will be inclined to believe that they deserve the bad things that happen to them. In saying this, however, he

ignores the importance of the causal connection between the person's badness and the *particular* thing for which he or she suffers: even bad people will get sympathy for a particular reversal if it is clear that it is not their fault. Such connections are sometimes in fact ignored—as when people who despise homosexuals view AIDS as a punishment for their alleged bad way of life; but the logic of compassion requires the person who withholds it to posit some sort of causal link; such links are often supplied by views of divine punishment.

16 *Endikôs men, all' agan,* 1259; and *epexerchêi lian,* 1346.

17 On the connection thus made between compassion and the Aristotelian notion of *hamartia,* see Nussbaum, "Tragedy and Self-Sufficiency: Plato and Aristotle on Fear and Pity," pp. 261–90, Halliwell, *Aristotle's Poetics,* and, for a superlative study of the word and its connection with blame and innocence, T.C.W. Stinton, *"Hamartia* in Aristotle and Greek Tragedy," *Classical Quarterly* NS, 25 (1975), pp. 221–54.

18 For further discussion of Hyllus' speech, and Bernard Williams' interpretation of it, see Nussbaum, *The Fragility of Goodness.*

19 See Clark, *Misery and Company,* Chapter 3, describing responses to a questionnaire about several examples of "bad luck," including a sexual assault and a job loss due to alcoholism. For the general evolution of attitudes on women's responsibility for sexual assault, see S.J. Schulhofer, *Unwanted Sex: The Culture of Intimidation and the Failure of Law* (Cambridge, MA: Harvard University Press, 1998).

20 Rousseau, *Émile,* p. 224; I have altered Bloom's translation in several places, in particular substituting "human being" for "man." I have retained "pity" for *pitié.*

21 See *Rhetoric* 1386a22–8, 82b26–7; *Poetics* 1453a5–6; for discussion, see Halliwell, *Aristotle's Poetics* and Nussbaum, "Tragedy and Self-Sufficiency," pp. 274–5.

22 See S. Bandes, "Empathy, Narrative, and Victim Impact Statements," *University of Chicago Law Review* 63 (1997), pp. 361–412, discussed further in Chapter 8.

23 Spinoza, *Ethics,* Part IV, Proposition 37, Scholium I: "I do not deny that beasts feel; I am denying that we are on that account debarred from paying heed to our own advantage and from making use of them as we please and dealing with them as best suits us, seeing that they do not agree with us in nature and their emotions are different in nature from human emotions." *The Ethics and Selected Letters,* trans. S. Shirley, ed. S. Feldman (Indianapolis: Hackett Publishing Company, 1982).

24 See Nussbaum, "Tragedy and Self-Sufficiency", R.P. Winnington-Ingram, *Sophocles: An Interpretation* (Cambridge: Cambridge University Press, 1980).

25 See R. Hilberg, *The Destruction of the European Jews* (New York: Holmes and Meier, 1985); J. Glover, *Humanity: A Moral History of the Twentieth Century* (London: Jonathan Cape, 1999), pp. 81, 345–8.

26 Glover, *Humanity*, p. 346: Rudolf Höss records how the sight of women and children caused men working in the crematoria to think of their own families. Christopher Browning, *Ordinary Men* (New York: HarperCollins, 1992), p. 113, describes a man who refused to take part in the shooting of Jews "[b]ecause there were children among the Jews we had brought and at the time I myself was a father with a family of three children."

27 Rousseau insists that Émile is ready to learn compassion only when budding sexual desire has already turned his thoughts outward toward others. He appears to be wrong about the development of compassion; and desire may lead to objectification as well as to the humanization of the object. Nonetheless, a humanizing effect is also possible.

28 Rousseau remarks that the emotion develops most easily where people live highly unstable political lives: thus the Turks, he alleges, are "more humane and more hospitable" than Europeans, because their "totally arbitrary government ... renders the greatness and the fortune of individuals always precarious and unsteady" (*Émile*, p. 224). One would not wish to draw normative political conclusions from this dubious observation. I have already argued that the perceptions of people who are inured to suffering and ill-treatment are very likely to be deformed by that experience—as Rousseau himself later argues. Maximizing the awareness of risk and vulnerability is not a morally valuable strategy—see Chapters 7 and 8.

29 As in Chapter 1, at this point in the argument sufficiency may be imagined either causally—these judgments produce whatever other constituents are also necessary for compassion—or by saying that these judgments are the only constituents there are. In both cases, however, we are considering the judgments as among the constituents of the emotion; each necessary to its being the emotion it is. I shall go on to argue that there are no further constituents that we should recognize as necessary in compassion.

30 Smith, *The Theory of Moral Sentiments*, pp. 17–18.

31 Rousseau, *Émile*, p. 222.

32 See my remarks on M. Stocker with E. Hegeman, *Valuing Emotions* (Cambridge: Cambridge University Press, 1996) in Chapter 1, note 62.

6 Reasons for Love

Robert C. Solomon

For the past 28 years, I have been pursuing the idea that the ancient opposition between reason and the passions is an insidious one. It is an idea that is now widely accepted in both philosophy and psychology, whether in broad terms as a claim about reasons and argument or in more specific conceptions about the "cognitive" constituents of emotions or the "emotional" grounds or "reasons" in rational deliberation. But I have found that the coupling of "reasons" and emotion hits a brick wall, however, when our romantic sensibilities are disturbed. In particular, there is stubborn resistance to the idea that *love* is based on reason and reasons. And that is what this essay is about.

How do I love thee? (Reasons for love)

Imagine proposing to (or being proposed to by) your beloved in the following terms:

It does not appear to me that my hand is unworthy of your acceptance, or that the establishment I can offer would be any other than highly desirable. My situation in life, my connections with the [appropriate] family, and my relationship to your own, are circumstances highly in my favor; and you should take it into further consideration, that in spite of manifold attractions, it is by no means certain that another offer of marriage may ever be made to you.

So said Mr. Collins, proposing to Elizabeth, in Jane Austen's *Pride and Prejudice.* I think that I would not be radically misrepresenting the most common reaction (and the one intended by the author) as repulsion, or at the very least, the sense that such an alternatively pompous, threatening and insulting proposal lacks any semblance of charm and romance.

Pressed to explain why, many people would be tempted by the response, "because you don't love someone for reasons. You just love them, or you don't." A particularly vulgar expression of this view, rendered with a rhetorical flourish, was recently published by the "person with the highest measured IQ in the world," Marilyn Vos Savant. She writes, "Can you imagine falling in love with someone for no reason at all? Of course you can!" The rhetorical emphasis at the end makes it clear that she considers the point self-evident. I expect that most philosophers are less thoughtlessly romantic, so they might simply say, "not for *those* reasons." But then, I myself wrote, not long ago, "Love goes wrong, but it would be a mark of perversity or cynicism to insist that love must therefore be prepared to defend itself with reasons." I would still maintain that a demand for *justification* may be perverse or cynical, but I no longer doubt the relevance of reasons in and for love, including a modest notion of justification (minimally, as "making intelligible").

Perhaps we should not talk about love at all in such contexts and rather talk about conjugal partnerships or something of that sort. But this, I want to suggest, is a bit too quick. In the romantic climate of the times, evidently not much appreciated by Mr. Collins, it would not be too much of a reach to suggest that, in order to best secure the acceptance he seeks, he intends that Elizabeth should indeed take these as reasons for love. In this essay, I would like to explore this notion, *reasons for love,* that is, loving someone for a reason or for reasons. While it is not my aim to evaluate or rank such reasons (nor to say what is "really" or "true" love and what is not), it will be clear in what I say that some sorts of reasons (and some sorts of love) are in several senses "better" than others. In particular, I would like to suggest that the most appropriate reasons for love, what I will call *Aristophanic* reasons, are very different from what most people might think of as reasons for love.

Philosophers have often talked about love, if more often the love of wisdom than erotic or romantic love. But Plato conflated the two, so that the love of wisdom became a version of erotic love.

Kant, by contrast, dismissed love as a sentiment as merely "patho-logical" and juxtaposed it to "practical" love that was defined by reasons. Arthur Schopenhauer, although he differed from Kant about both love and morality, thought that love (as so much else) was but the irrational striving of the will to live. Jean-Paul Sartre, never to be outdone in terms of perversity, argued that love was just another stratagem for manipulating "the Other." But despite these great thinkers, love seems to be an avidly avoided topic for most contemporary philosophers.

Nevertheless, love has undeniable attractions for philosophers, both because of its very special if often neglected place in ethics and the good life and because it is, at least in the popular roman-tic imagination, so delightfully unreasonable. That, of course, is what interests me here. "The love that defies all reason" is a staple of our literature. The very notion of "reasons for love" strikes many people as unintelligible. "If one loves for reasons, one does not really love at all," might be a simple way to put the objection. But love without reason, love without reasons, is an unintelligibil-ity too, of a different kind, suggesting psychotic obsession, blind, blithering, helpless attachment, or mere frivolousness. To be sure, love is often misdirected, with damage to the lover and consterna-tion, concern, or amusement for the lover's friends and family. But even misdirected love and love gone wrong must have their reasons, even if, all things considered, these reasons may be unreasonable.

Perhaps Mr. Collins was giving reasons why Elizabeth should accept his proposal of marriage and not reasons for her loving him. But what nevertheless rubs our romantic fur in the wrong direction are the *kinds* of reasons advanced by Mr. Collins and others like him. Loving someone for his or her money, or connec-tions, or status, or, for that matter, even for his or her looks seems like love for just the *wrong* reasons, or, rather, it usually turns out that one doesn't love the other person at all; one just loves the money and puts up with the person, or covets the connections or status and is willing to be not only tolerant but even affectionate in order to share them. It thus indeed looks as if love *for reasons* is not love at all but rather a strategy, a sham, a bit of hypocrisy.

Of course, part of the question, as so often with sham and hypocrisy, is who is fooling whom. A supposed lover who "happens" to love a very rich man or woman will probably not ever admit to him or herself, even in moments of deep self-scrutiny, the true object of his or her affection. More likely, the supposed lover will avow and report, in all sincerity, that he or she is indeed in love, or at any rate, loves. (I have discussed the dynamic of this impoverished language of affection elsewhere, the hair-splitting struggle between "loving" and being "in love" just one of the more obvious manifestations of this.) This doesn't jeopardize the idea of love for reasons, but it introduces a serious complication into the discussion. Must a reason for love be conscious or available for ready articulation? Or might self-deception be a common complication in loving for reasons? It might be argued to be, along something like the following lines: one may "love" for reasons. Indeed, as self-interested creatures, it may be impossible for us *not* to love for reasons. But love is understood as not about reasons at all, and so the lover must fool him or herself into believing that he or she *just loves* the beloved, that the reasons are peripheral or ultimately irrelevant. This is often captured in the plaintive lament, "I want you to love me *for myself*!" and its requisite if unconvincing rebuttal, "I don't care about the money, I love *you*." But is such a lament reasonable? Or (if not) is such assurance unnecessary?

"Because you're beautiful": loving someone for their looks

Is anything a more inviting reason for love than the fact that the beloved is beautiful? But loving someone for their looks is a difficult case insofar as one cannot readily separate a person from his or her looks as one can with some ease separate a romantic fool and his money. But do I love you because you are beautiful? Or are you beautiful (to me) because I love you? That's an awkward set of questions, to be sure. A phenomenologist might challenge both questions by insisting that (from the first person point of view) there is no distinguishing how I experience you and how you "really" are. A more hard-headed philosopher might insist that beauty involves objective standards, or, at least, it requires a third person or inter-subjective perspective. All of this is or should be irrelevant to the lover for whom "beauty is in the eye of the beholder." But is your beauty a reason for loving you? On the first interpretation ("I love you because you are beautiful") that seems to be exactly what it is. But if so (so the argument goes), do I really love *you*?

Wittgenstein famously noted that the best (and only) picture we have of the human soul is the human body. It follows that the best picture we have of the soul of the person we love, that is, the person *him or herself*, is his or her physical appearance. To love the person *is* to love the face, the shape, the body. On the second interpretation ("you are beautiful because I love you"), the answer is more confusing. Yes, I love you because you are beautiful but it is by virtue of my love that I view you as beautiful. Or, following Irving Singer, one might say that I *bestow* you with beauty. But then it seems odd to say that I love you *because* you are beautiful, i.e. that your beauty is a reason for my loving you. Your beauty is constituted through my loving.

Yet loving someone for their looks seems to most of us to be an exemplary case of loving for reasons, both because we are indeed such visual and beauty-bound creatures and because a person's looks are (as Wittgenstein noted) so inseparable from our conception of them. But what makes loving someone for their looks philosophically intriguing is both the complexity described above, namely, whether beauty is a reason for love or love is the explanation for seeing someone as beautiful, and the now cliched notion that "beauty is in the eye of the beholder." But what both the complexity and the cliche suggest is that beauty is not so much a property of the person but *a feature of the relationship* (even if it is an unrequited relationship) rather than simply a feature of the beloved. Philosophers have often tried to capture this phenomenon, from the ancient and medieval debates about "intentionality" to twentieth-century phenomenology and Simon Blackburn's contemporary notion of "quasi-realism." The usual way of putting the point is to say that such properties are in some sense "subjective," dependent on the perspective of the perceiver (the lover). What I want to suggest instead is that virtually all reasons for love are best understood as features of the relationship and not as simply properties-of-the-beloved. They are dependent not only on the lover's perspective but on the complex bonds between the lover and the beloved.

One of the standard arguments against beauty as a reason for love has much to do with the idea that love ought to be "eternal," and so its reasons should be timeless as well. I think that this is misconceived. Quite the contrary of timelessness, love is a *process* that develops over time. "Eternity" may be a poetic way of capturing a magic moment, but the very idea of our love's being "outside of time" is ultimately unintelligible. Reasons for love typically refer to temporal or even transient features of the beloved or the relationship. This is not in itself an argument against them, but I would argue that the problem with beauty does have to do with time. It is not that beauty is not eternal. The problem is that beauty, physical beauty at least, is not *historical*. It makes no reference to its history or origins. It makes no reference to the future (although some of its enthusiasts will quickly point out that it suggests immediate promise, of pleasure, for example).

We should reject both the idea that a passion is true only if it does not alter and cannot end and that a good reason for love is one that remains true over time. True, constancy is a virtue in love, and, true, beauty may "fade." But it does not follow that beauty cannot be at some point a reason for love though not at another. One might well fall in love for the sole reason that the beloved is beautiful but after several years find that beauty is among the lesser charms of the beloved. (Or, more complex, that the very conception of what is beautiful about the beloved has radically changed.) It may be only a matter of time until "the violet past prime, and sable curls are silvered o'er with white; when lofty trees I see barren of leaves ... Then of thy beauty do I question make" (Shakespeare, Sonnet XII). But it does not follow that I thereby question my love, nor does it follow that thy beauty was not indeed a reason if not the reason for my love.

There is another, harsher complaint against beauty as a reason for love, and that is, to put it in its usual form, that it is "superficial." True, beauty is only "skin deep" (though not even a surgeon would be much motivated to see quite literally beneath his or her lover's skin). But it does not follow that beauty is "superficial." Of course, the superficiality in question might be not that of the beloved's beauty but rather that of the lover who has only such "shallow" reasons. But I am not arguing for the dubious thesis that the beauty of the beloved is *by itself* a good reason for loving. I am only considering that far more plausible thesis that the beauty of the beloved is a good reason for loving. One would hope that all sorts of other reasons lie in waiting. Indeed, finding one's beloved beautiful is rarely a matter of physical looks alone (an attitude that is better called "fetishism" than love). It is common wisdom (promoted, for instance, by both Schopenhauer and Mark Twain) that by a modest age (say, 40), "one has the face one deserves." That is, a person's beauty is not just a matter of physical attributes but of the personality and character that "shine through." A face and a body reflect experience and grace (or the lack of it) learned by way of a certain style of life. So one could argue that the problem with beauty is not that it fades nor that it is superficial but that we too easily misunderstand what beauty really is. What comes to be beautiful in a relationship is no longer "looks" as such but a far more encompassing vision of a personality and a life together. (This, of course, is a plausible interpretation of what Socrates has in mind in his expansion of *eros* in Plato's *Symposium*.)

So none of this is to dismiss beauty or attractiveness as a reason for love. Even in an era of email and chatroom romances, how a person looks is the initial bridge to a relationship and love. And even in the maturity of a successful marriage or partnership, "looks" remain an essential part of the romantic package, even if only in the eye of the beholder. So, "is it OK to love someone for his or her looks?" Yes, so long as beauty is richly understood as all-encompassing and having as much to do with the nature of the relationship as it does with the properties of the beloved. Unfortunately, it is too often the case that loving someone's looks gets coupled with overt neglect or covert contempt for a good deal else of the person's intelligence and personality. This is not only a tragedy for both people involved in such a one-dimensional, "superficial" relationship. It is also a philosophical misfortune, as it supports the antagonism between mere looks and, as the word "superficial" suggests, some "deeper" aspects of the person.

Plato's problem

Which brings us to Plato's problem. Plato's problem gives rise to the sort of paradox that too often leads philosophers happily away from the subject at hand, that is, love with all of its messiness and sentimentality, to technical questions or logical analysis and ontology. Plato's problem emerges from Socrates' speech in the *Symposium,* where Socrates suggests, crudely stated, that one beloved is ultimately no different from any other beloved, that they all share a property in common, and that is beauty. We can ignore Socrates' rather outrageous conclusion, that the property shared is in fact an ontologically distinctive and independently existing Form and that the true lover is the lover of Forms, i.e. the philosopher, e.g. Socrates. But the argument itself raises some interesting questions about the nature of reasons for love.

The argument is that one loves for reasons, where the reasons are properties of the person loved. Thus one loves S because of properties a, b, c, d, and so on, and one would not love S if any or at any rate if all of these properties did not obtain. The paradox is that if one loved S because of some finite set of reasons a, b, c, and d, but then met T who also had a, b, c, and d, or to make it more dramatic, had *more* of a, b, c, and d, then logic would dictate that one would have no reason to prefer S over T (in the first case) or every reason to prefer T over S (in the second). This, of course, is nonsense. It is an argument that may work for computers, toasters, rental cars and business hotel suites but it does not work for love. The object of love—the beloved—is (to use a familiar legal term) *non-fungible.* No substitutions are allowed.

But Plato's problem is that substitutability seems inescapable, even for such seemingly good reasons as "because he/she is a terrific person." One must still raise the question, "why *this* terrific person rather than any other?" (Granted that the world does not have a surplus of them.) However we decide to resolve Plato's problem—by insisting (obscurely) that it is the person *as such* that one loves and not his or her properties, by arguing that some properties are such that they could not plausibly be shared with another (for example, a history of time spent together), or by appealing to the Forms or to God and conceding that the particularities of love are secondary—it is clear that our conclusion, at least once we step out of our self-made philosophical trap, must be that the love of a lover cannot be logically tied merely to properties of the sort considered here. But we should not thereby conclude that love is not of properties or that love has no reasons. Nor need one conclude that love is, as Alcibiades suggests to Socrates, merely an obsession in which the goodness of properties is of no real relevance whatever.

In Plato's problem the notion of reasons for love degenerates into a dubious dilemma: either one does love for reasons, such as "because she is beautiful," or one does not. On the first view, reasons turn out to be properties, and the properties most relevant to love seem to be only contingently true of the beloved or of the beloved alone. On the second view, one loves *the person* independently of any such properties, any of which (or all of which) might well be altered without altering love. Thus Shakespeare writes, "Love is not love which alters when it alteration finds." Much-quoted, perhaps, but (as I earlier hinted) its truth is rather doubtful. Love, as a process, changes, and it is not love when it is inattentive and indifferent to change. When love endures it is because it continues to find reasons (though, as I noted, these reasons may themselves change over time), and the love itself may "alter" accordingly.

The second view is psychologically if not ontologically dubious. What is "the person," apart from all of his or her properties? A naked soul? Can one in any erotic (as opposed to agapic) sense love an ontologically naked, property-less soul? Or a soul given any set of properties whatever? If you turn into a frog, not a Walt Disney cutesy talking frog but a regular *rana catesbeiana,* need I still love you? *Can* I still love you? Granted, I may try to provide you with a luxurious lily pad and a generous assortment of dragonflies and keep you safe from predators, but I doubt my "love" will even begin to approach the intimate affection that

I have for my mammalian pets, much less the love I *used to* have for you.

In line with the same romantic nonsense, we often talk about love being "unconditional." But if "unconditional" means "no matter what conditions," including "no matter what properties," then human love is rarely unconditional. (It may be more common in the love of children than of lovers, no matter how often it is held up as a false promise, as bait, to the latter.) A lover may stick with his beloved after she loses her youthful looks, perhaps even (for a while) after she has been turned by a witch into a duck. But to say that he loves her "no matter what" is surely a stretch. The question of reasons, and even the question of properties, is far more subtle than the simple-minded dichotomy *properties or die-Geliebte-an-sich* would suggest.

Reasons and rationalizations

There are several different senses in which one may have a reason for love. We can start with a crude distinction between reasons that actually explain or justify love, on the one hand, and reasons that are mere rationalizations of love, on the other. As starters, reasons that explain love are true, that is, the facts they cite are true or, at least, the beliefs they embody are believed to be true. Rationalizations need not be true nor even really believed. (The role of self-deception here is a topic for a different study.) Reasons that justify love are both true and persuasive. (Minimally, they make other people appreciate the *point* of one's love.) Rationalizations tend to be hollow and unpersuasive. It would make a mockery of my thesis here, that love has its reasons, to dismiss all reasons as nothing but rationalizations, that is, reasons (or excuses) mustered up after the fact, as if to make sense of one's love. I would also reject the "romantic" thesis that love is ineffable and reasons are nothing but rationalizations created after the fact to make one's love seem rational. My thesis is that love has its reasons, by which I mean not only that it can be described and explained but that it is also defensible and in a modest sense can be justified.

One may be fully aware of the reason why he or she loves someone. One may state a reason (for instance, by way of self-justification) while knowing that it is not "really" the reason one loves someone. And then there are reasons for loving someone that may be operative but may not be conscious or articulate at all. As Pascal so famously said, "*Le coeur a ses raisons, que la raison ne connait pas*" ("the heart has its reasons which reason cannot know"). Contrary to most philosophers, I would insist that reasons need not be articulated nor even articulatable, nor is this to say that they are only *explanations,* i.e. third person accounts of first person preferences and affections. There are circumstances when one feels forced to articulate reasons for loving someone, such as deciding to get (or stay) married, facing up to an existential crisis ("should I make the move to Boston with you, or keep my job here?"), having to choose between two love relationships, or defending one's love to skeptical friends or suspicious family members. Under such circumstances, however, it is by no means evident that one is simply articulating his or her own reasons for loving rather than manufacturing persuasive reasons in order to convince oneself or others.

It is by no means obvious that a *good* reason for loving someone is one's *actual* reason for loving someone. A proposed reason for loving someone might be a mere rationalization, an attempt to justify that does not really explain one's love. By contrast, one's actual reasons may be both inarticulate and sub-conscious. (These are not the same. A reason might be articulatable but unconscious, that is, not presently articulatable by the lover. And a reason might be quite conscious but difficult to articulate, for instance, "the feeling of affectionate familiarity I have when I am with you" or "the subtle anxiety I feel whenever I think of you.") I would argue that love (and all emotions) are developed through a lifetime of forgotten experiences, bad memories, cultivated and accidental habits. Waxing Heideggerian, one might say that love is always created against a background of emotional practices. These include the half-digested stories and movies and gossip of the culture, primal examples (one's parents, most obviously), and they determine not only the ability to love and the prototypes of love but the very structure of love. Consequently they also circumscribe the intelligible reasons for love, which in one culture might be an experience so inchoate that it resembles a passing mania while in another it can be understood only in terms of the most exquisite poetic inspiration. But the fact that such reasons (as comfort and discomfort, anxiety, and excitement) may be unconscious (that is, their exact nature and perhaps even their "object") and inarticulable does not in the least imply that these are not reasons. It is just that recognition and articulation of such reasons depends on an understanding of the larger cultural and psychological situation and do not at all yield the "privileged access" of some more straightforward psychic states. Indeed, some of these reasons might well be *bodily,* but this thesis would take us too far afield in this essay.

Nor need reasons be rational. Bad reasons, inappropriate reasons, wrongheaded reasons are still reasons—they are one's reason for loving—but they are not reasons that will stand up to rational scrutiny. Again, these are rationalizations and not good reasons. But what is a good reason? We should distinguish between a reason that is explanatory, that is, an actual "cause" of one's love, and a reason that is a *good* reason for love. There are also good reasons that are nevertheless only rationalizations. A bad reason may be an accurate description of a cause of love ("I love her because she's more perverse than I am"), and a good reason for love (when it is a mere rationalization) may not be one's reason for loving at all. The relation between good reasons, reasons as rationalizations, and truly explanatory reasons is complex and intricate and among other things harks back to the vibrant discussions in the late sixties about reasons versus causes and (explanatory) reasons versus a person's stated reasons. (As formulated by R.S. Peters many years ago (in his *Concept of Motivation*), the latter indicates a difference between "a reason" versus "his [or her] reason.") The relation of reasons to causes and the distinction between reasons and causes is of particular significance here.

In an article I published almost three decades ago, I supported Donald Davidson's then much-heralded argument that (*contra* one influential interpretation of Wittgenstein) reasons are causes and thus function in law-like causal explanations. Nevertheless, reasons obviously constitute a special case of causes. They necessarily refer to the perspective of the subject. But there is a very complex question about the extent to which this perspective must be comprehended or reflectively understood *by* the subject, whether he or she is capable of articulating or otherwise expressing this perspective, and the extent to which such a perspective may only be apparent by way of the explanation of behavior but not "known" as such to the subject at all. (I take it that virtually all non-primate animal behavior is like this.) When a reason (not necessarily provided by the subject) successfully explains one's loving behavior, I have no objection to calling it a "cause" of love. But the range of reasons is much broader than that, since reasons can function as attempted justifications and ways of "spelling out" one's feelings as well as causal explanations.

But we should be very careful about the notion of justification here. A reason for love presented as a justification does not imply that the reason is an attempt to get anyone *else* to accept that reason, much less to get anyone else to love the person in question. One of the journal referees suggested the following exchange: "Suppose someone gave reasons for loving Jill to an auditor, and the auditor said, 'OK; you're right, I love her too.'" One can readily imagine a seemingly parallel conversation: Someone invests in regional airline stocks, giving as reasons that the large airlines are in trouble, that local demand is more or less constant, and that the smaller airlines will benefit from this. His interlocutor responds, "OK; you're right, I will invest too." But what then does "justification" mean in the context of reasons for love? It cannot be of the form "I feel this, you should feel it too." What it does mean is more like "I think that this is a good reason for my feeling (that is, my loving so-and-so), you should think so too." But a good reason for me might not be a good reason for you, and what I think is a good reason might not seem like a good reason to you at all. What I am trying to do by stating my reasons is to justify my loving so-and-so, but this is "justification" in a modest sense indeed. It makes sense of my love but it says nothing about what anyone else ought to do or feel.

There are, of course, straightforwardly bad reasons for love. One's reasons for love may be bad in the obvious sense that they rest on false information, e.g. one's (false) beliefs that one's beloved has been sexually faithful, or has not spent time in prison, or is not a compulsive liar. They may also rest on false expectations, e.g. the expectation that the beloved, though lovable, can nevertheless be molded and re-shaped by the lover, or that he or she will make a good parent. But falsehood is not a reason not to ascribe a reason, so long as it is believed (and, again, not necessarily consciously believed) by the lover. That is to say, a false belief may nevertheless be the *cause* of a person's affection whether or not it would serve as a justification. Moreover, reasons for love may be *irrational* because they are unwarranted even if not exactly false. Varieties of inappropriate love, e.g. erotic love for a child or a younger sibling, would be based on reasons that are irrational even if they involve no false beliefs or expectations. They are perverse. Thus, again, the reasons might cite the *cause* of a person's affection but not serve as any justification whatever.

Some reasons for love seem to be bad reasons although they are neither false, nor unreasonable, nor obviously perverse. Loving someone for his or her money may in fact be one's reason for loving, but it is usually a bad reason. (As my ex-mother-in-law used to say, "Marrying for money is getting it the hard way.") It is a bad reason both because marrying for money is a very emotionally expensive way of getting money and because marrying for money is an extremely *unromantic* reason for loving. In other words, even if it serves as an accurate explanation of why one loves the rich person one does, it is in no sense a *justification* of one's love. It is an irrational reason both in the sense that it is (arguably) self-defeating and in that it is not a good reason *for love,* whether or not it might be deemed a good reason for marrying or forming some other kind of partnership. But I admit that as an example of a bad reason, loving someone for money is open to debate. As I shall argue below, it all depends on how we construe loving someone for money as a reason, and how we construe reasons for love.

Love as a reason for love

It is sometimes suggested that loving itself is a reason for love. That is, the fact that one already loves someone provides the reasons for loving them. Leaving aside the obvious paradoxes that might be derived from this suggestion, the idea itself has a certain sort of appeal. It is by now a trite movie scene, where the protagonist writes down in one column fifty reasons why he should leave his lover, and then in the other column simply writes "I love her!"—and that clinches the decision. (I remember doing this myself, towards the tail-end of a hopeless youthful romance.) The idea that love is its own reason or reason enough in itself is subject to several different construals. One reasonable interpretation is that already loving someone is a good reason to *keep on* loving them, all things considered. Another is that loving someone already provides any number of reasons (by way of the bestowal of beauty, for example, as discussed above). A more general construal would be the idea that love is a valued emotion that should be accepted and respected *so long as there are not good reasons against it.* Love may be a prima facie good, but it is nevertheless defeasible in the face of more persuasive reasons. But in this case, by hypothesis, there *are* good reasons, and presumably substantial reasons, against loving and thus the question becomes how to weigh these against reasons for love.

I am by no means arguing (what those who think that love is "intrinsically good" might mistakenly argue) that any reason for love is a good reason. I am only arguing that love has its reasons. That means, first of all, that love can be explained in terms of the lover's perspective. But it also means that love (on reflection) invites justification, and thus the reasons one may be challenged to produce in defense of his or her love may turn out to be good, bad, uninteresting, etc. Indeed, one might even press the cynical thesis that most reasons for love are self-deceptive, delusive, and therefore irrational. If that were so, then love would most often be irrational too.

Thus the question of reasons for love might be divided in two: (1) our reasons for thinking that love *as such* is a good and (2) our reasons for loving someone in particular. To be sure, the first set of reasons will supply something of a framework as well as provide some support for the second sort of reasons. If one's love for a particular person is to have any reason(s) at all (that is, reasons as purported justifications), there must be some virtue to being in love. But it is not the case that to have a good reason for loving someone it is also necessary to be able to produce good reasons for love. (Most people, even most philosophers, are quite incoherent if not speechless about producing good reasons for love. Quite a few of the speeches in Plato's great *Symposium* tend to such incoherence.) For that matter, most people are quite incoherent if not speechless about producing reasons for loving a particular person. But the reasons for love (in general) are not my focus here, although the nature of some such reasons will become evident as I explore the idea of reasons for (one's particular) love. And just to offset one possible pretension, finding good reasons for love (in general) will not provide a *sufficient* set of reasons for loving anyone in particular. (Those who are "in love with love" tend to ignore this point.)

One might argue that one's love of a particular person can have *good* reasons only if love in general can be justified. Thus a person can never be cruel for good reasons because cruelty in general cannot be justified. Thus one might argue that if the love of a particular person is to be justified, love in general must be justifiable. But consider this: I would argue that there is never a good reason for being envious because there is no justification for envy. But surely one can have reasons for being envious, and envy is unimaginable without them. (The reasons might include the perceived value of the object of envy, the person envied, the relationship between the subject and the object, the relationship between the subject and the person envied, and the more general circumstances in which the envy emerges.)

The example of envy gives some indication, I think, of the complex relationship between reasons and justification. It is important to keep these apart, although it is also important to see how they fit together. To have reasons is not necessarily to justify one's emotion, even if to justify one's emotion one must give reasons. And the justification of the emotion itself, in general, is not irrelevant to the justification of some particular instance of the emotion. To provide reasons for love, in particular, may be to justify one's emotion (for example, when challenged by friends), but the demand for reasons is nevertheless something less than the demand for justification. One might well protest, "why should I have to justify my feelings!?" but, of course, it is not just a matter of justification. It is also a matter of making sense of one's emotion, whether to oneself or to others.

Thus the question: *a reason* for *whom*? We have already alluded to this in our brief mention of Peters' distinction between "his (or her) reason" and "the reason." There is a difference between there being a reason to think someone is lovable and my having a reason *for me* to love that person. There may be a hundred reasons why you are lovable, but nevertheless I am not in love with you. They are not *my* reasons. Moreover, I have suggested that the issue of reasons for love stands in a complicated relation with questions regarding justification. Reasons for love may well be presented as an attempt at justification, but they certainly need not be. The quest for justification is, in general, a much stronger demand than the quest for reasons. (Thus the absurd confusion between reasons for loving so-and-so and reasons for investing in a certain sort of stock.) Reasons for love may also be (in the mind or mouth of the lover, secondarily for someone else) a further description of the love, a way of "spelling out" one's love, a clarification of what one feels and why. In this sense, following a distinction put forward by Peter Goldie, we might say that reasons for love render the emotion *intelligible* rather than rational, though I think that one can find many examples of both in people's presentations of their reasons for love. Spelling out one's love by giving reasons for love can be an important source of clarification, but it can also be a confirmation of the *rightness* of one's affection, both for oneself (to soothe over doubts) and to convince others. In other words, giving reasons may (but need not) involve *legitimating* love, demonstrating that it is *rational,* perhaps even suggesting some sense of *ought.* But it would be utterly mistaken to think that this is what all reasons for love try to do. Usually, it is enough that one makes his or her love intelligible, and with sufficient self-doubt or skeptical friends, this may be more than reason enough.

Illicit love, irrational love, all sorts of love that ought not to be nevertheless involve reasons, which is ultimately only to say that it can be further described and explained. It is virtually never the case either that "I simply *love* her" or "I simply love *her*." We have noted that reasons for love may also be (from the view of someone else, secondarily in the opinions of the lover) a kind of explanation, for instance, by way of the causal aetiology or source of the emotion. ("Because she looks and acts like his mother," "because he satisfies her need for feeling helpless.") This is one way (but by no means the only way) of understanding Peters' distinction between "the reason" and "his reason." But it should be evident that not all kinds of "the reason" explanations are relevant to us here. For example, there is the kind of explanation that is offered by biology and by evolutionary biology and sociobiology in particular. Such explanations point to the evolution of certain behavior patterns (and, presumably, the neurological structures and processes that cause them and the "feelings" that accompany them).

Such explanations apply to people in general and do not specify individuals, and so it is more of a generic explanation of love (narrowly considered as a biological phenomenon) than anything like a personal reason for one's particular love. (One persuasive reason for love consists of one's citing the intense feelings of attraction and affection that are triggered by the mere sight of the other person. But it is not evolution or for that matter neurology that is thus cited.) Such explanations are clearly examples of "the reason" rather than "his reason" explanations, and they can be defended quite apart of any beliefs or self-consciousness on the part of the lover (the "subject"), whether conscious or unconscious. Such accounts have often been abused and sensationalized, of course, not to mention their recruitment for all sorts of dubious political and social agendas. I would not for a moment deny that our biological make-up has a great deal to do with our feelings and behavior, but biological explanations have little to do with the sort of reasons that interest me here. And, I would add, it is by no means evident that biological imperatives give us any insight about *love*, as opposed to any number of possessive and protective (even affectionate) impulses. In the excitement over the new neuropsychology what is sometimes lost is the old idea that some "mental processes" make sense only because of the reasons we attach to them, not because of their neurological bases.

I would similarly exclude theological explanations of the sort "God created us as sexual, loving creatures," for just the same reasons that we exclude evolutionary explanations of sexual and romantic behavior, that is, insofar as these are simply accounts of "how we are and came to be that way" without reference to our beliefs and feelings. But insofar as such doctrines enter into the lovers' beliefs and feelings, they might very well be the basis of reasons for love (although I can't make much sense out of a similar claim in the case of evolution). A person or a couple who believe that God is love and sex is God's gift and that romance and marriage are their proper realization may have a host of reasons for love (both in general and in this particular relationship) which are quite distinctive. But I will not be discussing such reasons for love here.

Another third sort of explanation which I will not be considering has to do with all of those accounts of our phenomenology and behavior which properly belong in the realm of culture, or what these days is generally referred to as the "social construction" of (social) reality. There is little doubt that our enthusiasm about romantic love—as opposed to our drive to reproduce and our general sociability—is foisted on us through a lifetime of propaganda through literature, gossip, movies, peer pressure and love ballads. But here, as opposed to evolutionary explanations, there is some assurance that reflection and conscientious phenomenological and social criticism will disclose the structures of such social constructions and render these as full-fledged reasons—or as reasons for rebellion—as well as behind the scenes explanations. I say this because I want to be very clear that I am not, in this discussion, in any way denying the social and cultural determination of our concepts and consequently those sources of our reasons and rationale for love. They are just not themselves reasons for love, whatever powerful explanations of our behavior they may provide.

Beyond properties-of-the-person reasons for love

I think that much of the confusion surrounding discussions of love and its reasons has to do with a narrow focus on one particular kind of reason and a failure to appreciate the various kinds of reasons. All too often, the list of reasons is restricted to *properties of the person*, and quite a limited range of properties of the person at that. The question, "why do you love her?" typically gets answered with "because she is beautiful," or "because of her sense of humor," or "because of her wit and charm." And among these are the even more vulgar *materialist* answers (in Madonna's sense, not as meant by philosophers): "I love him because of his car" or "because his father's got enough money to buy Switzerland."

Right from the start, we might want to contrast such vulgar materialist reasons with *virtuous* reasons, such as "I love him for his courage" or "I love her for her love of knowledge," and lament the fact that, in most discussions, the selection of reasons tends to be mostly limited to materialist and other more vulgar than virtuous properties. But what I want to argue takes both vulgar and virtuous reasons as reasons of essentially the same kind, namely, reasons that cite *properties-of-the-beloved*. Nevertheless I want to suggest that there is a very different kind of reason—what I will call an Aristophanic reason, and that, furthermore, *properties-of-the-beloved-type* reasons are best construed as Aristophanic reasons. But first, I want to argue that what seems wrong with many such reasons—both vulgar and virtuous—is that they are covertly aimed at benefits and advantages for the lover.

Properties-of-the-person-type reasons for love when they are self-interested

Properties-of-the-beloved-type reasons for love are thought problematic, as in Plato's problem, because they tend to be fungible (or "repeatable") properties of the beloved. These are rightly suspect for not being "unique" to the person, but I think that there is an underlying objection to many such purported properties that is far more serious. Such reasons typically betray an ulterior motive, to satisfy the often selfish interests of the lover. "Because she buys me all sorts of presents." "Because she helps me with my homework." Such reasons are "self-interested" insofar as they (often covertly) invoke some personal advantage for the lover rather than a virtue or admirable feature of the beloved. I think that many of the objections to the very idea of "reasons for love" is based on the erroneous idea that all reasons for love are self-interested, that is, they cite some advantage for the lover and are therefore inconsistent with one of the most basic ideas about love, that in love one cares about the other person and considers his or her interests as important as one's own. (I think that this is an understatement, but it will suffice here. I would rather say that in love one takes the other's interests *as* one's own.)

Thus the real objection to such reasons is not that they are fungible but that they are *selfish*. The reason for loving someone who is wealthy (because he or she is wealthy, that is) is most likely due to one's expectations that one will get to share the wealth, or at any rate enjoy its benefits. This hardly needs to be said directly, although, if it is, the reason will be all the more offensive. Thus the fact that there is no hidden motive in such reasons as "because she buys me all sorts of presents" and "because she helps me with my homework" does not make the reason less but rather more dubious as a reason for love. One doubts their validity as reasons for love precisely because they are so explicitly self-interested, with little or no reference or regard to the interests of the other person. Of course, such reasons might be modified in some such way, for example, "because we enjoy doing our homework together and motivate each other" or "because we enjoy shopping together," but such reasons are still tangential to love at best and suspect, hypocritical, or devious at worst. Loving for one's own advantage seems to us not really loving at all.

But then again, many a mother has advised her daughter, "it's just as easy to fall in love with a rich man as a poor one," and we do not think her particularly crass or unromantic for doing so. Nor is it the case that wealth has nothing to do with "the real person," something one HAS rather than IS. It is said that money has nothing to do with personality or character, but it is obvious that making money presupposes some virtues which are germane to love (perseverance, knowing what one wants, a bit of cleverness, a bit of luck) and having money often provides a rich basis for such romantic virtues as a sense of elegance, a taste for the finer things, a good education and an ability to express oneself. But even where there is no plausible causal account of the link between money and virtue, there is an obvious temptation to exaggerate personal charm in the presence of wealth. As Humphrey Bogart reminds us in one of his lesser movies, "a man can look pretty good with his pockets on." If (as I shall argue) a good reason for love is one that ties two people together in a mutually inspiring, supportive and enjoyable relationship, then I'm forced to admit that wealth might count as a good reason for love in a consumer society where most couples spend far more time shopping together than they do making love.

The reasons for loving someone who is beautiful may be considerably more subtle. Beauty is attractive in its own right (indeed, that near tautology has often been used as a philosophical definition of beauty, e.g. in Plato). In that sense, a reason for love—"she is so beautiful"—is not apparently self-interested. Quite to the contrary, the reason for loving a beautiful person might just be, as Plato says, our natural love for beauty as such. The objection is rather that beauty is a fungible feature and in that sense impersonal. (Indeed, this is precisely Plato's point, that beauty is a universal and not just a feature of this particular person.) But, against Plato, we might well want to protest that the beauty of a particular person is not a fungible feature and that beauty is not an objective property. Even if a person is considered beautiful by the standards of the culture, indeed, even if he or she is considered beautiful by everyone, it is the lover's *finding* him or her beautiful that is the relevant reason for love. In other words, beauty does not specify so much a property of the person as it exemplifies a feature constituted in the relationship.

The reasons for loving someone who is beautiful may be subtle, but they, too, can be selfish as well as quite vulgar and "superficial." Insofar as one loves one's beautiful partner because one loves *being seen* with such a person and how that reflects on oneself—the "trophy wife" is an offensive example—such a reason is clearly self-interested and may have very little to do with any care or concern for the other person. ("You make me proud of myself," says Dolly Parton's date in the worse than mediocre movie *Straight Talk*.) Insofar as one's concern is one's own status in public appearances, one might argue that loving the beloved because he or she is beautiful hardly counts as a reason *for love* at all.

But few people, I hope, are quite so gauche. While being seen with beauty often does benefit our social status (although one must at least consider the problem of contrasts: "How can someone as beautiful as she is be seen in public with a little toad like him?"), being with someone beautiful enhances one's self-esteem, quite apart from any public considerations. Thus the thought, "she's so beautiful (that means that I must be pretty terrific myself)" is suspect, as is the more modest "he's so gorgeous (I'm so lucky!)." But here in particular the distinction between self-interested and un-self-interested (hardly disinterested) reasons is extremely evasive, and the whole range of motives for our enjoyment are obscure and perhaps unknowable. We enjoy beauty. And insofar as we enjoy the beauty of a person, that does indeed seem like a reason for loving, if not in itself a sufficient reason. But to what extent is our appreciation less than aesthetic and something other than the sheer enjoyment of being in the proximity of beauty a good deal of the time? To what extent do notions of "possession" and public display enter into our reasons, and are they, too, reasons for love?

Is sexual attraction a reason for love? Sexual attraction, of course, depends on physical cues, and insofar as we might simplify the description by calling this "finding someone attractive" we can understand how attractiveness is conducive to sexual desire and satisfaction and this in turn is a reason for love. Or is it? Sexual desire and satisfaction play a complex role in romantic motivation. If we are to believe Jean-Paul Sartre on the matter, sexual desire and satisfaction are intrinsically selfish and manipulative. (Then, again, so is love, according to him.) But it is by no means clear that sexual desire is in itself selfish, despite the fact that one wants, by the very nature of the desire, to be satisfied. Nor is it so obvious that sexual satisfaction is only a matter of one's own satisfaction. Leaving aside the rather elaborate accounts of sexuality in terms of evolution or "nature's" or "God's purpose," we may say that nevertheless what is desired is not necessarily one's own satisfaction and what satisfies is not simply to be understood only in terms of one's sexual desires. Thus sex becomes a reason for love.

If the argument against a good many reasons for love is their self-interestedness, this objection gets confused with the claim that such reasons concern properties that are inessential, extraneous to the person, detachable, fungible. This is obviously true of money, power, and certain sorts of benefits. It is not so obviously true of looks and personality (although one is more likely to lose the former than the latter). Nevertheless we can make good sense of the idea that someone would continue to love a once beautiful person long after his or her looks have faded. We also make good sense of the idea that someone would continue to love someone whose personality has disintegrated through Alzheimer's or some similar disease or trauma. And to say the obvious, one can probably get presents or help with one's homework from any number of people with whom one is not romantically involved. While one might well enjoy presents or academic help in a loving relationship, that is a very different matter than loving *because* one receives such benefits. Such self-interested reasons are subject to criticism not because they are readily detachable from the beloved but rather because they point primarily to the advantages of the lover.

But not all reasons for love are self-interested. What about what we called "virtuous" reasons?

Aristotle, in his *Nicomachean Ethics*, famously discusses three types of friendship, the first of which is clearly self-interested in the straightforward sense that it is a friendship of mutual advantage and benefits. But the second type of friendship discussed by Aristotle, the friendship of mutual enjoyment, is also self-interested in this sense. Thus, "because I enjoy her company" or (mutually) "because we enjoy each other's company" is a quite respectable reason for love. (The first might be considered self-interested, but the latter is more along the lines of the Aristophanic reasons for love that I want to endorse, which are neither selfish nor selfless but point to an essential aspect of the relationship.) Finally, however, Aristotle introduces his third type of friendship, which might be stated as *mutually inspiring one another*. Now mutually inspiring one another might seem merely utilitarian, but it is no longer vulgar or by any means merely self-interested. An excellent reason for love is "because we inspire one another." Again, this is neither selfish nor selfless but an aspect of the relationship. "Because she inspires me" doesn't have quite the ring to it, but neither is it selfish. It is, again, neither selfish nor selfless, and it seems to me to be a perfectly acceptable reason for love, despite the fact that it is, in one sense, a matter of my benefit. I might also love a person because I inspire her and I find it very rewarding to do so, but it is only a deep cynic or a philosopher with an ax to grind who would insist that such a reason is selfish or self-interested.

It is in this light that I want to consider "virtuous" reasons for love, for instance, "because he is courageous." Martha Nussbaum argues that such properties are what Plato has in mind as reasons for love, or, at any rate, for the best sort of love, the love exemplified by Socrates. Her analysis (based on the *Phaedrus)* is that "the best view of love bases it on a view of the individual as essentially constituted by values and aspirations." This way of putting the issue makes it quite clear that love is "best" based on *properties-of-the-beloved-type* reasons. Nussbaum expresses a number of reservations and objections to this analysis, including a suspicion that shared interests, aspirations, and values must somewhere come into the account, but she replies to these in Plato's name, leaving the basic claim pretty much intact. Now some of these virtues, of course, suggest an obvious benefit for the lover (e.g. generosity, wit and charm). Others, however, do not. But what I find problematic is not that such reasons sometimes tend to be covertly self-interested but that they tend to be reasons for admiration rather than love. Although Nussbaum provides Plato with a vigorous defense, I find it both unconvincing and unappealing, reinforcing my suspicion that Socrates, at least, remains something of a narcissist when it comes to love. To be sure, we *admire* people with virtuous qualities, and Socrates holds himself up as moral exemplar precisely because he exemplifies such qualities. But insofar as we *love* someone, his or her virtues are not merely to be admired. They are, in an essential sense, to be *shared*. This does not only mean that the *values* embedded in the virtues must be shared, as Nussbaum argues, but it is the mutual *effect* of the virtues on the lover and the beloved that makes the reasons for love. In other words, it is not the virtues as properties of the beloved but their inspiring influence on the lover that matters. Otherwise, what we have is mere admiration, or perhaps worship, but not love.

But notice again that quickly we are moving away from properties of the beloved and moving towards the nature of the relationship as the source of reasons for love, which is precisely where I want to shift our focus. To restate my main point bluntly, what most people find objectionable about reasons for love is that they tend to focus on a particularly narrow set of more or less self-interested reasons. But, again, not all reasons are self-interested or selfish nor are they restricted to mere properties of the person.

Aristophanic reasons for love

The second set of reasons I call "*Aristophanic,*" after the playwright who plays such a dramatic role in Plato's *Symposium*. It was Aristophanes who presented the classic myth about human beings as double creatures, cleft in half by Zeus and left to wander the earth "looking for their other halves." A reason for love, then, has to do with the way two people "fit" together, not with the features either of them might have nor even with features they might share. Of course, shared values and aspirations may make it much more likely that two people will fit together, but it is not the sharing of the values and aspirations that provide the Aristophanic reason for love. Moreover, it does not matter (as Socrates complains, as Alcibiades suggests) whether the features that "fit" are virtues or vices. One might call them "relational" in that they explicitly have to do with the relationship rather than just the person loved.

It may make us uncomfortable to think that evil aspirations shared may provide a good reason for love, but I think that it is important to refrain from "moralizing" love, as Socrates does. The first question is whether two people love one another and why. It is a secondary question, though perhaps more important, whether their love is a good thing or whether the two of them together are at all admirable, enviable, or a "role model" of a couple.

As I have argued, even self-interested reasons that look like properties-of-the-person reasons often turn out to be Aristophanic reasons. Paradoxically, I think that this is also what the critics of reasons for love complain about when they insist on "loving a person for him or herself." What looks like a problematic ontological claim is in fact a plea for a broader, not an ontologically more precious, set of considerations. The sense in which we love a person "for him or herself" rather refers us to the special role of the beloved *in the relationship,* not to a naked soul. Loving a person for him or herself is badly misconstrued as appealing to some sort of personal essence when it most often refers to something essential about the relationship and the unique role of the beloved in that relationship.

By explicitly talking about the relationship, we get to break through the troublesome distinction between the person, on the one hand, and his or her properties, on the other. We thus get to avoid Plato's problem (and the problematic metaphysics that goes along with it) by appealing to Aristophanes in the same dialogue. At the same time, however, I have a deeper aim. I am trying to break down another bit of misguided ontology that wreaks havoc in discussions of love. The misguided ontology is that the object of love is the beloved and his or her properties while love is the attitude or emotion the lover has *toward* the beloved. Thus Plato often employs the metaphor of attraction, but even in Plato, the paradigm of one person attracted to another encourages us to think in terms of the relationship between the two. This may not be apparent in Socrates' discussion of *eros*, but it is clearly the key to the story told by Aristophanes. The relevant properties of each person are defined only in relation to the other. There is no mention of the impersonal Form of Beauty. The beloved is defined in terms of his or her properties only insofar as these are identified in terms of their "fit".

To think about love in terms of Aristophanic reasons is not to deny that Aristophanic reasons can be trivial. As I have already indicated, I do not want to distinguish self-interested and Aristophanic reasons on the basis of the former's selfish vulgarity or superficiality and the latter's virtuousness and profundity. In Kanin and Gordon's screenplay, *Adam's Rib*, a would-be lover proclaims to the character played by Katherine Hepburn: "Do you know why I love you, Mrs. Bonner? Because you live right across the hall. You are mightily attractive in every single way—but I would probably love anybody just so long as they lived across the hall." That is a good, solid, Aristophanic reason for falling in love with Mrs. Bonner, but it is laughably inferior to "because you are attractive" or "because you are so witty" or "because you inspire me to do great things." Some Aristophanic reasons can also be cryptic. They seem to be property-of-the-person refer-ences, but they are in fact quite otherwise. For instance, a wife says (with a hearty laugh) of her husband—who just put his coat on inside out or walked out of the house with his face full of shaving cream—"that's what I love about you." Such endear-ments hardly count as a reason for love at face value, but they are clearly suggestive of a larger perspective of affection and tender amusement and thus they are good reasons indeed.

The most obvious and important example of an Aristophanic reason for love which is not a property (or a pair of properties) of either of the two people but of the relationship are those that have to do with the history of the relationship. The very fact of time together, to say the obvious, is not fungible. It cannot be replaced by anything else. One might spend an equal time with someone else, at a different time or (with some logistical difficulty) over the same period of time, but in an important and obvious sense, time together is unique to the relationship and can be a good reason for loving someone. I say "can be" because it might also be a good reason for not loving someone, as in "familiarity breeds con-tempt," or because time together can also result in a loss of novelty, a loss of interest, a restlessness for something or someone new. But this is only to say that any reason for love, even one that is unique to the couple, must be understood contextually and in terms of the particular dynamics of the relationship. But time together, even if it is not sufficient to yield a relationship with "depth" of feeling, is arguably a necessary condition for love (early love and love at first sight notwithstanding) and thus a good reason for love, whether or not it appears as an obvious candidate for such a reason.

There is, of course, a philosopher's trick. Suppose we came together just last week, or even five minutes ago, but with all of the same depth of feeling and extensive mutual knowledge that we have obtained over the last fifteen years. Wouldn't the reason for loving still be the depth of feeling and the mutual knowledge? Wouldn't the time together drop out as superfluous? Well, no. Love is a process, not a state, and it necessarily involves a narrative, a narrative of love. Love is not just the outcome but the whole process, and our reasons for love are bound up with that process. Here is the place to deal with the objection, "what about love at first sight?!" But love at first sight does not dispense with the process. It *anticipates* it. What make it *love* at first sight (as opposed to simple attraction, a "crush" or infatuation) is the fact that the relationship matures into love, and *in retrospect* it can be said that "we loved each other from the very beginning." Love, by its very nature, takes time.

Reasons for love can also be located in the future, in fantasies and possibilities in future plans and projections. A good reason for loving someone is the anticipation of what the beloved or the relationship will *make* of the lover. This can go awry, for instance in those men and women who see in their partner only what they would like to change. But *Pygmalion*, after all, does point to a familiar complex in love, and the fact that some people approach the beloved with the attitudes of a housing contractor facing a "fixer-upper" bespeaks the varieties of neuroses in love but it does not undermine its reasons. (Having children, though not necessarily part of romantic love, is obviously love that projects its reasons into the future.) Love is a forward-looking and not just a backward-looking narrative. So, too, our love may be part of a much larger theological, social, or political narrative, part of God's plan, playing a role in social transformation or in the revolution. Among couples who have been at the forefront of social change, it may well be that one of the main reasons for love is their joint role in that larger narrative.

The most important kind of Aristophanic reason for love, however, is one that cuts deep into the very nature of love itself, at least as I have come to understand it over the years. Referring back to the Aristophanes myth, "two halves of one complete whole," I have analyzed love in terms of what I call "*shared identity*." This is not at all a poetic or mystical notion. It refers to the way that lovers and spouses reconceive of themselves and redraw the boundaries of their identity and their interests with and through the other person. It is in this sense that I say that a lover takes the interests of the beloved *as* his or her own. To say that he or she takes the interests of the beloved to be as important or even as more important than his or her own is a much weaker claim. It is hard to put such reasons into words, since the "properties" or "features" of the relationship, the couple, or of either person are not what are usually considered properties or features. But Cathy in *Wuthering Heights* comes pretty close to the mark when she declares, somewhat hysterically, "I am Heathcliff—he's always, always in my mind—not as a pleasure, any more than I am always a pleasure to myself—but as my own being." Such are the ultimate reasons for love, I would argue. They do not mention properties of the beloved nor benefits to the lover nor even mere history together, which, after all, might just as well be a sitcom or a war story as a love story, or (most of the time, I reckon) a mix of all three. The focus is shared identity, misleadingly expressed in the declaration "I couldn't live without you." (This should not be understood as a statement of physical or mere emotional dependency, much less "co-dependency.")

Insofar as romantic love is a search for self-identity, the best reasons for love are those that highlight and consolidate self-identity. Repulsive traits and vices tend to work against this identity while attractions and virtues tend to work for it, but what makes a good reason for love as such is not any feature or characteristic of the other person. The question is rather how a trait or property fits into the relationship. Thus a person's vice can sometimes be a reason for love, tying two people together as firmly as any virtue. Plato's *Symposium* speakers make a special effort to decry such attachments, insisting that love is necessarily love only of virtue, but Alcibiades gives them a proper rebuke. Even repulsive features can provide reasons for love, if the lover finds them suitably endearing, amusing or self-gratifying. What's more, shared wealth can provide a sense of shared identity just as much as shared intellectual curiosity, shared moral virtues, shared sexual enthusiasm, shared humor or shared political opinions, whether or not (from some more objective standpoint) the identity in question may be dubious indeed.

In light of what I said earlier in this discussion, two objections present themselves. The first has to do with Plato's problem. The objection is that I have only shifted and not resolved the problem. Second, there appears to be a vicious circularity in the sorts of reasons I am now defending. I cast doubt on the idea that love is an intrinsic good or "its own reason," but now it seems that I have adopted some such position.

The Plato's problem objection is that one might love for Aristophanic reasons, where these reasons refer to properties of the relationship rather than properties of the beloved, but aren't these properties fungible as well? In other words, if I love U because of Aristophanic properties a, b, c, d, and so on, and I would not love U if any or at any rate if all of these properties did not obtain, would I not be logically compelled to love V if that *relationship* had or would have *more* of those same Aristophanic properties?

I do not see the force of this objection. The reason for rejecting Socrates' formulation of reasons was that they did not take account of the fact that properties of the beloved were reasons for love only insofar as they played a suitable role in the relationship. The question now is, but might not another relationship "fit" together just as well or better? Well, yes. And people do in fact move from one marriage to another on just this basis. When a person is widowed he or she faces the daunting prospect of either living alone or settling for a relationship that could not possibly have all of the features of "fit" that one enjoyed all of those years. But people do find new partners and form new relationships on the basis of quite different features of fit. It is not as if one relationship has fungibly replaced the other but rather that one romantic relationship has followed another and both of them have their harmonies and their virtues. (One can imagine the logistically complex but nevertheless possible co-existence of two such relationships, but here we run into deep problems about the constitution and unity of the self.) The fact that two very different relationships share the common property of "fitting together" does not say very much at all about the nature of the relationship—or about the reasons for love.

But, then, isn't there a vicious circularity in the notion of Aristophanic reasons, namely that the best reason for loving a particular person now becomes something embarrassingly close to "because I love him"? Well, yes again, in the sense that the reasons for loving this particular person do refer to the loving relationship in which these reasons earn their significance. But this is a far cry from the mystification of taking love as an intrinsic good or claiming that love is "its own reason." The reasons for loving a particular person presuppose that there are good reasons for love. But once we have accepted the idea that love is a good thing then the reason "because I love him" though trite and misleading does indeed point us to the many more informative reasons that are significant both because of the nature of love itself and exclusively within the domain of the on-going particular relationship.

Thus the ultimate reasons for love are concerned with the fact that we now share our *selves,* that my life is no longer imaginable without you, that there is a sense in which it is by way of your eyes and ears that I see and hear, in terms of your tastes and preferences that I gauge my own. That is love, and that is the ultimate reason for love. To say that our shared identity is a reason for love is, in this sense, a tautology, we love because we love. It is in this sense that we can understand how love might be its own reason after all, but we need not talk of "intrinsic goods" here. The shared identity of love can in some cases turn out to be a hateful, destructive, demeaning identity, and in such cases one would be hard pressed to say that love is a good at all. Nevertheless, in the pre-ponderance of happy cases, already loving is a good reason for love, in fact, it may be the best reason of all.

Some dubious and downright perverse reasons for love

I would not want to leave this discussion without bringing in some truly dubious or downright perverse reasons for love. This in-cludes an odd assortment of motives and concerns that are typified by a certain unsavoriness, but the charge is often graver than the self-interest charge levied against some of the more vulgar self-interested reasons (e.g. loving someone for his or her money). Typically, such reasons lay some claim on the relationship, but they also involve a generous dose of self-deception, although they need not do so and when they are not self-deceived, they are even more perverse. Many of them are neurotic. They are all dubious as reasons, at least, as reasons for love. Spurred by the belief that we should limit our reasons to undeniably virtuous or at least desir-able aspects of the other, we tend to ignore or deny many of the darker reasons that are operative in love.

For example, it is not unknown for a young woman to fall in love, not once but in an unmistakable pattern, with married men who will not abandon their wives and families. One (certainly not the only) reason for love in such cases—it eventually becomes evident—is the safety of such a relationship, the fact that it has built-in limits in terms of time and commitment. An unusually experienced and insightful woman might recognize this in herself as an operative reason for love, but this would be rare indeed. So too, the recognition that the beloved satisfies one's more neurotic needs—the need to be punished or martyred, the desire to take care of a truly pathetic human being, the need to play God with someone; these are some of the darker reasons for love that might be quite effective without ever being acknowledged. These might not be *good* reasons, but even a sick relationship is not without its reasons.

Then there is love that arises out of jealousy. This is its reason and, in the truly perverse cases, its sole reason. In the standard case, A has no interest in B until C shows an interest in B. As the rivalry heats up, it and not anything that has to do with B or the promise of a relationship with B, is the dominant or even sole motivation. But I want to be cautious here. It is a staple of sitcom romances that a little bit of jealousy (usually based on an easily resolvable misunderstanding) is good for a relationship. It reminds one of the contingency of this (or any) relationship. There is nothing perverse about that. A little bit of jealousy may also remind a lover of the virtues and attractions of the beloved, refocusing attention in a constructive and healthy way. There may be nothing perverse about that either. But both of these examples assume that the relationship already has its sufficient reasons, that the jealousy only serves to remind or redirect attention to reasons that are already operative. This is very different from loving someone (if that is the word) because someone else, perhaps someone who is already a rival, takes an interest.

A complex variation on love based on jealousy is what Jon Elster, borrowing from Stendhal calls *amour par pique.* "Jealousy desires the death of the rival it fears. A man suffering from pique, on the other hand, wants his enemy to live and above all witness his triumph." The rivalry predates the love, if it is love at all, which provides the means of getting back at the rival. It is the sine qua non of *amour par pique* that it lasts only as long as the rivalry lasts, and not a moment more. The relationship with the rival is complex. Elster describes it in terms of "A's belief about B's belief about B's counterfactual victory over A." But the supposed beloved, the object of the contest, does not appear in the formula at all.

There is also love out of fear. Stendhal writes, "the pleasures of love are always in proportion to fear," and La Rochefoucauld notes that "love ceases to live as soon as it ceases to hope or fear." Hope, not necessarily, but fear? The simple case is love out of the fear of leaving or being left alone. All other reasons for love may have faded, but the thought of being single again, or the thought of dating, or the thought of having to look for another apartment in a tight rental market, is sufficient to hold the relationship together. I think, again, we can seriously doubt whether such a relationship deserves to be called *love.* A more complicated but more interesting set of cases involve the fear of breaking up, the fear of resultant hostility, or the fear of hurting the other's feelings. Such considerations are clearly more relevant to the relationship than fear of dating or having to look for another apartment.

One could argue that the fear of hurting the other's feelings cannot be separated from affection and caring, whether or not we would say that such considerations necessitate love. By contrast, the fear of hostility, and in the worst cases fear of physical harm, are more problematic. Unfortunately, the psychopathology of abusive relationships seems to suggest that such fears can be confused with love, indeed, perhaps even give rise to love. I do not personally understand how this can be, but I think that you will agree that it is a perverse (and horribly self-deceptive) reason for loving someone.

What is not so perverse, but may become so, is love borne out of uncertainty and suspense. The passion that begins a relationship is certainly bound up with this (although here one might want to talk about the *cause* of the passion rather than its reason). One should not conflate uncertainty with fear, although the two may obviously support one another. It is said that "satisfaction is the death of desire." Whether or not this is always so (and I would argue that it is true only for a limited set of desires), it had better not be true of love. (Thus the naughty ambiguity of Juliet's lament to Romeo, "what satisfaction can I give you tonight?") Thus the continued provocation of love through jealousy, which is perhaps the most vicious (because so manipulative and humiliating) form of competitive uncertainty, may be innocent enough at the beginning of a relationship, when mutual expectations are so unsettled. But as love goes on it is rightly seen as an impediment, if not as sabotage. There is more than enough suspense in the inescapable uncertainty that is always the companion to passion, in the knowledge that we can never *really* get to know our beloved, her hidden dreams and fears and secrets, in the knowledge that *all* love is contingent and never "unconditional." But this isn't perverse. To the contrary, it is wisdom.

A different kind of dubious reason for love is this, although (again) there are traces of it in most good relationships. This is love out of obligation, loving someone because one is bound to do so. This one is tricky. Marriage, whatever else it may be—an expression of love, an excuse to have non-fornicating sex, the legitimization of children, a way to cut insurance costs—is a set of commitments and obligations. And I for one would certainly not say that marriage in any way compromises love. In my own experience, it provides love with fertile soil and room to grow. (I've also had other experiences, but let's not talk about those.) There are also arranged marriages, where the bonds of obligation precede any possibility of love. I have no reason to question such marriages as fertile ground for the development of love. (The original arranged marriage, at least in the Western tradition, was Adam and Eve. Trusting the wisdom of the arranger, whether it's God or parents or the village matchmaker, may itself be a good reason for love.) But the sort of perversity I have in mind is the more extreme case in which it is not only marriage but love itself that is conceived of solely in terms of obligation. Possibly there once was love, and now what remains is only obligation. Possibly one confuses obligation with love. (We can easily imagine Austen's Mr. Collins doing this, as perhaps does Kant, in an infamous passage.)

All of this is complicated further by the fact that the standard marriage vow includes the phrase "promise to love, honor and obey." The promise to obey can be objected to on other grounds, while the promise to honor sounds OK, if by "honor" we mean respect. But as for the promise to love, that seems to embody a number of philosophical confusions. Even if you embrace the idea of choosing your emotions (as I do, as most of my colleagues do not), the idea of promising to love seems incoherent. One can promise to abstain from activities that will endanger love. One can more positively promise to nurture conditions that are conducive to love. One can even promise to adopt or strive for attitudes and perspectives which are constitutive of love. But a promise to love, while it should open our minds to the possibility of "choosing love," is as such implausible, and feeling obliged to love is a very different matter than loving.

Love can be a mask for other, less affectionate emotions. Hatred, for example. Hatred shares many features with love, including the intimacy that I described as "shared identity." We have all seen people so consumed with hate that their lives turn on the activities and attitudes of their nemeses. It is a commonplace in romance novels that hatred may be a mask for love, although it is less commonly argued that love may be a mask for hatred, but the argument would be much the same. So, too, love may be a mask for envy, or resentment, or even contempt. The intricate and decidedly pathological tie between men and women who loathe women and men (respectively) but therefore insist on "loving" them is a familiar case in point. The question of whether or not one who uses love to mask such emotions can be said to actually love depends on the extent and the nature of the self-deception and whether there are other (possibly sufficient) reasons for loving. The idea that love and hatred, for instance, can sit side by side in the same soul (regarding the same beloved/foe) strikes most philosophers as something of an absurdity, except for the fact that it evidently happens. "Mixed feelings" may present us with a terrible personal quandary, but it raises no particular philosophical paradoxes. So, too, self-deception, against which many philosophers have raised apparently devastating objections, remains a regular part of all of our lives, and, especially, of love.

The idea that reasons for love might be unconscious and go unacknowledged opens up a vast territory of mysteries and accusations. Once it is allowed that one might not be aware of and even deny the reasons for loving someone, the way is cleared for all sorts of anxiety-inspiring theories about loving for revenge, loving because of infantile neuroses and unresolved Oedipal reasons, loving out of perversity and self-destructiveness. The theory of female "masochism" continues to enjoy dangerous currency, suggesting that women "really want" to be hurt and put down instead of looking for the reasons why many women's romantic situations are untenable or their images of love self-destructive in consequence rather than design. And too often, we dismiss the obvious in favor of the kinky, the mysterious or the degrading. A man or woman who is completely enamored with a young and beautiful face is diagnosed in the most dreadful clinical and moral terms. But sometimes, Freud himself insisted, a cigar is just a smoke, and so too the reasons for love may be just what they seem to be. Nevertheless, the most significant reasons may be the hardest to identify or to acknowledge.

These dubious reasons for love fail in many different ways, but at the core of them all is something like the complaint that they fail to take love as the love of a person and in a relationship. Now I already cast doubt on the idea that we love a person as such, the whole person or (in accordance with a familiar romantic declaration) *everything* about a person. Nevertheless, love's focus can be overly limited, and then it gives rise to that (usually benign) pathology called *fetishism*—loving someone for his or her wit or ability to do modal logic as well as the more celebrated sexual cases of foot fetishism, breast fetishism and penis envy. Even if one never loves "the whole person" in the grand holistic sense, nevertheless it is an ontological fact that in order to enjoy wit or intelligence or feet or breasts or penis, one should appreciate the person who has them. These dubious reasons, like most properties-of-the-person type reasons, latch onto one limited and perhaps tangential aspect of the beloved or the relationship. It is for this reason that one might insist that a good reason for love is one that fits into an ever expanding Aristophanic conception of both the beloved and the relationship.

Conclusion

"How do I love thee? Let me count the ways ..." writes Elizabeth Browning. But the "how" turns out to be a "why?" and the ways turn out to be reasons. When I first started writing about reasons for love, I thought that it would be simple business, explaining why loving someone for his or her money is frowned upon, why loving someone for his or her looks (but not *only* for his or her looks) deserves more respect than it usually gets, defending the importance of historical and other non-fungible features of the relationship as reasons for love. But it turned out to be much more complicated and intriguing. And this is even without getting into some of the deep phenomenological problems surrounding the "subjectivity" of love and the vicissitudes of self-deception. I hope that I have persuaded you that we do love for reasons, and that the best of those reasons are not of the sort usually noted as reasons for love.

Then again, to be convinced that there are reasons for love is not yet to insist that when in love we should flat-footedly say what they are. As George Eliot writes in *Middlemarch,* "We must not inquire too closely into motives.... they are apt to become feeble in the utterance." And as Nietzsche rather sexistly suggests at the beginning of his *Gay Science,* "Perhaps truth is a woman who has reasons for not letting us see her reasons" (p. 38). There are, to be sure, reasons for love, but there is good reason for us philosophers to abstain from overanalyzing them and rendering overly rational an emotion whose charm consists at least in part in the illusion that it cannot be explained by reasons.

7 The Value of Hope

Luc Bovens

> " … humankind
> Cannot bear very much reality."
> T.S. Eliot, *Burnt Norton,* 42–43

The concept of *hope* has received little attention in the philosophical literature outside of philosophy of religion. In contrast, hope, particularly hope in a secular context, has received much attention in the arts. Moreover, the kind of attention it has received is of a distinctly philosophical nature. In artistic explorations of hope, it is common to generate a tension with respect to the *value* of hope: on the one hand, hanging on to hope in trying times may be invaluable to one's survival, while, on the other hand, giving in to hope in trying times may stand in the way of one's survival. It is a scandal that a philosophical theme that is so central to how we should live our lives, and that has received so much attention in the arts, has gone virtually unnoticed in the philosophical community itself. To remedy this, I will set out on an exploration of the nature and the value of hope starting from a particularly insightful expression of this theme, viz., Frank Darabont's film *Shawshank Redemption,* based on a short story by Stephen King.[1] Similar results could have been reached by starting from, say, Henri Charriere's novel *Papillon*[2] or Eric Roehmer's film *Conte d'hiver.*

I Two puzzles of hope

Andy, a well-to-do New York banker, is wrongly convicted to life in prison for murdering his wife and her lover. In the Shawshank prison, he forms a friendship with Red who is also serving a life sentence for a murder he committed as a teenager. Andy sets up a money-laundering scheme under a false identity for a sleazy prison director. He succeeds in a spectacular escape and, at least in the film version, assumes the false identity that he has created, leaving the prison director with empty hands and the focal point of a scandal leaked to the press.

The story is told through the eyes of Red. The tension concerning the value of hope comes out most poignantly when Andy and Red discuss the value of music inside the walls of the Shawshank prison. Red gave up playing the harmonica, because "it does not make much sense" inside the prison walls. For Andy, it is here that music "makes the most sense," because music represents "something that they can't get from you, something inside that they can't touch, that is yours." Red feigns a lack of understanding, forcing Andy to lay out his cards and to acknowledge that music is a metaphor for hope in their discussion. This is the point that Red has been waiting for to present his views on hope: "Let me tell you something: hope is a dangerous thing, hope can drive a man insane, has got no use on the inside, better get used to that idea." Andy gets the upper hand in their discussion by the pointed three-word rebuttal: "Like Brookes did?" (Brookes, a fellow convict, was released on parole and hung himself being unable to get used to life outside prison.) Red, left without reply, walks out on the discussion. After his escape, Andy colors in his views on hope in a letter to Red: "Hope is a good thing. Maybe the best of things. And hope never dies." Red makes his point in picturesque ways at other junctions. When Andy tells him his dreams about going to Mexico, he starts dreaming along, but then catches himself and responds: "I don't think that you ought to be doing this to yourself. It's a shitty pipe dream. Mexico is down there and I am in here." Or, in the words that Stephen King (p. 72) puts into Red's mouth: "The whole idea seemed absurd, and that mental image of blue water and white beaches seemed more cruel than foolish—it dragged at my brain like a fishhook."

The story presents us with two puzzles with respect to hope. First, there is the practical question of how much one should hope in particular circumstances. Red knew that he would be doing himself harm if he were to hope in the way that Andy did inside the walls of Shawshank. He describes how Andy could wear "his freedom like an invisible coat" (King, p. 64), but is aware that he himself "couldn't wear that invisible coat the way Andy did" (King, p. 72). But also for Andy there are limits to how much hope he can support. Tommy Williams, a new inmate, provides Andy with the evidence of who killed his wife and her lover. This news releases a spurt of hope in Andy that no longer is beneficial to his survival in the Shawshank prison. Red observes that this is the one time when he knew Andy to "lose that [inner] light:" "… it was as if Tommy had produced a key which fit a cage in the back of his mind, a cage like his own cell. Only instead of holding a man, that cage held a tiger, and the tiger's name was Hope. Williams had produced the key that unlocked the cage and the tiger was out, willy-nilly, to roam his mind" (King, pp. 51–2). Hope seems to obey Aristotle's doctrine of the mean. To live one's life well one should not hope too much and not hope too little. But what is it that determines this mean in a particular situation and for a particular person? How can I assess how much room to allot to the tiger within, such that it will not suffocate, yet also will not raise havoc?

Second, there is a puzzle concerning the nature of inner strength and its relation to hope. Red disagrees with Andy about the place of hope inside the prison walls, but nonetheless has great respect for Andy's manner of comporting himself inside Shawshank. He knows that it is precisely this sense of hope that enables him to do so. It is hope that provides Andy with inner strength, but this inner strength is required to carry his hope in such a way that it does not drag him down. But what is the good of hope if its benefits are a prerequisite for its proper functioning? And what is the nature of this inner strength with which hope seems to be so tightly connected? Red fosters a sense of wonder and admiration for Andy's character. Andy never adopted "a prison mentality[, h]is eyes never got that dull look[, h]e never developed … that flat-footed, hump-shouldered walk" (King, p. 64). Red speculates that what Andy brought from the outside is a "sense of his own worth, maybe, or a feeling that he would be the winner in the end … or maybe it was only a sense of freedom … a kind of inner light he carried around with him" (King, p. 38). There seems to be a close connection between Andy's sense of self-worth and his hopes that soar beyond the prison walls. What is it about hope that supports this connection?

II Scepticism about hope

In trying to determine under what conditions it is rational to believe, the philosopher typically gives a voice to the sceptic who argues that we are never justified in believing anything. Subsequently the philosopher constructs a theory of rational belief as a response to the sceptic. I will follow this philosophical practice to deal with the topic of hope.

The sceptic about hope could put forward the following challenge to the rationality of hoping. Suppose that I want something and that I believe that there is some chance that it will come about. Now either it does or it does not come about. *Suppose it does not come about.* Then I would have been worse off having hoped than not having hoped, since I tend to be left with a greater sense of frustration after hoping than after not hoping. Witness expressions like "I do not dare to hope for ..." or "I should never have hoped for ..." *Suppose it does come about.* Then is there anything to be gained from having hoped for it? In hoping for something, I tend to fill in the contours in the brightest colors. Suppose that my hopes come true, but not precisely in the bright colors that I had pictured. Had I not hoped for anything, I would have been delighted. But having hoped as I have, I experience a sense of frustration rather than satisfaction. Either way, I would have been better off not having hoped for anything and so it is always irrational to hope for something. What the sceptic maintains is that Red not only has it right inside the walls of Shawshank, but that under *any* circumstances, a life in which one has no hopes is better than a life in which one does have hopes.

Towards the end of the story, Red is paroled and is having a hard time adjusting to life outside of the Shawshank prison. Encouraged by a letter from Andy, he decides to break his parole and take off to join him in Mexico. King concludes the novel with the following words in the voice of Red: "I hope Andy is down there. I hope I can make it across the border. I hope to see my friend and shake his hand. I hope the Pacific is as blue as it has been in my dreams. I *hope*" (King, p. 101). The moral of the story is that Red is no longer a sceptic about hope. In his newfound freedom, he has crossed over to Andy's side and embraced the value of hoping. But what is there to be gained from renouncing scepticism about hope? Why form a mental image of the blue of the Pacific only to meet with disappointment that its hue is less intense than one had hoped for?

Just like our beliefs and desires, our hopes are seldom under our direct control. Witness expressions such as "I could not bring myself to hope that ..." or "I could not stop hoping that ..." But just as this does not stand in the way of thinking about how we should set our beliefs and desires, it should not stand in the way of thinking how we should set our hopes. Even if direct control over our hopes is limited, our inquiry is still worthwhile in that it will inform us in how far to foster and discourage hopes in our children and how to adjust our own hopes through roundabout strategies of character planning.

III The instrumental value of hope

Hope is instrumentally valuable in that it has an enabling function, in that it counteracts risk aversion, and in that it spawns more attainable constitutive hopes. Let us take up each feature in turn.

a. The Enabling Function of Hope. The sceptic appeals to what is called a *dominance argument* in decision theory. I have a choice between hoping and not hoping for some projected state of the world. The state of the world may either come about or may not come about. Whether the state of the world does or does not come about, I am always better off not having hoped for it rather than having hoped for it. Hence, by dominance, I should not hope. What the sceptic forgets is that dominance arguments only hold if there is no causal dependency between states of the world and choices.

To see this, suppose that I have a choice between asking or not asking my daughter to help me out with some task. Two states of the world may come about, viz., either she does help me out or she does not help me out. Suppose she does help me out. Then I would have been better off not asking, since unsolicited help is better than solicited help. Suppose she does not help me out. Then I would be better off not having asked, since not being turned down is better than being turned down. Hence, either way, I would be better off not having asked and so, by dominance, I should not ask her to help me out. But this argument is clearly fallacious. My asking my daughter (who is not a teenager yet!) increases the chance that she will help me out. Dominance fails since the relevant states of the world are causally dependent on my choice.

Similarly, the sceptic's argument fails if there is a causal dependency between my hoping and the occurrence of the projected state of the world. Sometimes hoping can in no way affect whether the projected state will come about or not. For instance, I may hope all I want that the temperature will not drop below freezing on my camping trip. In this case, I have no argument (yet) with the sceptic. But sometimes hoping facilitates the realization of the projected state of the world. A hopeful rather than a defeatist attitude may at least be partly responsible for bringing some task to a successful end. It arouses a certain zeal and helps me explore alternative means to realize my goals. In this case, the sceptic has it wrong. Dominance fails since the states of the world (viz., whether I will or will not bring the task to a successful end) are causally dependent on my choice (viz., whether to hope or not to hope.)

b. Hope Counteracts Risk Aversion. A man and a woman are out for dinner. To provide for some evening entertainment, he takes out a coin and proposes the following gamble to her. If heads comes up, then he will pay her $200. If tails comes up, then she will pay him $100. She thinks for a while and says that she is willing to take up the gamble, but only if she can play this game at least one hundred times. The motivation behind this response is clear. By accepting this gamble for one game, she has a fifty-fifty chance of losing money. By accepting this gamble for one hundred games, she has no more than a negligible chance of losing money by the end of the evening. Should she accept the gamble in the one-off game?

If she is acutely short of money, we can well understand why she would not want to agree to the one-off game. In this case the gamble is a less than fair gamble. What can be won is $200, but what can be lost is not just $100, but, say, $100 and the humiliation of washing dishes all night followed by a ten-mile walk home.

But if she is not acutely short of money, then the gamble is a more than fair gamble. Now, suppose the offer were to play the game one hundred times, but spread out over a longer period at reasonably short intervals. And suppose that the chance mechanism and the payoffs were to vary, but always in such a way that the chance mechanism would yield roughly a fifty-fifty chance of winning and losing and that the relative values of the payoffs would mirror roughly the relative values of $100 and $200. It seems to me that none of these suppositions could provide good reason to back out of the game. But the game that she is facing now is not all that different from the game that real life has to offer. In life, we are confronted with a multitude of gambles of some kind or other, some less than fair and some more than fair. To accept the game under the suppositions stipulated above is not much different than to adopt a resolution to accept any more than fair gamble on the path of life. And since the one-off game is one such a gamble, she should accept it. If she should agree to play the game one hundred times, then she should equally agree to play the one-off game, since it is just one run in the sequence of more than fair gambles that life has to offer.

The players who adopt a resolution to accept life's more than fair gambles tend to come out as winners, while the players who resist such a resolution tend to come out as losers. And yet it is easy to succumb to myopia and to resist the more than fair gambles in life, because we are too fixated on the possible losses in each single gamble. Now the value of hope is that it makes us focus on the possible gains in more than fair gambles. It helps us overcome our myopic fixation on the possible losses in more than fair gambles. The resolution of accepting more than fair gambles will tend to be a winning strategy in the game of life at large.

But then what about fear? The value of fear is that it makes us focus on the possible losses in less than fair gambles. It helps us overcome our myopic fixation on the possible gains in less than fair gambles. The resolution to decline less than fair gambles will tend to be a winning strategy in the game of life at large. While hope is an antidote to the risk aversion that keeps us from taking up more than fair gambles, fear is an antidote to the risk proneness that makes us all too eager to take up less than fair gambles. The proper balance of hope and fear is instrumental in regulating risk-taking behavior to maximize our payoffs throughout life.[3]

c. Hope Engenders New Constitutive Hopes. The sceptic phrases his challenge in terms of hoping that some particular state of the world will come about. But what we are hoping for may have a much more complex structure. We hope that particular states of the world will come about because we take them to be constitutive of more general states of the world. For instance, I may hope that I will be awarded a particular prize because I take this to be constitutive of gaining recognition in the field and I may hope to gain recognition in the field because I take this to be constitutive of a better professional life. Now hoping can be illuminating in that it invites us to reflect and rearrange this structure. Through hoping we spend a certain amount of mental energy on the projected states of the world and we may come to realize that what we were originally hoping for is not worth hoping for after all. Our hopes are much more fluid than the sceptic envisions them to be. I may come to realize that there are other and better ways to gain recognition in the field than by winning the prize in question or that there are other and better ways to improve my professional life than by gaining recognition in the field. As I come to have such insights, I will set new constitutive hopes that I am more likely to realize because they are more in line with what I truly stand for, with my skills or with the limitations of my surroundings.

IV Hope and intrinsic value

If hope has instrumental value, then the sceptic loses ground in cases in which the realization of the projected state is dependent upon the agency of the person who is hoping. And this is true to a certain extent in *Shawshank Redemption*. But suppose that there was no escape possible for Andy. Suppose that, as with Red, his release was entirely dependent on the whims of the parole board. As for Andy's hope that he will some day be a free man again, we cannot appeal to instrumental value. Andy may hope all he wants, this will not affect his chances that he will some day be a free man again. Would scepticism about hope be vindicated, or could there still be a point to hoping under such circumstances? I will argue that there could still be a point to hoping due to its intrinsic value. But first we need to do some preliminary work and determine what it is to hope for something.

a. The Nature of Hope. An attitude of hoping for some state of the world is inconsistent with being confident that it will or will not come about. In other words, one cannot hope for some state of the world, unless one has a degree of credence that it will come about which ranges between some threshold value close to 0 for confidence that it will not come about and some threshold value close to 1 for confidence that it will come about.[4] Furthermore, one cannot hope for some state of the world, unless one has some desire that it will come about. But the conjunction of non-confident belief and desire is a necessary and not a sufficient condition for hope. There is no conceptual confusion in affirming one's desire for some state of the world and one's belief that this state may or may not come about, while denying that one is hoping that it would come about. Consider the following case. Sophie shows up late at some party and asks me very self-confidently whether I had been hoping that she would come. Now suppose that I did indeed believe that Sophie might come and that I consider her to be a welcome guest—i.e. I prefer her coming to the party to her not coming to the party. Still, it seems to me that it would be a lie to say that I had been hoping she would come, unless I had devoted at least some mental energy to the question whether she would or would not come to the party—e.g., I had been looking at my clock wondering whether Sophie would still come, I had been turning my head earlier to check whether Sophie was amongst some newly arrived guests, etc. Let us name this devotion of mental energy to what it would be like if some projected state of the world were to materialize "mental imaging."

There may be various reasons why I may not engage in mental imaging in the presence of the proper belief and desire, e.g., I may be preoccupied with other matters, my desire may be too weak to trigger the mental imaging or I may intentionally refrain from mental imaging to avoid future frustration. In none of these cases can I properly be said to be hoping. Mental imaging is no less a necessary condition for hoping than the proper belief and desire. Note how the metaphorical usage of "dreaming" for hoping—e.g., in Martin Luther King's famous words "I have a dream"— precisely capitalizes on the component of mental imaging that is present in hoping.

Is mental imaging in conjunction with the proper belief and desire a sufficient condition for hoping? I think so. It *would* be ludicrous for me to deny that I am hoping that Sophie would come to the party, while believing that she might come, desiring that she would come and not being able to keep my attention on conversations with the other guests. What else could there be to hoping that Sophie would come to the party? Hoping *is* just having the proper belief and desire in conjunction with being engaged to some degree in mental imaging.

One might be tempted by the following objection. Just as there are two kinds of beliefs, viz., latent and occurrent beliefs, there are two types of hopes, viz., latent and occurrent hopes. My description is an accurate description of occurrent hopes. For latent hopes it is sufficient to have the proper beliefs and desires. Furthermore, latency is an explanation of why, just as we can be mistaken about our beliefs, we can also be mistaken about our hopes.

I grant that I can be hoping for something while it is not the case that I am engaged in mental imaging at that very moment. Thus far it is meaningful to draw a distinction between latent and occurrent hopes. But I must have at least some intermittent episodes of mental imaging before I can be said to be hoping at all. In this respect, hoping is different from believing. There is no conceptual confusion in saying that I believe some proposition but I never gave any thought to it whatsoever. There is a conceptual confusion in saying that I hope that some state of the world will come about but I never gave any thought to it whatsoever. Suppose that upon meeting Sophie last week, I had an occurrent belief that she has hazel eyes and I had an occurrent hope that she would come to the party. But since then, I did not give a moment of thought to Sophie's hazel eyes or that she might come to the party, although I still consider her to be a welcome guest. Then, assuming that my memory is not failing me, I still have a latent belief that Sophie has hazel eyes, but it would be false to say that I still have a latent hope that Sophie will come to the party.

I do not deny that we can be mistaken about our hopes. But, unlike in the case of beliefs, latency is not a sufficient explanation for being mistaken about our hopes, since even for latent hopes there must be intermittent episodes of mental imaging. We *can* be mistaken about our hopes because we do not correctly assess one or more of their constituents and hence explanations can take on various forms. Consider a scenario in which I do indeed hope that Sophie will come to the party but refuse to acknowledge my hope. This can come about because I incorrectly assess my belief that there is some chance that she might come. It may come about because I incorrectly assess my desire that she will come. Or, most comically, it may come about because I misread my mental imaging. When my friends tease me that I can hardly quit talking about the upcoming party, I point out that this is so because I am excited, say, about the band, but not because Sophie might come. Yet curiously enough, it is when Sophie bails out and not when the band bails out that I lose all interest in the upcoming party.

b. The Pleasures of Anticipation and the Epistemic Value of Hope. Once we agree on what it is to hope for something, two points emerge. First, hoping has intrinsic value in that mental imaging provides for the pleasures of anticipation and this can be especially important in times of hardship. The mental play that is constitutive of hoping provides a satisfaction that one cannot attain from attending to one's actual circumstances. In times of hardship, there is welcome respite in hoping.

Second, I argued earlier that the mental play that is constitutive of hoping permits us to restructure our hopes which can be conducive to realizing our more general hopes. But restructuring our hopes does not only have instrumental value. It is also conducive to an increased self-understanding. We restructure our hopes by reflecting on what it is that we truly want and what is attainable in our lives. Returning to our example, I may start off hoping to win the prize in question in order to gain more recognition in the field, but through mental imaging I may come to realize how unattainable or how futile my pursuits really are. As I shift my hopes to more attainable and meaningful pursuits that are no less constitutive of a better professional life, I have come to learn something about myself and my place in the world.

All other things being equal, a life with hope is a better life than a life without hope due to the pleasures of anticipation and the illumination that hope provides. But the sceptic may point out that all things are not equal because a life with hope is vulnerable to frustration and the concomitant pangs of disappointment. Certainly these have a place in the equation but it is important to give them no more weight than is due. The pleasures of anticipation may outweigh the potential pangs of disappointment. Furthermore, our hopes are fluid and often do not need to be abandoned in the face of frustration. Rather they painlessly leave the stage of our mental lives as we learn and shift our hopes towards states of the world that are more attainable or that are more in line with what we truly want. The knowledge that hope affords can safeguard us from frustration and the concomitant pangs of disappointment.[5]

c. Hope, Love and Self-Worth. There is a close connection between love on the one hand and hope or fear on the other hand. Suppose that I believe some state of the world may come about that would detract from the well-being of some person and I desire that it not come about. It would be odd to say that I love the person in question yet do not spend at least some amount of mental energy contemplating the possibility that the state of the world may or may not come about. I fear for the well-being of a loved one as my mental imaging sways more towards the former, while I hope for the well-being of a loved one as my mental imagining sways more towards the latter. Hoping and fearing for the well-being of a loved one are constitutive of loving.

Robert Adams[6] describes a case in which a passionate art lover is unable to tear himself away from a visit to the Cathedral of Chartres and is forced to do many hours of night driving, has trouble finding a place to sleep, etc. It would be a better world if our art lover would be able to enjoy art to the same extent as he actually does, but see a few sculptures less and allow himself some time to make comfortable arrangements for the night. Adams' point is that such a character is not attainable. The passion of the art lover is closely connected with his imprudence. If our art lover were to become the kind of person who could tear himself away from the sculptures in order to give himself ample time to make comfortable arrangements, then he would no longer be the passionate art lover that he was before (Adams, pp. 239–40). Similarly, in certain cases, it might be a better world if one could love to the same extent as one actually does and not have to subject oneself to the hazards of hoping and the agonies of fearing. But such a world is simply not attainable. When hoping and fearing are considered in isolation from their connection with other character traits, it may be the case that there is little to be said for them. But their close connection with love is what vindicates attitudes of hoping and fearing.

The argument so far is limited. It vindicates hoping when it is a case of hoping for the well-being of a loved one. Can the argument be extended to hoping for one's own future well-being? If hoping and fearing for another person's well-being are constitutive of loving him or her, then hoping and fearing for one's own well-being may well be constitutive of loving one's own self. And at least on some understanding of the concepts involved, what such loving one's own self amounts to is precisely having a sense of self-worth. Hence, just as locally irrational hopes and fears for another person's well-being may be vindicated because such attitudes are constitutive of love, locally irrational hopes and fears for one's own future well-being may be vindicated because such attitudes are constitutive of a sense of self-worth.[7]

What is the nature of these connections? I take it that hoping and fearing for someone's well-being are contained in a cluster of features that are constitutive of loving and that hoping and fearing for one's own future well-being are contained in a cluster of features that are constitutive of having a sense of self-worth. There is a presumption that a person who loves or has a sense of self-worth satisfies the features in the respective clusters. This presumption may be violated in special cases. The love of a parent for a child may persist after the child has passed away and this love is not contingent on a belief in an after-life. A terminally-ill cancer patient may block out her hopes and fears for the future and decide to live for the moment without losing her sense of self-worth. We ask for an explanation if someone says that she loves but does not hope or fear for the loved one's well-being, or that she has a sense of self-worth but does not hope or fear for her own future well-being, but it is short of being incoherent. However, it would be incoherent if someone were to say that she loves or has a sense of self-worth but does not have any of the constitutive features contained in the respective clusters.

My vindication of hope through love and a sense of self-worth rests on the assumptions that love and a sense of self-worth are attitudes that themselves have intrinsic value. I believe that these are plausible assumptions. All other things being equal, a life in which one enters into loving relationships is a better life than a life in which one does not. All other things being equal, a life in which one has a sense of self-worth is a better life than a life in which one does not. If an attitude of hoping and fearing is indeed constitutive of love and one's sense of self-worth, then hoping and fearing are valuable precisely in this constitutive role.

V Hope and epistemic rationality

To believe that some states of the world may or may not come about is to assign a subjective probability (or range of subjective probabilities) to these states of the world. The strength of our beliefs—i.e. the magnitudes of these subjective probabilities—should be determined by the available evidence. This constraint of epistemic rationality is violated in the phenomenon of wishful thinking. The wishful thinker raises the subjective probability of desirable states of the world beyond what is warranted by the available evidence and lowers the subjective probability of undesirable states of the world below what is warranted by the available evidence.

The danger of any type of mental imaging—whether in hoping or fearing—is that the invitation of wishful thinking becomes so much more difficult to resist. This is not to say that it is impossible to hope or fear, while remaining epistemically rational. But just as it is harder to exercise self-control when the peanuts are within reach, it is harder to remain epistemically rational when one hopes or fears.

But why would this be so? I can see two reasons. First, too much mental imaging may obscure the line between reality and fancy. Consider how difficult it is to determine whether our images of early childhood incidents are constructions on grounds of stories that were told to us at an older age or are memories of actual incidents. In the same way, the distinction between reality and the mental constructions we form in hoping are easily obfuscated. And in the absence of this distinction, our capacity to form beliefs on grounds of the available evidence vanishes.

Second, hoping seems to carry with it an illusion of agency. Imagine the following strange coincidence. In an unguarded moment of boredom, I catch myself gazing up at an airplane and hoping for its downing just seconds before it actually occurs. It would not be untypical that this would elicit a sense of shame and that, in working through this sense of shame, I would need to remind myself that my hoping really had nothing to do with the tragic event. Furthermore, hoping carries with it a stronger illusion of agency than mere desiring. Consider the following cases. Suppose that my closest friend races cars and that I attend various car-racing events. Some day I come to realize that I only attend races on the more dangerous circuits, place myself at locations that provide a good view of dangerous corners, etc. It becomes clear from my behavior that deep down I have a *desire* for an accident to happen. However, I cannot be said to *hope* for an

accident to happen, since I do not find myself devoting much
mental energy to what it would be like if such and such accident
were to occur. Contrast this with a case in which I find myself
acting in precisely the same way, but in addition my mental space
is filled with unbridled thoughts about what it would be like if such
and such accident were to occur, the stories I would be able to tell
my friends, etc. In this case, I am not just *desiring*, but I am *hoping*
for an accident to happen. Now, suppose that an accident does
happen in which my closest friend is killed. I think it would not be
untypical for me to encounter a greater sense of shame in the case
in which I was hoping than in the case in which I was just desiring
for an accident to happen.[8] Why would this be so?

This difference in degree of shame can be fully warranted.
Though I do not want to exclude the possibility of akrasia and self-
deception with respect to our hopes, hoping typically involves
more of a conscious endorsement of the value of the projected
state of the world than mere desiring. As such it permits for more
opportunities to recognize the shamefulness of our attitudes and to
reform. Hence, our failure to do so weighs heavier in the case of
hoping than in the case of mere desiring. But the difference in
degree of shame can also have a strictly psychological explanation.
In the case of hope, unlike in the case of desire, our shame tends to
become tainted with a sense of "*if only I had not ...*" Hoping has
something in common with prayer in that it builds on an illusion
of causal agency. When two of our close friends are engaged in
a bitter and painful relationship, we either hide or report with a
slight sense of shame that, at one point, we were hoping that they
would fall in love, as if we see ourselves as being responsible for
bringing them together and causing their pain.

But why does hoping as opposed to desiring have this aura
of agency about it? My conjecture is that we attend to a feature of
hope in circumstances in which hoping does affect our performance and does raise the probability of the occurrence of the projected state of the world and we mistakenly generalize this feature
to hoping at large. What we overlook is that there are strict constraints on the domain in which hoping is instrumentally rational.
Indeed, sometimes hoping makes things so—or, at least, helps

make things so. It is an understandable error that this feature of hoping is then generalized to cases of hoping in which even the most fervent hopes cannot change the probability that the projected state of the world will come about in any way. Now, if hope may carry with it this illusion of causal agency, then it is understandable that hope may lead one to overestimate the subjective probability that the state of the world will come about.

VI Resolving the puzzles of hope

The sceptic has got it wrong. It is not true that it is irrational to hope under any circumstances. Hoping is instrumentally valuable in that it helps me realize the projected state of the world, it cures me of a myopic evaluation of more than fair gambles, and it aids me in adjusting my constitutive hopes. Hoping is intrinsically valuable in that it provides for the pleasures of anticipation and respite in trying times, it helps me gain self-understanding, and it is constitutive of intrinsically valuable attitudes such as loving and having a sense of self-worth. But the sceptic does have a point. Hoping increases my frustration about missed opportunities and colors the desired states of the world in such detail that it increases the likelihood of frustration. Furthermore, hoping is an open invitation for wishful thinking and can interfere with my epistemic rationality. This analysis of the pros and cons of hoping provides a complex response to our first puzzle, i.e. the practical question of how much a particular person should hope for in a particular situation. We should evaluate the good-making features and the bad-making features of hoping for the person in question and within the situation in question. For instance, a person with low frustration tolerance should be cautious about hoping in case the projected state of the world is unlikely to come about. On the other hand, there is a clear invitation to hope in a situation in which hoping can provide for the necessary zeal that will affect the likelihood that the projected state of the world will come about. The economy of hoping requires a careful balancing act between these good-making and bad-making features and how much one should hope is a function of the circumstances, the object of hope and the character of the would-be hoper.

This analysis also provides insight into our second puzzle, viz., what is the good of hoping if the inner strength that it provides is a prerequisite for its proper functioning? There is a fast response to bypass this challenge to the value of hope. Suppose someone were to question the good of foreign exchange offices, since, after all, one needs money in order to get money. Well clearly, it is sufficient to point out that one needs one kind of money in order to get another kind of money. Similarly, the kinds of inner strength that hoping requires are different from the kinds of inner strength that it provides. What is *needed* to hope well is (i) a sense of groundedness not to fall prey to epistemic irrationality and (ii) a degree of frustration tolerance not to let failure drag one down. What hoping *affords* is (iii) welcome respite through mental imaging, (iv) an increased self-understanding and (v) a sense of self-worth.

But this response is too easy-handed. Notice that there are intricate connections between the kinds of inner strength that hoping affords and the kinds of inner strength that hoping requires.

First, epistemic rationality and the development of a sense of self-worth are connected through the concept of *self-respect*. A person cannot respect herself unless she develops a sense of self-worth. And, in wishful thinking, a person violates the norms of self-respect. To provide a theoretical account of the relation between epistemic rationality and self-respect is a difficult endeavor. I take the following Kantian line to be promising. The wishful thinker violates the teleology of epistemic agency—i.e. the gathering of knowledge. Hence, she treats her epistemic agency as a means to some further end—say, a semblance of peace of mind—rather than as an end in itself. In treating her epistemic agency as a means to some further end, she treats herself as a means to some further end and not as an end in itself.

Second, self-understanding and a sense of self-worth are closely connected to frustration tolerance. A fine-tuned self-understanding combined with a sense of self-worth provides for a backbone to deal with failure. Low frustration-tolerance is typically associated with incertitude and a lack of self-worth.

Third, the capacity to enjoy the respite from mental imaging is closely connected to the capacity not to succumb to wishful thinking. If mental imaging comes to deteriorate into wishful thinking then, in Red's words, it starts dragging at one's brain like a fishhook and it can no longer perform the function of revitalizing one's inner strength.

Considering these intricate connections, the types of inner strength that are required to hope well are tightly linked to the types of inner strength that hope affords. And so, through hoping, inner strength can get caught in vicious and virtuous cycles. For those who do not have sufficient inner strength to hope well, hoping can jeopardize the little resources they have. For those who do have sufficient inner strength to hope well, hoping can solidify these resources. Inner strength, in its relation to hoping, is very much subject to the biblical adage: "The man who has will be given more and the man who has not will forfeit even what he has" (Mark 4:25).

Notes

I am grateful to Stephen Leeds, Iain Martel, Christopher Shields, two anonymous referees of this journal, and especially to Graham Oddie for their inspiration and/or comments.

1 "Hope Springs Eternal—Rita Hayworth and Shawshank Redemption." In *Four Seasons*, (Bergenfield, New Jersey: Viking Press, 1982).

2 Translated from the French by Patrick O'Brian (London: Hart-Davis, 1970).

3 Graham Oddie drew my attention to hope's corrective role for risk aversion and fear's corrective role for risk proneness.

4 I resist the more inclusive requirement that one must have a degree of credence which ranges between 0 and 1, or, in other words, that one must be short of being *certain* that the state of the world either will or will not come about. As to the upper bound, it seems to me that once I am confident, even if short of being certain, that some state of the world will come about, then I no longer hope for it, but rather look forward to it. The lower bound is somewhat more tenuous. Could I not hope for world peace in my lifetime and yet be confident that this will not come about? It is notoriously difficult to make sense of utopian hopes. Either, the projected state in utopian hopes functions as a guiding ideal. But then, what I am hoping for strictly speaking is that the world will move closer towards peace in my lifetime and it is not true that I am confident that *that* will not come about. Or, utopian hopes may require a divided mind. Upon reflection, I admit that the evidence warrants confidence that world peace will not come about

in my lifetime, but a part of me resists this confidence and this is what enables me to continue to hope.

5 The ideas in this section originated with some stimulating comments by an anonymous referee of this journal.

6 "Motive Utilitarianism." In J. Glover (ed.) *Utilitarianism and its Critics* (New York: Macmillan, 1990) pp. 236–49.

7 Cf. M.S. Quinn (1976) "Hoping." *Southwestern Journal of Philosophy* 7, p. 63, for some suggestive remarks to this effect.

8 One might object that it may be more accurate to describe my hope as the conditional hope that if an accident were to happen then I would see it and that there is no reason for shame in the face of conditional hope. This *may* indeed be the case, but there are ways of telling whether my hope is merely conditional or not. Suppose that I tend to be in a remarkably better mood after car-races in which there had been an accident and I saw it than after car-races in which there had been no accident whatsoever. Or, suppose that I am offered a seat which gives me a clear view of all the curves on which an accident might occur, so that I can be confident that if there is an accident, I will see it. However, I still continue to experience hope. Under these suppositions, I can no longer exculpate myself by saying that my hopes are merely conditional.

8 Patience and Courage

Eamonn Callan

Suppose your friends had to ascribe a single vice to you in large measure, along with any virtues that could be coherently combined with that salient vice. Suppose further that the vice had to be either cowardice or impatience. Which would you choose?

I believe almost everyone would choose impatience without hesitation. There are sound moral as well as purely self-regarding reasons for despising cowardice, and to that extent our preference would be reasonable. If we say that a man who is a coward is also compassionate, we know that his compassion cannot be relied upon in any circumstances where it must contend with fear, and if he has a sense of justice, that will be useless if oppression has to be resisted. We cannot even expect him to pursue his own good whenever he perceives that to be hazardous, and so even the self-regarding virtues are corrupted by his dominating vice. On the other hand, a pronounced impatience may seem to be compossible with abundant virtue. Those who are just but cannot patiently endure tyranny are perhaps the most formidable threat to tyranny, and people who boldly go out to seize their own good often fare rather better than those who patiently await its arrival.

Cowardice and impatience are vices of deficiency in relation to courage and patience respectively. The relevant vices of excess would be a reckless bravado and a sort of witless passivity in the midst of avoidable suffering and hardship. The seeming superiority of courage over patience is evident here as well. For the vice that pulls one beyond a judicious courage seems less contemptible than the vice of excess that distorts the patience worth having. There is often something almost flattering in our ascriptions of recklessness. It is as if we prize courage so highly that even its thoughtless extremities may not altogether extinguish our admiration. But patience seems perilously close to a kind of weakness, and any excess provokes pity or contempt. So it is not altogether surprising that when modern moralists talk about the virtues, they have much to say about courage and little or nothing to say about patience. The cowardice that subverts courage threatens the good life at its very core; impatience is, at worst, a forgivable peccadillo, or so we are apt to think.

Our contemporary ethical understanding does not merely marginalize patience while exalting courage; we are also apt to assume that there is some serious friction between them. Consider Sabina Lovibond's revealing response to Iris Murdoch's suggestion that our moral paragons might be found among "inarticulate, unselfish mothers of large families":

> It is not to be expected that an ethical theory which finds moral goodness, above all, in "simple people" ... will favour the unrestricted development of the moral "imagination" of these people—the unrestricted advance, that is, of the process by which they come to see things from unfamiliar points of view. The process can only result in their becoming less simple, with consequences no one can predict. For example, it might turn out to be a bad day for "moral reality" if the women whom Murdoch singles out for praise were to learn to conceptualize their possible resentment of the conditions of their life.... ("If I hadn't been so inarticulate I wouldn't have had ten children," they might say in a moment of heightened dialectical acuity.)[1]

Lovibond alludes to a distinctively modern contrast between supposedly rival moral postures: there is the individual who has reconciled herself to the "moral reality" of her life, forgoing the anger and resentment that would destroy her patient endurance; and there is the individual with the imagination to conceive a better life, the self-respect to see that the better life is her due, and the courage to do what is necessary to achieve it. It would be unfair to suppose that Lovibond can acknowledge no place whatever for a patient acceptance of suffering and hardship, but what is striking is Lovibond's assumption that because Murdoch would assign an exemplary status to that patience she must thereby overlook the importance of resentment towards being used and the courage to assert one's rights. It is as if the distinction between true patience and its vice of excess were a matter of virtual indifference to Lovibond, so that anyone extolling the virtue is presumptively guilty of recommending the vice. I shall return to the question of what might explain this attitude toward the end of the essay.

The exaltation of a courage that is sharply contrasted with patience, and the marginalization of patience in our commonsense catalogue of the virtues, are serious mistakes. There is no less reason to prize patience than there is to value courage, and no less reason to despise impatience than there is to loathe cowardice. Moreover, to understand these reasons is not to find grounds for valuing things that must be possessed by the virtuous in some deep and ineradicable tension; it is instead to arrive at a view of the harmony of patience and courage in the good life.

I

We think of courage as the paramount virtue of self-control. Indeed, we are more than a little tempted to speak of it as the only virtue of self-control. This grossly underestimates the importance of patience. Some attention to cases can correct the error.

A man grows blind in the prime of his life. There is nothing that can bring back his sight, and many of the projects to which he had been devoted must be discarded or conceived anew. The potential for a good life remains. He is healthy, prosperous, surrounded by people he loves who love him. But the man does not re-create a good life. He remains in the grip of a despair and rage that will not abate. There is something wrong here. What is it?

It might be that the man lacks courage. That possibility would be borne out if certain additional things were true. He is fearful of how others will regard him now that he is blind. He has always pitied the blind, and the thought of being a pathetic spectacle to others is terrifying. His fear of humiliation makes him hide from the world. Though others reassure him that independence and competence can be regained with effort and flexibility on his part, he doubts his own capacity to learn a new way of life. Trying and failing to learn is more frightening than failing by not trying at all, and so he drifts helplessly. Given these facts, it makes sense to impute a kind of cowardice because there is a paralysis of the will to pursue the good in the face of fear. This man might still have a fulfilling life if only he mustered the will to act in spite of his fears, and mustering that will requires a courage he does not have.

Then again the man's rage and despair might not be symptomatic of fears he cannot or will not find the courage to fight. Suppose he is more or less indifferent to how others view his blindness, and he knows that with time and perseverance he could learn to regain the competence and independence he had lost. Yet he still rages against his blindness because the good that is now available to him is not enough. Of course, it may sound more than a bit smug and censorious for those who are sighted simply to say that what is available *is* enough. But one may still have reason to judge that it is enough, and the time may come when his failure to acknowledge that it is becomes an ethical failure.

On this version of the man's story, one might say that what he lacks is fortitude in the sense that Sidgwick specified—the disposition "to bear pain unflinchingly."[2] But this may not be so. The man's anger and despair could well be endured without any complaint or childish self-display. He does not flinch. Yet he can still find no good in contact with those whom he loves because he cannot see them, and the intensity of his suffering deprives all his other endeavors of hope and joy. Attributing a lack of fortitude mislocates the problem because it suggests that the difficulty has to do with the way the man bears his suffering when in truth it has more to do with why he suffers so much in the first place. If he could grow to accept the good that is available, he would not suffer so much in his blindness, and hence the need for fortitude would not be so great. The blind man in my story has no patience for the moral task his blindness has set him, and no amount of courage or fortitude can compensate for the absence of that virtue. Patience is what he needs because it entails a discipline of those particular emotions that threaten to loosen or destroy one's hold on the good in circumstances of this kind. In courage, there is discipline of the fear that would make us cowards and the overweening confidence that would make us reckless; in patience, anger and despair are the things to be controlled if we are to cleave to the good against the temptations of impatience or a dejected passivity.

Simone Weil wanted us to think of our whole lives as a matter of waiting for the good rather than seeking it.[3] No doubt that greatly overstates the case once the theological background to Weil's claim is rejected. Yet there is much at the core of our lives that calls us to await something we cannot seize in a grand moment of courage or accept a more limited good than we had hoped for or taken for granted, and patience is what we need there. Patience is needed because in waiting for what is good, or accepting less than we craved, our power is thwarted, the limits of our capacity to shape the world to our liking humiliatingly exposed, and the despair and anger we are vulnerable to in that predicament threaten to alienate us from what matters in our lives. In rearing or teaching children, for example, the virtues and accomplishments we want for them have to ripen, and we must have the patience to allow that to happen. Being a decent parent or a good teacher may sometimes require courage, though it is hard to see how that could be a routine requirement. Other things being equal, patient cowards would seem to be a better bet as parents or teachers than impatient paragons of courage. Furthermore, time may show that what we had wanted for our children is not possible, and then we need the patience for something else: the patience to endure as new and more modest hopes can develop in us or, if even modest hopes are out of place, the patience to find a way of living with or without the child that is neither hopeful nor utterly despairing.

There is heroic patience in matters of this kind, though I admit that phrase has a slightly paradoxical flavor. The protagonist of Wordsworth's *Michael* is an example. Michael is a poor farmer who becomes a father for the first time in old age, and he takes to the task of raising his son with a maternal solicitude.

> For oftentimes
> Old Michael, while he was a babe in arms,
> Had done him female service, not alone
> For pastime and delight, as is the use
> Of fathers, but with patient mind enforced

> To acts of tenderness; and he had rocked
> His cradle, as with a woman's gentle hand.[4]

When his son grows up Michael must send him to work in the city. Before he leaves, the son lays the first stone of a sheepfold that will be a covenant to their love. The son is corrupted by life in the city, and his father never hears from him again. Michael continues to build the sheepfold, but many times he goes there and sits the whole day "And never lifted up a single stone."[5] For Lionel Trilling that line evokes the authenticity of an immense grief.[6] For me it suggests something more. Michael's gesture has a heroic quality, and no amount of grief makes anyone heroic.

> There is a comfort in the strength of love;
> 'Twill make a thing endurable which else
> Would overset the brain, or break the heart.[7]

Wordsworth plainly does not mean that Michael's love is above a certain threshold of intensity beneath which disappointed parental hopes will leave you merely demented or heartbroken. Borrowing an apt phrase from D.Z. Phillips,[8] one might say that Michael has "given himself" to love in such a way that love does not merely survive terrible disappointment but in some way continues to console despite its hopelessness.

The aptness of Phillips' phrase might be understood in this way. There is much in the good of parental love that is ready to hand in that a father might enjoy it without "giving" himself to love in ways that are especially hard for ordinarily selfish human beings. I have in mind such things as what Wordsworth calls the "pastime and delight" of fatherly affection, vicarious pride in a child's growing accomplishments and hopes for future successes, and so on. But suppose all this readily accessible good is destroyed, as it is in Michael's case. Others who might love as intensely as he would be overwhelmed by anger or despair. Yet the readily accessible good of love does not exhaust its value, and the deeper, residual value—the sheer good of loving that remains if one can endure through anger and despair—is open to Michael because he has given himself so wholly to love. This is not to say that his grief is not immense; it is only to say that his love has not been reduced to grief, and what love makes possible beyond that grief is a great good. It seems right to say that what makes Michael's achievement possible is heroic patience, and his sheer passivity in the sheepfold is a haunting image of that virtue.

II

Yet there is something odd about the idea of heroic patience. What is it? The contrast with courage is instructive here because I think it helps to disclose much of what lies behind the prejudice that courage matters to a degree that patience does not begin to approximate.

Our culturally dominant intuitions about heroism revolve around the notions of the glorious and the great. The paradigmatic heroic act attests to the striking potency of the self in seizing the good, and that potency is most clearly expressed when fearful thoughts of our weakness and susceptibility to harm do not deflect us from our course. That is why there is an affinity between heroism and courage. The self seems magnified when it proves undaunted by (or impervious to) thoughts of its own limits and vulnerability that would deter typical, ethically diminutive mortals from hazardous action. And the appearance of magnification may persist when courageous action fails to achieve its immediate end, results in death or serious harm to the agent, or even when it slides into sheer recklessness.

This relation between courage and the heroic magnification of the self can be seen in a passage from Milan Kundera's *Life Is Elsewhere*. Kundera's novel is a tragi-comedy about a young poet, Jaromil, who longs for greatness. His longing is expressed in a dream sequence where he becomes Xavier, a superman who in one episode takes leadership of a revolutionary group that is being pursued by the police:

He was repelled by the pettiness that reduced life to mere existence, and that turned men into half-men. He wanted to lay his life in a balance, the other side of which was weighed with death. He wanted to make his every action, every day, yes, every hour and minute worthy of being measured against the ultimate, which is death. That was why he wanted to lead the file, to walk the tightrope over the abyss, his head illumined by a halo of bullets, to grow in everyone's eyes until he had become as immense as death itself.[9]

The relation of the self to the good here is the exact opposite of Michael's. Instead of giving himself to the good, Jaromil wants to take it for himself. For Michael to find a comfort in the strength of love, the importance of his disappointment in the scheme of things—and hence his own importance—must recede in the way he experiences love, and patience is what makes that recession possible. The self seems to diminish as it gives itself to the good. In Jaromil's case, the self aspires to enlarge itself in prevailing against the immensity of death. This is surely the source of what may intoxicate us in courage of a certain kind—the heady sense that in defeating our fears we wax stronger and greater than "half-men" who shy away from danger and wallow in the pettiness of mere existence. The intoxication does not strictly require public recognition, but public recognition certainly intensifies the effect. In the most spectacular cases, the mere mortal self is elevated in the eyes of others to a semi-divine status, its head "illumined by a halo of bullets."

It is ironic that the image Kundera uses to express Jaromil's aspiration to greatness—the halo of bullets—conflates the concept of Christian saintliness with the classical understanding of heroism as primarily a martial accomplishment. For one might say that the deepest difference between Michael and Jaromil is that Michael achieves a kind of saintliness whereas the foolish Jaromil represents the desire for (a degenerate version of) pagan heroism. What makes the idea of heroic patience sound slightly paradoxical is precisely our declining cultural sensitivity to the kind of heroism that saintliness can embody. This may seem an inevitable loss for those of us who can no longer ask questions about good and evil against the background of religious faith, but that is not so. After all, one can be moved by the story of Michael, and moved in a way that depends on seeing his distinctive sensibility as more than a notional ethical possibility, without seeing that sensibility as witnessing to anything transmundane.

William James claimed that among the psychological features of saintliness are "A feeling of being in a wider life than that of this world's selfish little interests ... A sense of the friendly continuity of the ideal power with our own life, and a willing self-surrender to its control ... An immense elation and freedom, as the outlines of the confining ego break down."[10] Notice that feelings akin to these are what one might be inclined to ascribe to Michael, with or without the theistic baggage that James would attach to them. So one might think that Michael's love is such that he seems to live a wider life than even the more honorable selfish, little interests of the world will permit; his self-surrender to love makes what is ethically deep in love central to his identity (i.e., his life becomes continuous with the "ideal power" of love); and though the depth of his grief makes James' saintly elation and freedom utterly inapplicable, it does seem that in his self-surrender the outlines of the confining ego are in some way muted. On the other hand, if we are in thrall to the kind of heroism to which Jaromil aspires, a regard for such feelings could not be internal to our admiration for the exemplar of heroic courage because it is precisely the appropriation of value by the potent ego that Jaromil's fantasy is directed toward.

I have distinguished two kinds of heroism, the self-enlarging and the self-surrendering, and I have associated these with courage and patience respectively. What exactly do these associations amount to? It might be that courage and patience are virtues which, so far as they can be developed and exercised in a single life, must co-exist in some deep and abiding tension. Each subsumes a set of cognitive and motivational dispositions that will tend to press the agent's interpretations and choices in opposing directions. Call this the Conflict View. So if one wants, say, some alliance of egalitarian justice, imagination and courage at the centre of the moral life, then one might, like Lovibond, find outrageous the suggestion that our moral paragons are to be found in examples of saintly endurance. The outrage would be justified, given that view of the basic values of the moral life, because the emulation of saintly endurance would pull against the interpretations and choices that the priority of these values requires. The

Conflict View might also be endorsed by those who would elevate patience over courage or by those who would see the good life or the good society as the site for an edifying friction between allegedly opposed virtues like courage and patience. Alternatively, one might argue for a way of seeing patience and courage in a good life that marginalizes neither of them without inviting a destructive level of psychical discord. Call this the Unity View. In what follows I argue for the Unity View.

III

An interesting defence of the Conflict View can be constructed on the basis of a thesis about the virtues that Amélie Oksenberg Rorty has advanced.[11] According to Rorty, so far as particular virtues are socially prized and developed in our lives they tend to take on imperialistic tendencies, conquering the psychological territory that might be occupied by other, perhaps highly functional traits. There are three interlocked aspects to the imperialism of the virtues. First and fundamentally, virtues entail habits of interpretation that make some considerations salient to the agent while thrusting others into the background, or beyond the reach of attention altogether, and where these marginalized or unnoticed considerations are such that rival virtues would make them salient, the operative virtue can be seen as driving out its rivals. Second, virtues tend to be magnetizing in that one is drawn to situations where they can be exercised. Third, virtues tend to be self-activating by inclining one to promote or create the occasions that require their exercise.[12]

Rorty is acutely wary of the imperialistic tendencies of courage in particular. But she thinks the more obvious ways we might try to cope with the problem—by building restraints on the impetus toward expansion into its criteria or by postulating some master-virtue that will exert the necessary restraint—are both unpromising solutions. Trying to redefine courage will dissolve it into a heterogeneous congeries of virtues, and all plausible candidates for the role of master-virtue will also subsume a wide diversity of constitutive dispositions. That being so, the problem of the imperialism of

virtue is postponed rather than solved in the absence of argument
to show that the motley dispositions that compose a revised
courage or the favored master-virtue do not themselves harbor
imperialistic tendencies.[13]

There is a third possible solution. Rorty says that the necessary
restraint on the imperialism of a given virtue is often secured by
its conflict, with other virtues. The courageous are drawn toward
"oppositional confrontation," they tend to see actions as victories
or defeats and are inclined to resist cooperative, compromising
attitudes.[14] So other traits are needed whose motivational and cognitive pressures will be pitted against these dangerous propensi-
ties that courage feeds. Although Rorty does not mention patience
as a trait that might exist in salutary conflict with courage, it is
plainly a prime candidate for that role. An impatient courage is
just what one might expect of those who are drawn to oppositional confrontation, who interpret everything as victory or defeat
and resist cooperation and compromise. And an impatient
courage is also what one would expect of those whose courage,
like that of Jaromil's Xavier, is fastened to a conception of
heroism as self-enlargement.

But as an intra-psychical solution to the problem, Rorty's third
alternative obviously has severe drawbacks. For she admits that if
virtues are really opposed their standard outcomes will tend
to undermine each other, or the development of one will tend to
obstruct the development of the other, and this would seem to rule
out a stable condition of conflict between radically opposed virtues
within a given life. That is to say, conflict will tend to produce
winners and losers among the contending virtues in the individual's character rather than an enduring equilibrium. Even if it
were possible to sustain over a long period two opposing virtues in
a single life, each developed to a high degree, and each with
conflicting cognitive and motivational habits, this would invite an
intolerable level of psychological discord unless there were some
master-virtue to break deadlock. Therefore, it is not surprising that
Rorty has recently presented the idea of salutary conflict between
the virtues primarily as an inter-psychical solution to the problem
of their imperialism. We all benefit from the moral diversity of a

society in which the virtues exist in varying patterns of dominance and recession across different lives because the expansive tendencies in the partialities of moral vision and inclination of some will be balanced by the opposing partialities of others.[15] So it might seem that we can render unto Murdoch what is Murdoch's and unto Lovibond what is Lovibond's. This is a more appealing version of the Conflict view than alternative versions, but there are good reasons to be sceptical.

Consider again the first and most basic of the imperialistic tendencies that Rorty ascribes to the virtues: the entrenchment of interpretative habits that entail patterns of salience and thereby blind us to much that is morally relevant in our lives. For Rorty it is as if such habits were spotlights which can only come on when others are dimmed or turned off. But an analogy with the development of interpretative capacity in another area suggests a different possibility.

Suppose I am teaching poetry to a child. I come to realize that despite a lively responsiveness to imagery, she is insensitive to rhythm. My efforts to correct this are an attempt to establish a new habitual alertness in the reading of poetry. Yet it would be bizarre for me to worry that by encouraging an ear for rhythm this will of itself tend to make a certain narrow range of things salient to the reader and thereby weaken receptivity to other matters, like the significance of imagery. The educational point of trying to instill the new habit would be to *expand* the range of relevant things the child is alive to in reading poetry; the point would not be to turn on a new spotlight, so to speak, while dimming or turning off others.

It is not clear why we cannot see the development of whatever interpretative habits are internal to patience and courage along similar lines. The understanding the courageous have of fear as an emotion that may deflect them from their good gives them a distinctive alertness to certain possibilities in their lives concerning the need to take risks and face danger. But it seems plausible that the habits they might acquire in achieving a parallel understanding of their susceptibility to anger and despair in relation to the good could readily cohere with the cognitive habits that go with courage.

The two sets of habits would thus form a mutually supportive whole, like the integration of a responsiveness to imagery and a sensitivity to rhythm in an educated capacity to read poetry, rather than a pair of combatants jostling for perceptual salience.

The idea that the interpretative habits entailed by courage and patience will tend to operate in radical conflict only looks appealing so long as we focus on the primitive form they might take when one tries to explain the virtues to a very young child. And if that is true, the problem of the "imperialism" of courage seems vastly overblown. The child might be incapable of grasping anything more subtle than the thought that the courageous are undeterred by fear in pursuit of their ends and that the patient will calmly endure what others will not. So a puerile conception of courage might seem to require someone to be on the lookout for dangers and obstacles with a view to overcoming them, whatever they might be, while the patient scan their lives for hardships to be borne with equanimity. This is a stark conflict indeed. But the more developed our understanding of courage and patience, the more vaporous the conflict seems to become. For obstacles and dangers must be construed against the background of a deepening understanding of the goods and evils our lives contain, and that understanding will inevitably throw into relief much that has to be borne with patience as well if our commitment to what we cherish is to remain constant. After all, the story of Michael is as much about courage as it is about patience. Sending his son to the city to secure a future for him without hopeless poverty was an act of courage. It is implausible to think of the Michael who rocked the cradle and sat silently in the sheepfold as gripped by one habit of ethical interpretation and the Michael who sent his son to the city as governed by another, conflicting habit. Michael's courage and patience do not entail what Rorty calls "tensed" cognitive dispositions,[16] each pulling into the foreground of thought and feeling what the other would shove into the background; on the contrary, his courage and patience are twin aspects of the one love. To recognize this is not to deny that an imperialism of courage or patience may afflict many of our lives because we hold puerile conceptions of such virtues. But if that is what the Conflict

View must depend on, it would seem also to require an extravagantly pessimistic attitude toward a moral education that could lead people beyond puerile conceptions of the virtues toward a more discriminating and inclusive ethical perspective.

If we can acknowledge Michael's courage as well as his patience, we can also see how easily and inconspicuously courage thrives away from the conception of heroism as self-enlargement. Courage is not a routine moral requirement of parenthood, but neither is its moral necessity a rarity there. As Peter Geach once observed,[17] childbirth is typically an act of physical courage. The conduct of women who have shown that virtue in giving birth to many children is unlikely to be explained by the imperialism of their virtue. The sheer desire to put on another display of parturient valour would seem an uncommon motive.

Of course, there is a very obvious difference between parental courage and the courage of Jaromil's Xavier because high social recognition is only accorded the latter. This may incline one to think that if courage in childbirth were given the same recognition, it too would acquire the imperialistic tendencies that go with a self-enlarging heroism. But it would only acquire these so far as social recognition induced women to lose their hold on the wider moral context of motherhood. "I'm going to show how brave I am, regardless of consequences" is a thought whose temptation is decreasingly strong the greater one's appreciation of the importance of the consequences. Again, what seems to reveal the imperialism of courage, and hence the reasonableness of some version of the Conflict View, really discloses a task for moral education that we should be able to approach with some modest confidence—the task of teaching children that social recognition has its seductive side, and helping them to see and resist that seduction.

I have argued that courage of a familiar kind can flourish without the imperialistic tendencies spawned by a particular view of heroism, and that courage of that kind can happily coexist with an abundant patience. To that extent, the Unity View would seem vindicated. Yet its vindication might hold only for a restricted range of endeavors. Much of our lives takes place within practices where conflict is acute and pervasive, where relations tend to be competitive and adversarial, and success is highly contingent on risk-taking. Child-rearing and teaching are not like this. But commerce is, and so too is a large part of politics as we know it even under the most civilized conditions. Warfare is the conflictual practice par excellence, and there Rorty's claims about the imperialism of courage seem most plausible. In conflictual practices, it might be said, the Conflict View holds. The nature of the practice is such that it calls for a courage that is naturally if not inevitably allied with a self-enlarging heroism and opposed to dispositions that would incline us toward a patient acceptance of what we have—or what we are soon going to lose because we are so patient. To agree with this is not to commend conflict. Our lives may often be bad because of the conflictual character of the practices that absorb us, however successful we are according to their internal standards, and perhaps with enough imagination we could reconstruct many of these practices so as to mitigate their conflictual character. Any philosopher with feminist sympathies will be sure to press these points. Be that as it may, they do not undermine the claim that so long as a practice is conflictual, the patience and courage that might be appropriately displayed therein will fit the Conflict View.

I think the Conflict View is false even for conflictual practices. Another example is needed to show this. Consider the following passage from Primo Levi's *If Not Now, When?* Levi is describing how Mendel, a Jewish partisan fighting behind the German lines, compares the two men in whose bands he has fought:

... the only quality they had in common was courage, and this wasn't strange, because a commander without courage doesn't last long. But even their courages were different: Ulybin's courage was stubborn and dull, a duty courage that seemed the fruit of study and discipline rather than a natural gift. His every decision and his every order arrived as if coming to earth from heaven, charged with authority and tacit menace; often the orders were reasonable, because Ulybin was a shrewd man, but even when they weren't, they sounded peremptory, and it was hard not to obey them. Gedaleh's courage was extempore and varied; it didn't spring from a school but from a temperament that chafed at bonds and was hardly inclined to study the future; where Ulybin calculated, Gedaleh flung himself as into a game. In him, Mendel recognized, well fused as in a precious alloy, heterogeneous metals: the logic and the bold imagination of Talmudists, the sensitivity of musicians and children, the comic power of strolling players, the vitality absorbed from the Russian earth.[18]

Despite its studied quality, Ulybin's courage is in some ways very like the *andreia* of the godlike Achilles, with its anger and ruthlessness. It is a courage that comes "from heaven" rather than a recognizably human source, and it menaces even those who would follow its direction. Gedaleh's courage is altogether different from this. The point is not that Ulybin and Gedaleh are divided by contrasting dispositions over and above the one substantive virtue they held in common. There simply is no common virtue, save at a level of deceptive abstraction, because "even their courages were different." Moreover, though there are tendencies within Gedaleh's character that lend themselves to a certain impatience— his resistance to external discipline and his reluctance to calculate carefully—his courage is far more congenial to the patience he needs, and other virtues as well, than Ulybin's dour ferocity. His capacity to take delight in the moment, his nonchalance and sociability, his playfulness and sense of the comic—all these enable him to lead his band with a gentle patience for their lapses and squabbles that Ulybin is wholly incapable of. It is not as if Gedaleh's courage exercises a magnetizing power pulling him in the direction of Ulybin, a power effectively countervailed by other forces in his personality that draw him in contrary directions. If that were so his courage would be a source of deep and abiding psychological conflict, but it plainly is not: as Levi notes, these "heterogeneous metals" were fused into a single precious alloy.

Yet if we cannot explain Gedaleh's patience with his sometimes querulous and incompetent band by an inner resistance to the expansive tendencies of his courage, it is not clear that we can explain Ulybin's conspicuous vices by invoking the same tendencies. Notice how odd it would be to explain one of Ulybin's bouts of rage with his men by saying "He's just *so* courageous, he cannot resist doing this sort of thing." It is true that the courage of people like Ulybin might be contingently connected with certain vices or partialities of moral vision which, were they corrected, would precipitate the erosion of courage. But it hardly follows that we should explain this by the imperialistic tendencies of the virtue that is preserved by an unholy alliance with vice. The dark and destructive side of Ulybin's character has nothing to do with courage per se and everything to do with irascibility and ruthlessness, even if without irascibility and ruthlessness *his* courage would be undermined.

The seamlessness of Gedaleh's courage and patience is like the seamlessness of Michael's courage and patience, notwithstanding the fact that in Gedaleh's case the twin virtues are deployed in the conflictual practice par excellence. Like Michael, Gedaleh gives himself to the good his life offers where others would succumb to despair or the corrosive rage that drives Ulybin. To be sure, the kind of character Ulybin represents may be less obviously evil in warfare (on the right side) than elsewhere, but even there, as W.H. Auden noted, its ethical liabilities are immense:

Righteous anger can effectively resist and destroy evil, but the more one relies on it as a source of energy, the less energy and attention one can give to the good which is to replace the evil once it has been removed. That is why, though there may have been some just wars, there has been no just peace. Nor is it only the vanquished who suffer. I have known more than one passionate anti-Nazi who went to pieces once Hitler had been destroyed. Without Hitler to hate, their lives had no *raison d'être*.[19]

The moral failures of war may be those without the patience to survive great anger as well as those without the courage to resist great fear. It is certainly hard to see a man like Ulybin, given the blind rage and pugnacity war has evoked in him, easily finding a *raison d'être* in a post-war Soviet Union, unless it was some suitably aggressive role in the maintenance of an unjust peace.

IV

There is a worry about patience, however, which I have not so far directly addressed, and it is surely what lies behind Lovibond's animadversions on Murdoch's penchant for selfless mothers of large families. There are psychological traits that increase the ease with which we can be mistreated by others, and these may be extolled as virtues by those who would do the mistreating, palliate its evil or deny its avoidability. Patience can ensure compliance among the victims of exploitation, and so, unsurprisingly, it has often been recommended to the poor or to women as a virtue that befits their station and its duties. The affinity I noted earlier between patience and the idea of giving oneself to the good may seem to expose the problem in an especially vivid way. If I am to construe my relation to the good as a matter of service, I must learn that the despair or anger I might experience in bearing the burdens of service are to be resisted as emotions that threaten to alienate me from the good. By allowing such emotions to engage my thoughts and actions, I cease to give myself to the good. So a woman, say, who yields to anger in circumstances of domestic exploitation has failed to evince the patience that befits a conception of the good in which the giving of the self is the paramount moral demand. My attempt to restore patience to parity of status with courage among the virtues of self-control ignores its prominent role in the maintenance of injustice, or so an obvious line of objection will go.

Part of my response to this should be as obvious as the objection. It is only a puerile, coarse-grained patience that could motivate a blanket impassivity towards evils that are fit objects of indignant resistance. One cannot reasonably argue against the ethical centrality of patience by dwelling on the deficiencies of its least discriminating versions any more than one can make a decent case for the marginalization of courage merely by noting the moral hazards of a naïve bravery. But there is perhaps something deeper at work in the objection. The more we assume that the hardships or evils we experience can be set right with enough justice or courage the less room there is for the reasonableness of a moral posture that counsels acceptance of the limits of our capacity to make the good we crave our own. So the very idea that the relation of the self to the good might in some important way be a matter of giving, of service and sacrifice rather than appropriation, comes to have an air of antiquated false consciousness, like patience itself; and when such giving or service is lauded, as it is by Murdoch, it is tempting to think immediately of *abused* selfless mothers of large families and tempting to infer that the praise is morally obfuscating. Yet the limits of our capacity to make the good we crave our own are often intractably narrow. The unabused parent of a family, large or small, is likely to have much need for a selfless patience, and the tragedies of child rearing are not so rare that a patience that borders on saintliness is not often a necessary ethical aspiration.

The same point applies to patience in those public and conflictual practices where the notion of serving the good sounds similarly archaic. So long as our civic life is fraught with hopes that are commonly disappointed, ideals compromised and diluted in the process of realization, so long, that is, as our politics are not utopian, a patience will be needed to carry on that is grounded in a sense of the goods of public life as objects of service rather than brute appropriation. It is no accident that Jaromil becomes a literary apologist for a Communist dictatorship that promises to bring about Utopia. A man who thinks of his own good as perfect self-fulfillment is predisposed to think that the purpose of public life is the same value writ large. The essential rottenness of that sensibility is what *Life Is Elsewhere* is brilliantly about.

The Unity View I have defended is not the grandiose thesis that all virtue is one. Patience and courage exhibit a unity only in the modest sense that both can and should be developed to a high degree in any given life without precipitating some disabling level of inner conflict. But pointing to that modest unity would still seem a useful thing to do at a time when cultural fashion has largely discarded patience and sensible philosophical talk about the diversity of values often yields hasty conclusions about the fragmentation of value.[20]

Notes

1   Sabina Lovibond, *Realism and Imagination in Ethics* (Minneapolis: University of Minnesota Press, 1983), p. 199; Cf. Iris Murdoch, *The Sovereignty of Good* (London: Routledge, 1970), p. 53.

2   Henry Sidgwick, *The Methods of Ethics*, 7th edn (Indianapolis: Hackett, 1981), p. 332.

3   E.g., Simone Weil, *Gravity and Grace* (London: Routledge, 1952), p. 105.

4   Wordsworth, *Michael*, 152–8.

5   Ibid., 466.

6   Lionel Trilling, *Sincerity and Authenticity* (Cambridge, MA: Harvard University Press, 1978), p. 93.

7   *Michael*, 448–50.

8   D.Z. Phillips, *Through a Darkening Glass* (Notre Dame, IN: University of Notre Dame Press, 1982), p. 102.

9   Milan Kundera, *Life Is Elsewhere*, trans. by Peter Kuzzi (New York: Knopf, 1974), p. 78.

10 William James, *The Varieties of Religious Experience* (Cambridge, MA: Harvard University Press, 1985), pp. 219–20.

11 Amélie Oksenberg Rorty, "The Two Faces of Courage" and "Virtues and Their Vicissitudes" in *Mind in Action* (Boston: Beacon Press, 1988), pp. 299–329; and Amélie Oksenberg Rorty, "The Advantages of Moral Diversity," *Social Philosophy & Policy*, 9, no. 2 (1992): 38–62.

12 Rorty, "Virtues and Their Vicissitudes," pp. 316–7.

13 Rorty, "The Two Faces of Courage," pp. 308–10; "Virtues and Their Vicissitudes," pp. 318–24.

14 Rorty, "The Two Faces of Courage," pp. 301–2.

15 Rorty, "The Advantages of Moral Diversity," pp. 38–62.

16 Rorty, "Virtues and Their Vicissitudes," p. 323.

17 Peter Geach, *The Virtues* (Cambridge: Cambridge University Press, 1977), p. 151. Geach is quoting Chesterton, though he does not tell us where Chesterton said this.

18 Primo Levi, *If Not Now, When?* trans. by William Weaver (London: Michael Joseph, 1986), pp. 140–1.

19 W.H. Auden, "Anger" in Angus Wilson *et al.*, *The Seven Deadly Sins* (New York: William Morrow, n.d.), pp. 84–5.

20 I am very grateful to Margaret Buchman and Pat White for helpful comments on an earlier draft of this paper.

9 Forgivingness

Robert C. Roberts

I Introduction

Virtues are personal traits that fit us to live our life well in its distinctively human dimensions, and especially in its social ones. Thus the virtues of truthfulness (intellectual honesty, sincerity, promisekeeping, forthrightness) are dispositions to live well with respect to our powers to represent ourselves and features of our world in language and gesture. The virtues of will power (courage, perseverance, self-control, etc.) are powers to act, feel, and think well despite the urges, desires, emotions, and habits which tend to undermine proper action, feeling, and thought. Generosity, gratitude, and justice are dispositions to live well (act well, think well, be properly affected) in contexts where things can be given or received—things as diverse as material goods, the use of one's home premises, praise, and attention. In the present paper I want to describe the virtue of forgiveness—which I shall call forgivingness, to distinguish it from the act or process of forgiveness in which this virtue is typically exemplified. "The forgiving person" refers to the person with the virtue of forgivingness.

Why regard the disposition to forgive people their offenses against oneself as a virtue? Anger (the emotion that forgiveness characteristically overcomes) can be destructive in several obvious ways. It is reputed to be a cause of medical problems such as hypertension and its ramifications. It also tends to reduce effectiveness in the pursuit of tasks that depend on relationships with fellow workers, clients, employers, etc. But more importantly for ethics, it is often a significant factor in the destruction of friendships, marriages, and collegiality. Forgiveness has the advantage over mere control of anger that it involves a genuinely benevolent (generous, giving, loving) view of the other person and thus fosters attitudes, and not just behavior, characteristic of the various kinds of happy relationships. And unlike condoning offenses, forgiving them does not compromise the moral integrity of the offended one.

Forgiveness is virtuous because one's anger is given up without abandoning correct judgment about the severity of the offense and the culpability of the offender. I argue that acts of forgiveness, in which one lets go of one's anger without thereby abandoning the relevant judgments about offender and offense, are possible because of a certain looseness of fit between the judgments that constitute the cognitive content of an emotion, and the emotion itself. The emotion is a special kind of *perception* in terms of the cognitive content, such that if considerations of certain other kinds are brought to bear on the offender and/or oneself, the judgment in which this content is affirmed may be retained without the anger (that is, without the alienating special kind of perception).

So an enduring disposition to the act or process of forgiveness will match the definition of a virtue as a trait that fits one to live one's life well in some distinctively human dimension—or it will do so at least within moral frameworks in which relationships like friendship are important, yet must be maintained without the compromise of integrity. Of the philosophical writings on forgiveness that I have read, two refer to forgiveness as a virtue, and one of them has a couple of pages of analysis of the concept;[1] but most of the literature is about the act or process of forgiveness, rather than forgivingness. In what follows I shall argue that forgivingness is the disposition to abort one's anger (or altogether to omit getting angry) at persons one takes to have wronged one culpably, by seeing them in the benevolent terms provided by reasons characteristic of forgiving.

Thus the two main issues in the analysis of forgiveness are anger and the reasons for which it may be aborted. In section 2 I compare anger with some neighboring emotions that philosophers have proposed as characteristically overcome in forgiveness, and sketch briefly my account of what anger, and emotion more broadly, is. In section 3 I canvass a number of possible reasons for forgiving which, when incorporated into one's perception of the offender, dissipate one's anger at him. Exploration of these considerations suggests that the forgiving person is characterized by discomfort at alienation from others and by a sense of justice and self-respect. Presumably the forgiving person is not an indiscriminate forgiver; she may sometimes properly hold onto her anger. So I sketch, in section 4, roughly the considerations that guide the forgiving person as to when to forgive and when to withhold forgiveness. In a concluding section I delineate the character of the forgiving person using insights that have emerged in sections 2–4.

II The emotion that forgiveness overcomes

It is mildly controversial just which emotion is characteristically overcome in forgiveness, though it is widely agreed to be something in the neighborhood of anger. Aurel Kolnai[2] makes it out to be indignation, and Bishop Butler[3] seems to be behind the idea that it is resentment, with several recent writers following Butler in this.[4] Jean Hampton[5] suggests that the emotion relevant to forgiveness is "moral hatred." In the present section I canvass these suggestions to refine our understanding of the emotion that forgiveness overcomes and begin sketching its relation to forgiveness. I argue that we do not have a word that denotes the emotion and the only emotion that forgiveness characteristically overcomes, but that "anger" is the least troublesome term, and we can use it as long as we stipulate a rather simple circumscription. Before I survey the philosophical claims, let me state what I take emotions, and more particularly anger, to be.

I have argued that emotions are best thought of as concern-based construals,[6] that is, perceptual states analogous to the ones we are in when we view the gestalt figures in certain psychology books, or hear a snippet of melody as part of the subject of the C minor fugue in Bach's *Well-Tempered Clavier*. To have an emotion is to perceive a state of affairs in certain terms that define the emotion type (nostalgia, embarrassment, romantic melancholy, indignation) and give the emotion its particular "object," but always on the basis of concerns (desires, attachments, carings).

The concerns basic to an emotion are to be numbered among its terms—they do not just move to action, but color how things are "seen." Among the terms of human emotions are almost always to be reckoned certain propositions or language-dependent thoughts. Such propositions are often, though not always, believed; but even when they are believed, they figure in emotion only to the extent that the subject "sees" in terms of them. Emotions are more perceptual than mere evaluative judgments.

Anger, on this account, is a construal of a situation as containing an offender and an offended. The offender is construed as culpable for the offense (otherwise the emotion is only irritation, annoyance, vexation, regret, grief ...), which is construed as morally significant (important, serious); and the offender is construed as having punishment coming to him. Thus the subject would like to punish the offender, even if only with a harsh word or a dirty look, or would take satisfaction in seeing punishment meted out to the offender by some third party, or even by Fate. That the offender *appears* to the victim to be offensive and worthy to be punished is particularly relevant to forgiveness, inasmuch as it is this appearance that drops out as forgiveness supervenes. Also, the angry person (who may or may not be the offended) construes himself as in a moral position to render judgment—that is, in a position of moral superiority. This we learn from noting that anger can be undermined by getting the subject to construe himself as on a moral footing with the offender (see section 3, *Moral commonality*). It shows that forgivingness is a dispositional attitude concerning oneself, and not just offenders; it involves a particular kind of self-understanding.

The tradition I follow, of interpreting forgiveness as the overcoming of an emotion, is exemplified in the modern philosophical writings with which I interact, as well as in the Judaism and Christianity of the Bible from which our contemporary concept chiefly derives. But sometimes forgiveness is not a forswearing or avoidance of emotion. A graduate school colleague of twenty years ago phones you out of the blue and asks forgiveness for once enviously slandering you in the presence of some other students and a professor. Nothing came of the slander and you were unaware of it until now; knowing of it, you are emotionally indifferent. Your forgiveness in this case is not much of a psychological process at all, but simply the act of saying "I forgive you." This kind of case does not undermine the defining place of anger in the concept of forgiveness. First, it is uncharacteristic. Second, the offender feels the need for forgiveness because he feels guilty, and guilt can be regarded as self-directed anger or as a sense that the offended one should be angry or would be justified in being so. Third, while forgiveness, in the present case, is not a withdrawal of anger, it is an act of assuring the offender that one is not disposed to be angry. In these ways forgiveness' reference to anger remains even in this nonstandard case.

Indignation. Kolnai selects indignation as the emotion that forgiveness dispels, perhaps because to be indignant is to be especially confident of being morally right and to see the offense one is angry about as especially morally aberrant. As a strongly "moral" and retributive form of anger, indignation fits forgiveness, which applies paradigmatically where the offended one emotionally ascribes moral guilt to the offender. But many cases of indignation actually rule out forgiveness, since one can be indignant about an offense that is not against oneself, but one can only forgive offenses against oneself.[7] And forgiveness is appropriate to many cases where there is no indignation or even the possibility of it, but only, say, resentment or some milder or less confident form of anger.

Resentment. One reason to favor resentment as the emotion relevant to forgiveness is that it accords with the logic of forgiveness inasmuch as it is limited to offenses against the resenter. (I could not, as a white North American, have forgiven the Afrikaners for their offenses against South African blacks; in parallel it would be bad English to say that I resented their offenses, while it is perfectly natural to say that I was angered by them or indignant about them. Perhaps African Americans, in an attitude of strong identification with native South Africans, could resent the Afrikaners' actions.) But I think resentment is in a worse position than indignation since "resentment" is reserved for anger that is to some extent brooding and defensive. The resenter not only construes himself as culpably offended against in some matter of importance; he also construes himself as to some degree impotent or restrained in the matter of avenging the offense. Thus the suggestion that resentment lasts awhile, and that the resenter harbors his anger, and only reluctantly, or perhaps indirectly, expresses it. So to take resentment to be always the emotion that is overcome in forgiveness seems to rule out a powerful and frankly angry person's forgiving his offender. To take the extreme case, it rules out God's ever forgiving anyone, since God is too much in control for his wrath ever to be resentment.[8]

Resentment appeals to some theorists because of its durability or grudge-bearing quality; some of the most dramatic cases of forgiveness are ones in which a person triumphs after struggling with a recalcitrant, gnawing, destructive anger. These cases also appeal to people who emphasize that forgiveness is a kind of therapy for the forgiver. But such dramatic and therapeutic cases are not the only ones, and in a discussion of the *virtue* of forgiveness, this kind of case will not take center stage. Forgivingness will tend to shorten the anger, and in some cases forgivingness is exemplified without there being any actual anger to be overcome, aborted, forsworn, or abandoned. I conclude that because of resentment's passivity and durability, making it *the* emotion overcome in forgiveness artificially narrows the field of forgiveness.

Moral hatred. Jean Hampton suggests that the emotion relevant to forgiveness is moral hatred. On Hampton's analysis, moral hatred differs from two other kinds of hatred, malice and spite.[9] Malice springs from low self-esteem and seeks (in vain) to establish one's own worth by diminishing that of the offender, who is construed as having diminished one's worth or shown it to be low. Malice is self-defeating because it is essentially competitive (I'm OK insofar as I'm better than my offender) but since its strategy is to show or cause the offender to be worthless, then insofar as it succeeds, it fails to show the malicious one to be worth much. Spite is similar, except that instead of seeking superiority to its object, it seeks to bring the object down to its own miserable level. Hampton's example is the AIDS victim who seeks to feel better about herself by infecting others. On Hampton's view, you cannot have forgiven someone if you still feel spite or malice towards him, but spite and malice are not the emotions characteristically overcome in forgiveness because forgiveness applies to *moral* offenses and *moral* offenders, and in malice and spite we construe our offenders too little in moral terms and too much in terms of their relevance to our own status.

What Hampton calls moral hatred seems to be not so much an emotion on its own, as a dimension of what she calls indignation. It seems to me that at this point her phenomenology is right but her vocabulary is not well chosen. "Indignation" is too narrow a word for the emotion that includes "moral hatred," and "moral hatred" is too strong for this aspect of the emotion. An example of her own illustrates both points.[10] A normally self-possessed mother whose young child lies to her will protest the wrong, which is also an insult to her (and her sense of the insult and her motive for protest will be anger, though Hampton does not say this). As Hampton notes, because of the mother's position and self-confidence it will be improper to say that she resents the child's action. But it seems equally inappropriate to say the mother is indignant towards the child. If she is indignant, she has exaggerated the moral seriousness of the offense. It seems better just to say that she's angry.

If she forgives the child, it seems too strong to say that she has overcome her "moral hatred" of him. But on my account of emotion it is clear enough what Hampton has in mind with this phrase. In the anger-construal the moral offense is synthetically locked onto the offender so that he looks offensive, alien, and unwelcome; he looks guilty[11] and deserving of suffering (punishment); he has decidedly *not* the look of a friend (even if he is a friend), and in the extreme case he has the look of an enemy. As it dawns on the mother of the little liar that she has been offended against in this matter of importance, her vision of her son—however fleeting, in whatever degree of intensity, and whatever the degree of conviction or disbelief she may attach to her perception—comes into the focus of anger and she sees an offender, one who needs, not to be hugged and cuddled, but to be held at a distance, to be shunned and punished. It is this vision of the other as properly alien on grounds of guilty offense that, it seems to Hampton and me, is characteristically overcome in forgiveness. Hampton is right to think this vision of the offender is separable from the issues surrounding what she calls malice and spite, issues of wounded self-esteem interpreted in a matrix of invidious comparison and competition. Whatever other perceptual features may be present in such special versions of anger as indignation and resentment, they share this experience of the offender as alien, unworthy, and due to be punished.

An advantage of the view of emotion that I am trading on is that it clarifies how a victim can fully believe that his offender has culpably wronged him in a morally significant way and even deserves to suffer punishment for her offense, yet without being angry at her. Since emotions are construals (instances of "seeing-as"), their cognitive or propositional content is not just whatever the subject happens to believe about the object of his attention. They are a matter of "seeing" in terms of one or another proposition, and for this purpose only *some* of the occurrently believed propositions will be picked out. When the victim succeeds in forgiving his offender he does not see her, in that specially vivid and concern-based way that constitutes anger, in terms of his beliefs about her offense against him; instead he sees her in other, more benevolent terms that derive from his reasons for forgiving her. The victim's forgiveness consists in his overcoming the retributive emotion, not by ceasing to make the retributive judgment, but by becoming undisposed to the alienating retributive construal. A non-emotional analogy may help convince the reader that my distinction between judging a proposition to be true and seeing in terms of it is not gratuitous. A famous gestalt figure can be seen, alternatively, as a pretty young woman or an old lady. You can look at the figure and currently judge that there is an old lady to be seen in the figure, without actually seeing her.

I propose, then, that the emotion overcome in forgiveness is anger, and that the facet of anger that makes it important sometimes to overcome it, even in its morally purest forms, is the *view* of the offender as bad, alien, guilty, worthy of suffering, unwelcome, offensive, an enemy, etc. We do need to circumscribe the concept of anger as forgiveness applies to it, in a way that people were probably trying to do in making resentment the emotion overcome in forgiveness: forgiveness applies only to anger about offenses against oneself.

In forgiveness the perception of the offender as alien, evil, etc. is abandoned not just in any way, but on the basis of considerations of a certain type or types which promote a benevolent perception of the offender. Thus our next task in the analysis of forgiveness is to clarify how the angry vision is overruled, and I do so by examining kinds of considerations that may undermine anger at an offender. The concepts of anger and forgiveness will be clarified by determining just what bearing these considerations have on anger, and by determining which of the possible ways of dispelling one's anger are characteristic of forgiveness. Our explorations will also make clearer the concept I have been expressing with such words as "overcome," "give up," "abandon," "abort," and "dispel."

III Considerations favoring forgiveness

The chief considerations favoring forgiveness are 1) repentance of the offender; 2) excuses for the offender; 3) suffering of the offender; 4) moral commonality with the offender; and 5) relationship to the offender. Forgivingness consists in sensitivity to such anger-reducing considerations; self-management in forgiveness consists in exploiting such considerations with a view to reducing one's anger. Such exploitation can be more or less intentional and self-conscious. The more intentional form may be called self-control; as it becomes more automatic we may speak of increments in the virtue of forgivingness. Though forgiving self-control clearly differs from forgivingness, the line between them is not clear. Without sensitivity to the forgiveness considerations, forgiving self-control won't work; and even the person who is most mature in forgivingness will have to employ some forgiving self-control since, as I shall argue in section 5, the forgiving person is not unsusceptible of anger.

Repentance. That the offender has expressed remorse for the offense and sought forgiveness is perhaps the paradigm reason for forgiving. It is instructive to see why. When the offender asks forgiveness he is showing that he takes (roughly) the same position of moral disapproval of the offense as the offended one takes. He invites the other to construe him as in attitudinal solidarity with her, as on her own side with regard to evaluating the offense. In the last section we saw that anger envisages the offender as an alien, someone opposed to oneself, and his repentance goes a long way toward overcoming this impression.

The paradigmatic status of repentance as a reason for forgiving suggests that the aim of reconciliation, a return to the status of being fellows, is basic to forgiveness. It suggests too that being fellows is largely a matter of attitudes, and in particular emotions—of how we view each other, from the heart. Forgivingness and the practice of forgiveness are at home in an ethic of community or friendship—one underlain by a sense of belonging to one another. But they require that there be strong differentiation of individuals as well, so that the one can bear responsibility for offending the other, and the other can choose to forgive. The centrality of repentance tells us that the forgiving person has an underlying proneness to see others as fellows, a concern to live in peace with them. She may get angry and alienated from people, but she remains uncomfortable with that. The more encompassing the class of people she feels this way about, the greater the scope of this virtue in her. Some ethical outlooks, say a warrior or honor ethic, assume that having enemies is natural and appropriate; others, like Christianity, assume that all enmity is unnatural, abnormal, and inappropriate. Paradigm individuals from these traditions will differ in the scope of the disposition to feel discomfort at having an enemy, and this will be an important difference in the structure of their forgivingness.

Kolnai says at one point that forgiveness is "reacceptance," and Norvin Richards objects[12] that if so, then to forgive a person one offense is to forgive him all his offenses against oneself; but sometimes we forgive a person one injury, but not another, so forgiveness cannot be reacceptance. This objection does not touch my claim, which is not that forgiveness *is* reconciliation, but that it *aims* at it. If S has committed two wrongs against me, W_1 and W_2, and I have forgiven S for W_1, but not for W_2, I am still alienated from S, despite forgiving him for W_1. Nevertheless, my forgiving S for W_1 will be motivated by a concern for reconciliation. Another objection *would* touch my claim:

> Consider the stranger whose car drenches you with mud…. She stops to apologize, insists on paying your cleaning bill, and so on. Surely it is possible to forgive this woman, just as it would be if she were an equally repentant friend. But to call this "reaccepting" her or "reestablishing our relationship" is rather strained: there was no relationship, and there is none after she drives away.[13]

Richards is too quick to say there was no relationship. Some moral outlooks make it quite explicit what that relationship is: members of a kingdom of ends, brothers and sisters, children of God, fellow sojourners upon this earth; and even people who do not explicitly share in such a tradition may be shaped in their vision of others by some such conception. The stranger's injury of the pedestrian disrupts this relationship: he is angry at her for having injured him, she is alarmed at having done so; the repentance and forgiveness reestablish the disrupted relationship. Forgivingness belongs in an ethic in which at least some people are conceived as in a relationship that can be disrupted by injury and anger; insofar as forgiveness can be extended to strangers, they too are construed (if only subliminally) in this way. I speak of a *vision* of the other as in this community with oneself, or the *sense* that these offenders ought not to be one's enemies, because this is not just a *belief* of the forgiving person, but a basic form of his vision of himself and other human beings. As an emotionally integrated belief, it is the stuff of which virtues are made. One welcomes the repentance of offenders, is on the lookout for possibilities of reconciliation. The more generally susceptible the forgiver is to this reason, the more deeply forgiving a person he is, other things being equal.

Excuses. From the cross Jesus of Nazareth prays, referring to those who have crucified him, "Father forgive them, for they know not what they do." Jeffrie Murphy, thinking Jesus has misunderstood the grammar of forgiveness, suggests an improved formulation. Jesus should have said, "Father *excuse* them for they know not what they do."[14] It is true that Jesus is excusing his offenders;

does it follow that he cannot be forgiving them? It would, were Jesus excusing them of *all* wrongdoing. In that case there could be no question of forgiving them, because forgiveness applies only to culpable wrongdoing. But it is implausible to think that Jesus regarded his crucifiers as guilty of no wrongdoing. They surely noticed they were crucifying a man, and knew this was wrong; perhaps they even knew he was innocent. But still, they did not know what they were doing: crucifying the Holy One of God. Jesus' words suppose some offenses to be more forgivable than others. There are mitigating factors, degrees of guilt, and corresponding to these, degrees of forgivability. A good excuse may show an offense to be more forgivable—that is, less properly angering—than it seemed.

Forgivability may be ethical or psychological. It is an ethical matter that the crime of crucifying an innocent man is more forgivable than crucifying the Holy One. It is a psychological matter that some people may be unable to forgive a certain kind of offense against themselves—unable to overcome their perception of its perpetrator as detestable and alien—but able to forgive another, that strikes them, emotionally, as less terrible. In either case, excusing the crime may render it forgivable by reducing its perceived offensiveness, either bringing it into the range of offenses that are ethically forgivable, or bringing it within the forgiver's psychological range. Both kinds of forgivability are relevant to forgivingness. The person with the virtue of forgivingness will be one whose psychological range is relatively more encompassing than that of people who are less forgiving, up to the limit of ethical forgivability.

In the last subsection we saw that the forgiving person is open to the repentance of his offender, because he is uncomfortable being alienated from fellow human beings, or from the particular human being who has alienated him. For a similar reason, the forgiving person is open to excuses for his offender, indeed is prone to look for such excuses. But openness for the offender's repentance and for mitigations of his guilt are *special moral* forms of the disinclination to stay angry, ones that show sensitivity to the moral weight of the offense. They are to be contrasted with an inability to recognize offenses for what they are, which might result from being undiscerning, or from a perverse self-image, perhaps in the form of one of Thomas E. Hill's character-types, the Uncle Tom, the Self-Deprecator, or the Deferential Wife.[15] But moral stupidity, though it effectively reduces one's disposition to anger, is as far from being characteristic of forgivingness as the disposition to bear grudges is. The forgiving person's higher tolerance of offenses must be a *morally intelligent* tolerance. It must be characterized by an ethically concerned practical wisdom that enables the forgiver to recognize the offense as an offense, and also to know, at least virtually, a reason why he does not take offense. An excuse that makes the offense more forgivable is such a reason.

Another way not to take offense is condonation. Like the excuser and unlike the morally stupid, the condoner recognizes that a wrong has been done; but he neither forgives nor mitigates the wrong with an excuse. Like the forgiver, the condoner gives up his anger or doesn't get angry, doesn't seek retribution. But unlike the forgiver, the condoner's failure to get angry is sub-morally motivated: by an aversion to getting upset, by a fear of the consequences of angry behavior, by a distaste for effort or trouble. An example would be employees who quell their tendency to get angry at their employer's injustice towards them out of fear of losing their jobs. That such motives prevail against the sense of offense indicates a lack of the moral seriousness, or integrity, characteristic of forgivingness. The forgiving person's interest in her offender's repentance and in excuses for his action springs not only from a discomfort with being alienated from him, but also from a robust concern for justice and a robust self-respect.

Suffering. Brand Blanshard remarks:

Malice in others, particularly if they pose as our friends, is of course deplorable. Still as a rule it is far more damaging to the malicious person than to his victims; and as a reflective man contemplates it steadily, he sees that most of his resentment against it is a waste of his own substance. Malice is the symptom of moral disease, the sign of a maimed and disfigured spirit. It always has its causes in frustration, inadequacy, self-misjudgment, and the like. To the master of serenity, like Marcus Aurelius, it has seemed a more appropriate object of compassion than of anger....[16]

Blanshard does not tie these remarks to forgiveness proper, but we can see here four possible reasons to forgive. If we take the reference to disease in a strong sense, connecting it with the supposed "causes" of malice, then we may see the malicious person as a patient *rather than* as an agent, as a victim rather than as a criminal. This gives us a compelling reason not to be angry at the offender. But Murphy is right: this is not forgiveness, but excuse.[17] The second reason is suggested by Blanshard's remark that resenting others' malice is a waste of one's own substance. Therapeutic motivations in this egoistic form seem to be outside the spirit of forgiveness, which is a species of generosity.[18]

The third reason is more explicit in the following from Butler:

> ... though injury, injustice, oppression, the baseness of ingratitude, are the natural objects of indignation, or if you please resentment ...; yet they are likewise the objects of compassion, as they are their own punishment, and without repentance will for ever be so. No one ever did a designed injury to another, but at the same time he did a much greater to himself.[19]

Butler's point is that the disfigurement resulting from malice is adequate *punishment* for the crime. In my anger I wish retribution—that the offender suffer as he deserves. Then I reflect that by his malice he has maimed himself, and satisfy my thirst for his punishment by noting that he got what he deserved. This is not forgiveness either, but pure retributive justice. Forgiveness involves suppressing, forgoing, aborting, starving, or by-passing the anger, whereas the present reflection dispels it by *satisfying* it. One who habitually satisfied his anger by this mental strategy might give the appearance of being forgiving, since he would feel no impulse to vindictive *behavior*. But if he expressed this strategy openly by saying, for example, "That jerk deserves his misery, and I feel OK about what he did to me, when I consider that he is as miserable as he deserves to be," no one would regard him as displaying forgivingness.

The fourth reason for forgoing anger at an offender we might call compassion pure and simple. It is compassion, because it construes the offender in terms of his damage, weakness, suffering, inadequacy, etc.; it is pure because it does not vindictively regard this harm as his rightful punishment for the offense, but something to be regretted and if possible corrected for his sake; and it is simple because it adds no rider that the offender is a mere patient, but allows that he has responsibility for what he has done. Because in compassion we wish the offender well, having compassion for him is at odds with being angry at him, in which we wish him punitive harm. A moving example of forgiveness motivated by the suffering of the offender is found in Leo Tolstoy's *War and Peace*. Prince Andrei Bolkonsky's marriage to Natasha Rostov must, at his father's insistence, be delayed a year. Prince Andrei departs for a time, and while he is away the rake Anatole Kuragin alienates Natasha's affections and they attempt to elope. The elopement fails, but in Prince Andrei's view it destroys any possibility of marrying his beloved Natasha. Prince Andrei pursues Kuragin to Petersburg and into Turkey with the intention of provoking him to a duel, but does not find him. At the battle of Borodino, Andrei is severely wounded and carried into a tent-hospital where he is laid on one of three tables. On one of the other tables lies a man sobbing and choking convulsively, whose leg has just been amputated. Gradually, Prince Andrei recognizes him as Kuragin.

He remembered Natasha as he had seen her for the first time at the ball in 1810, with her slender neck and arms, with her timid, happy face prepared for ecstasy, and his soul awoke to a love and tenderness for her which were stronger and more pulsing with life than they had ever been. Now he remembered the link between himself and this man who was gazing vaguely at him through the tears that filled his swollen eyes. Prince Andrei remembered everything, and a passionate pity and love for this man welled up in his happy heart. Prince Andrei could no longer restrain himself, and wept tender compassionate tears for his fellow-men, for himself and for their errors and his own.[20]

Forgiveness here is a matter of refocusing the wrongdoer: while "remembering everything," Prince Andrei switches from seeing Kuragin in terms of the harm he had done him and his desert of punishment—the terms in which he had pursued him for months—and now sees him benevolently in the suffering and weakness of his humanity. The crisis created by the battle activates a disposition to forgive that neither Andrei nor anyone else knew he had. Note that in this example the compassion seems to work without the aid of the other two considerations we have looked at: Kuragin does not repent, nor does Prince Andrei learn or reflect on any excusing circumstance.

It seems clear what this reason for forgiveness implies about forgivingness. An important dimension of the virtue will be an ability and disposition to take the viewpoint of sufferers, in particular of sufferers who have offended against us. It is an ability to transcend, or detach ourselves from, our own position as one who has been harmed, and take the position of the other almost as if it were our own.

Someone may grant that compassion dispels anger in the way I have described, and even that when this happens it may be genuine forgiveness, but object to my talk of compassion as a *reason* for forgiveness. Prince Andrei does not consult a reason for forgiving Kuragin, but is simply *caused* to do so by the vision of Kuragin's suffering. I invite the reader to consider the following. As a construal, an emotion may be a reason for doing something or (as in the present case) for not feeling another emotion, because a human emotion is typically a propositionally determined perception. If asked why he has a medical check-up yearly, the fifty-year-old may say he fears latent diseases, which on my view of emotion is to say that he sees himself in terms of the proposition (among others), *I am under threat from latent diseases.* Similarly, if we ask Prince Andrei why he is no longer angry with his offender, he may say, "Look how miserable he is." And in saying so, he commends to our perception the proposition in terms of which he construes the offender. But to speak of reasons here is not to exclude talk of causes. The occurrence of compassion *causes* anger to fade, in much the way that seeing the duck-rabbit as a duck excludes, for the moment, the view of the duck-rabbit as a rabbit.

The forgiving person is one in whom such reasons as the offender's suffering and weakness habitually cast into the shadow legitimate reasons for being angry. Consideration of the significance of repentance and excuses in the two preceding subsections has suggested that a basic aspect of forgivingness is a concern for benevolent, harmonious fellowship with others. The relevance to forgiveness of compassion—a disposition to care about others in their adversity—seems to point in the same direction.

Moral commonality. The concern for harmonious relationship is also reflected in the forgiver's proneness to appeal to moral commonality with his offender as a reason that resolves his anger. The following story is told of Moses, called the Robber or the Negro, who before he became a monk lived by robbery:

> A brother at Sects committed a fault. A council was called to which Abba Moses was invited, but he refused to go to it. Then the priest sent someone to say to him, "Come, for everyone is waiting for you." So he got up and went. He took a leaking jug filled with water and carried it with him. The others came out to meet him and said to him, "What is this, Father?" The old man said to them, "My sins run out behind me, and I do not see them, and today I am coming to judge the errors of another." When they heard that, they said no more to the brother, but forgave him.[21]

Since they finally forgive the brother, we can assume that his fault was some offense against the members of the council. As a reason to forgive him, Abba Moses invites his fellow monks to consider their own faults. But how is this a reason?

We can dismiss a common but spurious inference: That if we all do some wrong, it is less reprehensible than if only some of us did it. Abba Moses seems to suggest, instead, that a sinner is *not in a position to judge* another sinner. What can be meant by "judge" here, and what has it to do with granting or withholding forgiveness, with being angry or forswearing one's anger? The judge sits in a superior position vis-à-vis the defendant; as judge, he is removed from the defendant, so it is incongruous for one criminal to sit in judgment of another. Abba Moses is inviting the council to see themselves as on the "same level" as this offender.

This interpretation is borne out by something in the logic of anger. Anger takes the superior, "judgmental" position. The angry one construes himself as in the position of judge and the offender as defendant, as in the inferior position—at least with respect to the matter about which he is angry. Anger is thus a down-looking emotion. This need not be an invidious or contemptuous looking down; pride and contempt have a significantly different grammar from anger. But the social ordering ingredient in anger explains why resentment is so unpleasant and thus often unconscious: being a form of anger, it has the compulsion to look down, but it is also a construal of oneself as impotent with respect to the offender—as looking up at him. So an aspect of the grammar of anger is undercut by the recognition that one is guilty of offenses similar to the offender's, and this recognition is a reason for forgiving the other. This is why humility is closely allied with and supports forgiveness. One who is inclined to insist on the moral difference between himself and offenders—a haughty or self-righteous person—will be unsusceptible to this consideration and more likely to remain angry.

In some moral outlooks, such as Judaism, one's likeness to the offender is always a reason to forgive, and one is seriously deficient in forgivingness, to the extent that one lacks humility.[22] This is so because of a doctrine (or insight) that before God we are all in the wrong, even if there may be *people* we have not sinned against. By contrast, in an outlook like Aristotle's, where some people may very well be perfectly good and one may legitimately have a strong sense of one's moral superiority to others, this reason for forgiving will be available only on some occasions. Insofar as reasons to forgive become embedded in a person's habitual perception of offenders, Jewish forgivingness differs, as a virtue, from Aristotelian forgivingness.

A related reason to forgive is that the offended one has himself been forgiven some similar offense. Jesus of Nazareth tells a parable about a servant who owed his king a sum of money so vast he couldn't pay. The king resolved to sell him into bondage to raise money for the debt, but the man begged patience and out of compassion the king forgave him the whole debt. The servant himself was owed a small sum by a fellow servant, but when the latter asked for patience the servant had him thrown in debtor's prison. Hearing of this, the king summoned the servant and said, "You wicked servant! I forgave you all that debt because you besought me; and should not you have had mercy on your fellow servant, as I had mercy on you?"[23] Literally the parable is not about the forgiveness of offenses, but about the remission of debts—a matter having nothing to do with overcoming anger and the alienation it entails. But it is probably to be read as saying that God's having forgiven us our offenses against Him should be a compelling reason for us to forgive those who offend us. Let us read the "should" as a virtue-should—as saying that one who is properly formed emotionally will find, in his being forgiven, a compelling reason for forgiving others. Because the servant was insensitive to this consideration the king takes him to be "wicked."

How does somebody's forgiving me become a reason for me to forgive somebody else? What is the wicked servant's defect, that blinds him to the connection between his receiving forgiveness and his being called on to give it? Is there a principle of justice here, to the effect that I owe as much forgiveness as I receive? Or does this reason collapse into the one just discussed, namely that it establishes my being on the same "level" as my offender and thus militates against my being angry at him? (In this case my having *received* forgiveness is not the reason for forgiving, but rather my *needing* it.) Neither of these interpretations is quite right. It is neither justice, strictly speaking, that the servant lacks, nor simply humility (though he does lack that).

The servant lacks gratitude and empathy. By involving the forgiver's benevolent beneficence towards the forgiven, acts of forgiveness exemplify a kind of generosity. So the attitude which properly receives and acknowledges forgiveness is gratitude. But gratitude requires humility, in that it is a glad response to a one-down situation, that of being indebted.[24] The servant, however, takes the king's grace for granted. That is, he forgets or emotionally underrates the magnitude of his debt, and thus the goodness of the king. Generosity can be exemplified by cancelling a debt; gratitude, however, is not a disregard for the debt, but a glad dwelling in it and gracious acknowledgment of it. The grateful person construes himself as indebted to his benefactor, even though, and precisely because, the benefactor has canceled his debt. If the servant sees these things clearly, he will see himself, with a certain gladness, as being unrepayably indebted to the king. Grasping this more than intellectually, he will be sensitive to the commonality between himself and his own debtor—that is, will identify with his own debtor, see him as like himself and be concerned for him on analogy with his concern for himself. This attitude is called empathy. But instead he regards himself as scot-free, forgets his former debt and the king's goodness, and thus fails to perceive the analogy between his own situation and the other servant's. That connection, then, can be expressed in the following proposition: *In his indebtedness to me, my fellow servant is like me in my (now canceled) indebtedness to the king; and my fellow servant's faring well, like mine, is important.* The virtues by which such a proposition can move a person to forgive—virtues which lie therefore in the background of forgivingness—are gratitude and empathy.

Relationship. In our discussion of the previous four reasons for forgiving, it has emerged that the teleology of forgiveness is reconciliation—restoration or maintenance of a relationship of acceptance, benevolent attitude, and harmonious interaction. So it comes as no surprise that close, non-instrumental relationship is one of the most important reasons people give for forgiving: "I forgive her because she is my friend (sister, wife, daughter, mother, colleague)."

We can distinguish two ways that a person may desire reconciliation, one that has the offender in benevolent view, and another that is purely instrumental. Imagine an estranged couple, angry and alienated over marital crimes against one another. Though Piet is still very angry at Tieneke, he wants to be reconciled with her. But what does he want, in wanting that? They have three young children, and Piet believes the children will suffer psychological damage if he and Tieneke are not reconciled. So he has an *instrumental* desire for reconciliation with her: reconciliation with her is a means of protecting the children. As long as this, and nothing more, remains Piet's reason for seeking reconciliation, Piet cannot forgive Tieneke. He may succeed in putting away his anger at her, and he may live with her in a kind of harmony that is better for the children than divorce, but he cannot forgive *her*. Piet is over his anger, all right, but the *way* he is over it is not forgiveness.

I noted at the beginning of this section that a kind of self-control is often involved in forgiveness, a more or less intentional management of one's anger by reference to the considerations characteristic of forgiveness. But there are other ways of controlling anger that do not replace it with a benevolent view of the offender. For example, Piet reminds himself that 200 years from now Tieneke's offense against him will matter to no one, least of all to him, or he tells himself that no one can really hurt him unless he consents to be hurt, and thus he takes upon himself responsibility for his injuries. Or he convinces himself that the course of the world is inevitable (including the vicious actions of Tieneke). Or he construes Tieneke as literally beneath contempt and her hatred or disregard of him as meaning nothing. The ability to mitigate or dispel anger in such ways as these is self-control, but these ways of overcoming anger are not the self-control characteristic of forgiveness, even if they result in one's getting along well enough with the person one was formerly angry at. Such a control of anger does not have the *offender* in benevolent view.

This is not just control of the *behavior* characteristic of anger—scowling, yelling, insulting, etc.—but control of the view that one takes of the offender. The Stoic and Nietzschean exercises mentioned in the preceding paragraph are designed to dispel the perception that is (I hold) identical with anger. In the one, Piet sees the offense as unimportant, in another he sees himself as invulnerable to hurt, in another he sees Tieneke as non-culpable or merely contemptible rather than deserving punishment, etc., etc. But even though the anger itself is dispelled, none of these cases is forgiveness, because the motivation characteristic of forgiveness (desire for a benevolent relationship with the offender) and the replacement perception characteristic of forgiveness (the view of the other as friend, fellow, lover) are absent.

This non-forgiving self-control of anger may promote forgiveness. If Piet succeeds in controlling his anger at Tieneke, even if only for the sake of the children and using Stoic strategies, Tieneke may respond by becoming lovable, and as a result he may begin to regard her with genuine benevolence. Or Piet's demeanor of non-anger towards her may transform his construal of himself into that of a person benevolently disposed towards her, and what was a simulacrum of benevolence changes gradually into the real thing.

IV Withholding forgiveness

The forgiving person has in him anger-defeating principles—sensitivities to forgiveness considerations. But he is capable of anger, and the anger-defeating sensitivities don't always apply—don't always meet with fit objects. The patterns of affordance and refusal of forgiveness define the virtue no less than the nature of anger and anger's interactions with the considerations characteristic of forgiveness that undermine it. So, briefly and with an imprecision befitting the subject matter, we must indicate when the forgiving person will *withhold* forgiveness. Let us look for proper limits to forgiveness corresponding to the five considerations favoring forgiveness, reversing, however, the order of the first two considerations.

Severity of the offense. Fyodor Dostoevsky's Alyosha Karamazov is a paradigm of forgivingness (see his response to being stoned and bitten by the boy Ilusha[25]). But he has his limits. His brother Ivan tells of a gentleman general who lords it over his serfs. An eight-year-old serf boy throws a stone in play and hurts the paw of the general's favorite hound. The general orders the boy locked up. The next morning

the general comes out on horseback, with the hounds, his dependents, dog-boys, and huntsmen, all mounted around him in full hunting parade. The servants are summoned for their edification, and in front of them all stands the mother of the child. The child is brought from the lock-up. It's a gloomy, cold, foggy autumn day, a capital day for hunting. The general orders the child to be undressed; the child is stripped naked. He shivers, numb with terror, not daring to cry.... "Make him run," commands the general. "Run! Run!" shout the dog-boys. The boy runs.... "At him!" yells the general, and he sets the whole pack of hounds on the child. The hounds catch him, and tear him to pieces before his mother's eyes![26]

Ivan challenges the mild Alyosha to say what should be done with the general, and Alyosha murmurs reluctantly that he should be shot. It is no doubt the heinousness of this crime—its despicable pettiness, calculation, and cruelty—that blocks Alyosha's access to the considerations that characteristically soften the anger response in him.

Alyosha is not properly in a position to forgive the general, since the general's crime was not committed against Alyosha. If the murdered boy were Alyosha's little brother, then Alyosha would himself be in a position to forgive or withhold forgiveness. Given what we know about Alyosha, it seems clear that the despicableness of the crime is not an absolute barrier to forgiveness. Imagine that the general comes to Alyosha and begs his forgiveness for murdering Alyosha's little brother. At first Alyosha is skeptical about the depth of the general's repentance, but as a token of it he is willing to divide his property among his serfs and adopt the life of a mendicant. He does this, and Alyosha receives him as a brother.

Unrepentance. Lesser offenses may properly remain unforgiven, at least for a time, because of the offender's unrepentance. Your brother is a (supposedly) recovering heroin addict. He calls you up, says he needs a place to live and a job and can you help him out. You invite him, along with his girlfriend and their baby, to come live with you while he gets on his feet. You lay down some house-rules: No smoking indoors, no drugs, look hard for a job, regular Bible study at the rehab center, cooperate in the family life (the house is really too small for two families). A couple of weeks into their stay, you have incontrovertible evidence that they've been smoking pot in the house and that some of the job-hunting excursions were used to find heroin. Confronted with the facts, your brother lies to you at first, but then concedes that it's all true. You're a forgiving person and you love your brother but you're mad, and not by any deficit of virtue. You judge that this is not the time for forgiveness.

The justification for remaining angry is that the offender is currently active in his offense. Any gestures of allying himself with your moral position seem to be more or less shameless manipulation and persistence in crime. It would be a sign of moral flaccidity to forgive at the moment. Here your forgivingness is not displayed in forgiving, but consists in a *readiness* to forgive whenever real repentance becomes evident.

What if repentance is not forthcoming? Fed up with your brother's unwillingness to do what needs to be done, you turn him out of the house. Three years later he is still a miserable addict, and has not even apologized for the deceit and the six fruitless weeks of freeloading. Maybe he even resents your not giving him another chance. I judge that in a forgiving person the anger will have faded to sadness under the bleaching influence of compassion and brotherly affection.

So it seems that for the forgiving person neither the heinousness of the offense nor the absence of repentance is enough by itself to prevent forgiveness. Together, they may very well be. With no deficit of forgivingness, the mother of the serf boy may find herself unable to forgive the general if he remains unrepentant. But if her forgivingness consists in a dispositional desire to live in benevolent and harmonious relationship with all persons, she will feel uncomfortable with her enmity, and so will be disposed to hope for his repentance and the possibility of forgiveness.

Lack of suffering. The suffering of the offender can evoke a compassion that dispels anger without changing the forgiver's judgment about the offender's culpability and desert of punishment. So in some cases forgiveness does not occur because the offender does not suffer or is not perceived to do so. We can well imagine that without the experience in the hospital tent, or something similar, Prince Andrei would not have forgiven Kuragin. But the lack of suffering of the offender is not a consideration that characteristically moves the forgiving person to withhold forgiveness. The effectiveness of such a consideration seems to suppose a vindictiveness inconsistent with forgivingness.

Lack of commonality. Our fourth consideration favoring forgiveness is the moral commonality of the forgiver, and so we may ask whether a lack of such commonality might block the forgiving person's forgiveness. Might the uprightness of the offended party— the moral distance between himself and the offender—be a reason for not forgiving the offender? Applied to the case of Ivan Karamazov's general, the mother's thought would now be not, "the crime is too heinous to be forgiven without extraordinary repentance," but "he is, morally, so different from me that I cannot receive him as a fellow human being; were I more of a sinner, perhaps I could…." Whether this consideration ever properly blocks forgiveness seems to vary with moral outlook. In a Christian framework it rings false because of the teaching that *all* are in very deep moral trouble if rated on their own merits. But in an outlook from which such teaching is absent—say, Aristotle's—perhaps the moral merit of the forgiving person could sometimes supply him a reason for withholding forgiveness from an offender.

Lack of relationship. Something analogous can be said about the possibility that lack of relationship of offender to offended might justify withholding forgiveness. In some moral outlooks—say, Nietzsche's—two people may be naturally foreign to one another if one is, say, a naturally slavish sort of person and the other is naturally noble. If at the center of forgivingness is a concern for harmonious and benevolent relationship with (certain) others, then the fact that an offender does not belong to the class of persons with whom it is fitting to have that kind of relationship provides a good reason for withholding forgiveness. In outlooks that recognize no moral classes, such a consideration would be unavailable to justify withholding forgiveness. Still, if "he is my brother" favors forgiveness, could not "he is not my brother" be a reason for withholding it, in some imaginable circumstances? Even an egalitarian morality may recognize more and less proximal relationships. If we have duties to our families that we have not to the population at large, might the forgiving person also be disposed to forgive family members in circumstances, and for offenses, in which he would withhold forgiveness from less closely related persons? Imagine that you take some refugees into your home, and they exploit you just as severely and intentionally as your brother does in our example. And let us continue to assume that you are an ideally forgiving person. It would seem to follow from our discussion in section 3 that their being less closely related to you might lead you to forgive them somewhat less readily than you forgave your brother, since one of the anger-defeating sensitivities that that situation called into play may not be called into play here.[27]

Forgiving persons do not always forgive, any more than the courageous always take action in the face of danger, or the generous always give lavishly, or the compassionate always help. Like these other virtues, forgivingness is a complex disposition to respond to complex circumstances. It is not possible to delineate with precision the practical wisdom possessed by the ideally for-giving person, but the foregoing discussion begins to indicate the boundaries.

V Concluding overview

Let me summarize our results. The act or process of forgiveness is a dispelling of justified anger at one who has offended against oneself, in particular a dissolution of the victim's retributive gestalt of the offender. It is, however, not just *any* such dispelling or dissolution, but one in which the judgment ingredient in the anger—that the offense is significant and the offender culpable—is retained,[28] and the emotion is dispelled by any of a set of con-siderations that bear, in various ways, on the concern to be in a benevolent and harmonious relationship with the offender. I have suggested that an understanding of how the judgment characteris-tic of anger can be retained while the anger itself is overwhelmed by the benevolence-considerations depends on having a view of emotions in which a person's emotions can change without change in her judgments.[29] The account of emotions as concern-based perceptions or construals meets this requirement. Thus when the angry one construes her offender in terms of the offender's good-will as expressed in repentance, or compassionately in terms of the offender's suffering, or in terms of the offender's close relationship to the victim, or in terms of the victim's moral commonality with the offender, with perhaps the help of mitigating excuses for the offender, the retributive construal is apt to be supplanted by a more benevolent one. But this new way of seeing the offender by no means rules out the judgment that the offender is culpable of a significant offense and deserves some punishment. The emotional state is rather a matter of what features of the situation are *percep-tually salient* to the victim, in this special "seeing-as" sense of "perceptual." This, then, is my account of forgiveness as an act or process. Forgivingness is a disposition for this act to be performed or the process to occur. What then is the psychological make-up of a person with this virtue?

A dispositional concern to be in benevolent, harmonious relationship with others is basic to forgivingness. The forgiving person tends to feel uncomfortable with the alienation from others that his own anger at them brings. In general, the wider the range of persons to whom this concern applies, and the stronger the concern, the more forgiving will the person be, other things being equal. One thing that may not be equal is the person's dispositional concern for justice and the related sense of self-respect. Someone who is willing to pay any price to be in harmonious relationship with others does not have the integrity requisite for forgivingness. He will be a condoner and will tend toward moral stupidity. So the concern for harmonious relationship must coexist in the personality with a disposition that makes one prone to anger. H.J.N. Horsbrugh seems to deny this when he says, "a perfectly forgiving person has no occasion to forgive since he is animated by such a forgiving spirit that no conceivable injury can destroy his good-will or give rise to feelings of resentment or hostility towards his injurer."[30] This description fits better the morally stupid person than the perfectly forgiving. Sometimes an eminently forgiving person will exemplify the virtue by feeling no anger at all. But it is wrong to make the obviation of acts of forgiveness generally characteristic of the perfectly forgiving person. Such unsusceptibility to anger would undermine forgivingness. The eminently forgiving person has it in him to become angry on occasions when this is called for.

So the forgiving person will at times engage in active self-control of her anger; in some moments of anger *she* will activate the kind of anger-mitigating considerations that we explored in section 3. After all, anger may be quite intense, and is a disposition against benevolence. Thus forgivingness involves a certain amount of self-awareness and self-management skill. The forgiving person has to "know," for example, that her anger can be reduced by finding excuses for her offender, by considering her own moral resemblance to the offender, by focusing compassionately on the offender's misery, by remembering her own indebtedness; and she has to be somewhat practiced in turning her mind to these considerations. Sometimes her concern for benevolent,

harmonious relationship will dispose her mind in these directions, so that she just finds herself automatically free of the anger;
at other times she will struggle to deny herself, and will have to
draw on her repertoire of anger-mitigating considerations. But
most importantly—and here I return to the fundamental insight
of section 3—she must have the basic concern for harmonious
relationship with her offender that motivates a susceptibility
to these considerations and a willingness, when this is difficult, to
transcend her anger.[31]

Notes

1   R.S. Downie in "Forgiveness" *Philosophical Quarterly*, Vol. 15 (1965),
    pp. 128–34, and Jeffrie Murphy in *Forgiveness and Mercy* (Cambridge:
    Cambridge University Press, 1988), co-authored with Jean Hampton, cited
    hereafter as Hampton and Murphy. See pp. 133–4 of Downie for the analy-
    sis. Murphy confuses forgivingness with forgiveness as an act, for he says
    that "forgiveness is not always a virtue" (p. 17). It is not always appropri-
    ate to forgive—to perform an act of forgiveness, or allow a process of for-
    giveness to proceed. But if forgivingness is a virtue, then it is always a
    virtue—barring a radical change in our environment. (As Hume points
    out, distributive justice would not be a virtue in a world of complete
    abundance, and similarly forgiveness would not be a virtue in a world
    lacking moral offenses.) That compassion should occasionally be withheld
    does not mean that compassion is sometimes not a virtue; courage is not
    sometimes not a virtue just because sometimes it is better not to act
    courageously.
2   "Forgiveness" in *Ethics, Value, and Reality: Selected Papers of Aurel
    Kolnai* (Indianapolis: Hackett Publishing Company, 1978), pp. 211–24.
3   Bishop Butler, *Fifteen Sermons* (New York: Robert Carter and Brothers,
    1860; reprinted in facsimile by Ibis Publishing, Charlottesville, Virginia,
    1987), Sermons 8 and 9, "Upon Resentment" and "Upon Forgiveness
    of Injuries." Butler reverses what I take to be our contemporary usage,
    and makes anger a kind of resentment: "Resentment is of two kinds:
    hasty and sudden, or settled and deliberate. The former is called
    anger...." (p. 94). Indignation is likewise made out to be a form of
    resentment: "it is resentment against vice and wickedness" (p. 95f).
    But he does not insist on his terminology: "It hath been shown, that
    mankind naturally feel some emotion of mind against injury and

injustice, whoever are the sufferers by it; and even though the injurious design be prevented from taking effect. Let this be called anger, indignation, resentment, or by whatever name any one shall choose; the thing itself is understood, and is plainly natural" (p. 102). Since 1962 the focus on resentment may also have been encouraged by Peter Strawson's influential paper "Freedom and Resentment" in which he makes some tangential comments on forgiveness. The essay is reprinted in P.F. Strawson, ed., *Studies in the Philosophy of Thought and Action* (Oxford: Oxford University Press, 1968), pp. 71-96. In the *Oxford English Dictionary*, definition 3 of "forgiveness" is "To remit (a debt); to give up resentment or claim to requital for, pardon (an offence)." And definition 4 is "To give up resentment against, pardon (an offender)."

4 For example, Jeffrie Murphy in Hampton and Murphy; R.J. O'Shaughnessy, "Forgiveness," *Philosophy*, Vol. 42 (1967), pp. 336–52; Paul Lauritzen, "Forgiveness: Moral Prerogative or Religious Duty?" *Journal of Religious Ethics*, Vol. 15 (1987), pp. 141–54; Anne C. Minas, "God and Forgiveness," *Philosophical Quarterly*, Vol. 25 (1975), pp. 138–50.

5 Hampton and Murphy, pp. 79-87, 147-57.

6 See *Emotions: An Essay in Aid of Moral Psychology* (Cambridge: Cambridge University Press, 2003), especially Chapter 2.

7 Some exceptions to this last claim are noted by William Neblett in "Forgiveness and Ideals," *Mind*, Vol. 73 (1974), pp. 269–75; see p. 270.

8 Anne C. Minas points out the oddness of ascribing resentment to God, "God and Forgiveness," pp. 147-8.

9 Hampton and Murphy, pp. 60-79.

10 Ibid., p. 55.

11 To be distinguished from "looks as though he feels guilty."

12 Norvin Richards, "Forgiveness," *Ethics*, Vol. 99 (1988), pp. 77-97, p. 79.

13 Ibid. The connection of forgiveness with reconciliation leads John Wilson to think it strictly impossible to forgive an offender who does not repent. "Why Forgiveness Requires Repentance," *Philosophy*, Vol. 63 (1988), pp. 534-5. Forgiveness is "a bilateral ... operation" (p. 534). But this is to confuse forgiveness with reconciliation. Forgiveness is an attitude of one person towards another, not a pattern of interaction between them. Often, the benevolent putting away of anger precedes repentance, or persists in the face of unrepentance.

14 Hampton and Murphy, p. 20, Murphy's italics.

15 Thomas E. Hill, "Servility and Self-Respect," *Monist*, Vol. 62 (1979), pp. 87–104.

16 Brand Blanshard, *Reason and Goodness* (London: G. Allen & Unwin, 1961), p. 445.

17 See Hampton and Murphy, p. 20.
18 For a discussion of forgiveness as therapeutic, see chapter 10 of my *Taking the Word to Heart: Self and Other in an Age of Therapies* (Grand Rapids: Wm. B. Eerdmans, 1993).
19 *Fifteen Sermons*, p. 111.
20 Leo Tolstoy, *War and Peace*, trans. Rosemary Edmonds (Penguin: Harmondsworth, Middlesex, England, 1982), pp. 967f (Book Three, Part Two, Chapter 37).
21 Benedicta Ward, ed., *The Sayings of the Desert Fathers* (Kalamazoo: Cistercian Publications, 1975), p. 117.
22 On Jewish humility, see Daniel M. Nelson, "The Virtue of Humility in Judaism: A Critique of Rationalist Hermeneutics," *Journal of Religious Ethics*, Vol. 13 (1985), pp. 298–311.
23 Matthew 18.23–35.
24 This is no doubt why Aristotle's great-souled man has difficulty with gratitude. See *Nicomachean Ethics*, 1124b10. For an elaboration of the emotion and virtue of gratitude, see my "The Blessings of Gratitude" in Robert A. Emmons and Michael McCullough, eds, *The Psychology of Gratitude* (New York: Oxford University Press, 2004), 58–78.
25 Fyodor Dostoevsky, *The Brothers Karamazov*, trans. Constance Garnett (New York: Modern Library, 1995), Book IV, Chapter 3.
26 Ibid., Book V, Chapter 4.
27 For simplicity's sake I ignore the fact that the closer relationship provides not only an extra reason for forgiving, but also extra reasons for anger. If we took that factor into consideration, it might turn out easier to forgive the strangers than to forgive one's brother. This fact is presumably behind William Blake's comment that "It is easier to forgive an enemy than to forgive a friend."
28 Though it may be revised. See the discussion of excuses.
29 For moral psychologists who think that change of emotion necessarily involves a change of judgment, see Gabriele Taylor, *Pride, Shame, and Guilt* (Oxford: Oxford University Press, 1985), chapter 1 and *passim*; Hampton and Murphy, the Introduction; Robert Solomon, *The Passions* (Garden City, N.Y.: Anchor/Doubleday, 1976) and "On Emotions as Judgments," *American Philosophical Quarterly*, Vol. 25 (April, 1988), pp. 183–91; and Martha Nussbaum, *The Therapy of Desire* (Princeton: Princeton University Press, 1994), chapter 10. For an author who rejects the judgment theory, see Patricia Greenspan, *Emotions and Reasons* (New York: Routledge, 1988).
30 "Forgiveness," *Canadian Journal of Philosophy*, Vol. 4 (1974), pp. 269–82, p. 281. Downie makes a similar comment, p. 133.

31 I gratefully acknowledge help from the National Endowment for the Humanities in providing a summer stipend to write this paper, and support from the Pew Charitable Trusts during its final revision. An anonymous reviewer for the *American Philosophical Quarterly* suggested important revisions, as did my colleagues in the philosophy department at Wheaton College.

10 Trust as an Affective Attitude

Karen Jones

I Introduction

In this article I defend an account of trust according to which trust is an attitude of optimism that the goodwill and competence of another will extend to cover the domain of our interaction with her, together with the expectation that the one trusted will be directly and favorably moved by the thought that we are counting on her. The attitude of optimism is to be cashed out not primarily in terms of beliefs about the other's trustworthiness, but rather—in accordance with certain contemporary accounts of the emotions[1]—in terms of a distinctive, and affectively loaded, way of seeing the one trusted. This way of seeing the other, with its constitutive patterns of attention and tendencies of interpretation, explains the willingness of trusters to let those trusted get dangerously near the things they care about. This account is presented and defended in the first two sections of the article.

Any account of what trust is sets constraints on what can be said about the justification conditions of trust. Thus, if a theorist analyzes trust as (perhaps among other things) a belief that the one trusted will have and display goodwill toward the one who trusts, then that theorist has committed herself to saying that trust is justified only if the one who trusts is justified in forming the belief constitutive of trust. In the fourth section of the article, I take up the question of the justification conditions of trust. While a full account of the justification conditions of trust is beyond the scope of this article, I identify the key variables affecting the justifiedness of trust. An account of trust that makes affect central has an unexpected payoff: it is able to view a wide range of our trustings—including many of those undertaken for instrumental reasons—as justified. Moreover, it is able to do this without taking a stance on evidentialism, or the doctrine that we should not believe anything without sufficient evidence. Since trust is not primarily a belief, it falls outside the scope of the evidentialist thesis.

It is necessary, first, to get clearer about the target of my investigation. The word "trust" is used in a variety of expressions, ranging from "Trust you to do something like that!" to "We trust you have enjoyed your flight with Air New Zealand," to "Othello's trust in Iago was misplaced." In the first sentence "trust" is used ironically, although it brings with it from its non-ironic uses the idea of expectations having been met, while in the second it politely conveys something intermediate between an expectation and a hope. Sometimes the word "trust" is used to convey any sort of delegated responsibility, especially one where checking up is difficult or precluded. Thus a politician of such egregious ethical turpitude that she has long since ceased to be trusted by any of her constituents can nonetheless, on the exposure of some new failing, be said to have once again violated the public's trust. My task is thus not to explicate the meaning of the word "trust" wherever it occurs, since there is no one common phenomenon that all uses of the word "trust" pick out. Instead, my target is the sense conveyed in our third example: "Othello's trust in Iago was misplaced." That is to say, my target is interpersonal trust. But this is not a narrow target: it is the trust always found in friendship, often found between professionals and their clients, sometimes found between strangers, and sometimes, even, between people and their governments. My task is therefore an explanatory task, the success of which is to be tested by how well it lets us understand this everyday phenomenon—how well, that is, it can account for the similarities and differences between interpersonal trust relations of the sorts just listed.

II An account of trust

A. *The basic model*

Trusting is composed of two elements, one cognitive and one affective or emotional. (I say "affective" rather than "noncognitive" because affective states can themselves contain a significant cognitive component.) Roughly, to trust someone is to have an attitude of optimism about her goodwill and to have the confident expectation that, when the need arises, the one trusted will be directly and favorably moved by the thought that you are counting on her. If A's attitude towards B (in a given domain or interaction) is predominantly characterized by optimism about B's goodwill and by the expectation that B will be directly and favorably moved by the thought that A is counting on her, then A has a trusting relationship with B (within that domain). There can be moments of trust within relationships that are not, in general, characterized by trust, although if the attitude and expectation are too fleeting, it would not be correct to say that A trusts B. The attitude and expectation characteristic of trust combine to explain why trusters are willing, when the need arises, to rely on those they trust.[2]

In the standard case, the confident expectation that the one trusted will respond directly and favorably to the thought that the truster is counting on them is itself grounded in the attitude of optimism; thus the attitude of optimism is central. This account of the two aspects of trust requires further elaboration and refinement. It also needs to be shown why we should think that both are necessary for trust and why we should think that together they amount to a satisfying account.

First, though, I should explain what I mean by "optimism," for the word has connotations that are apt to be misleading. The attitude of optimism is directed at the goodwill of another. I can trust someone with whom I'm engaged in a very difficult endeavor even though I have no optimism about the success of our joint task; thus, trust does not involve a general tendency to look on the bright side. However, trust does lead one to anticipate that the other will have and display goodwill, and this is the aspect of optimism that I want to highlighty—the way optimism leads us to anticipate a favorable outcome. Throughout the article, though, I do not want "optimism" to suggest a general tendency to look on the bright side. With that in mind, we can turn to the task of refining our characterization of trust.

At the center of trust is an attitude of optimism about the other person's goodwill. But optimism about goodwill is not sufficient, for some people have very good wills but very little competence, and the incompetent deserve our trust almost as little as the malicious. (Almost, but not quite, for the incompetent might sometimes get things right, whereas the malicious will get things right only to the extent that they are incompetent.) Thus, we should say that trust is optimism about the goodwill and *competence* of another. The position requires additional refinement: except perhaps with our most trusted intimates, the optimism we bear is seldom global. This is not to say that the optimism itself is qualified and instead of being unreserved optimism is a qualified or restricted optimism. What is qualified is not the optimism itself, but the domain over which it extends. So, for example, the optimism we have about the goodwill and competence of strangers does not extend very far. We expect their goodwill to extend to not harming us as we go about our business and their competence to consist in an understanding of the norms for interaction between strangers. For a man to run up at full speed behind a woman on an ill-lit street is to display a lack of such competence, and, even if he was simply out for a late night run and meant no harm, he has given the woman reason to distrust him. When we trust professionals, from plumbers to physicians, we expect of them a technical competence (and minimal decency). However, the competence we expect in trusting need not be technical: when we trust a friend, the competence we expect them to display is a kind of *moral* competence. We expect a friend to understand loyalty, kindness, and generosity, and what they call for in various situations.

There are a number of reasons why we might think that a person will have and display goodwill in the domain of our interaction with her. Perhaps she harbors friendly feelings towards us; in that case, the goodwill is grounded on personal liking. Or perhaps she is generally benevolent, or honest, or conscientious, and so on. The formulation is meant to be neutral between these reasons for thinking that a person's goodwill extends to cover the domain of our interaction.

It might be thought odd to claim that trust centrally involves an affective *attitude,* but this analysis is borne out by considering distrust. Distrust is trust's contrary and is synonymous with wary suspicion. Distrust is pessimism about the goodwill and competence of another (again, relativized to a certain domain), but to be pessimistic about someone's goodwill is to expect that it is likely that she will harm your interests, and thus to treat her warily and with suspicion.

The analysis is further borne out by considering a parallel between trust and self-confidence. It seems intuitively correct to say that self-confidence involves an affective attitude. To have self-confidence is to be optimistic about one's competence (in the domain in question) and to have the expectation that one will be able to bring about a favorable outcome. Sometimes we use the phrase "trust yourself" as roughly interchangeable with "be self-confident." There seems, though, to be an important difference between the two: with self-confidence, and its lack, self-doubt, we are worried about our capacity, rather than our will. "Trust yourself" has application precisely because parts of ourselves can sometimes stand in the kind of external relation to other parts that makes their interaction more like the interaction between two persons. We need to trust ourselves when we are worried about the possibility of self-sabotage, about the possibility that some not fully conscious part of ourselves might be operating from motives other than our professed ones.

While trust essentially involves an attitude of optimism that the goodwill and competence of another will extend to the domain of our interaction with her, it is not exhausted by such an attitude. The affective element of trust needs to be supplemented with an expectation, namely, the expectation that the one trusted will be directly and favorably moved by the thought that someone is counting on her. Being directly and favorably moved by this thought may not give the one trusted an overriding motive; acting on such a thought, could, for example, be tempered by other concerns or by thinking that what the one who trusts is counting on is not, under the circumstances, in her own best interests. Nevertheless, one is not trustworthy unless one is willing to give significant weight to the fact that the other is counting on one, and so will not let that consideration be overruled by just any other concern one has. For this reason, one would not trust if one thought that the fact that one was counting on someone, while always being taken into account, would nonetheless be reliably overridden by other considerations. Were that the case, then, from the point of view of the truster, the other would appear unwilling to give enough weight to the thought that she was counting on her. If someone thought another would give this much weight and not more to the thought that she was being counted on, then she would not willingly rely on her if the need to do so were to arise. However, the truster's expectation need not amount to an expectation of actual performance in every case. Someone doesn't show herself untrustworthy simply because there are occasions on which the thought that someone is counting on her is not a consideration that she can let prevail. Further, when the attitude and expectation lead the truster to willingly rely on the one trusted, there may be (though there does not have to be) some vagueness about what it is the truster is counting on her for. There may be a number of ways of adequately responding to the thought that you are being counted on, which is why trusting is associated with discretionary powers.[3]

The qualification "directly" in "directly and favorably moved by the thought that someone is counting on her" is required to distinguish trusting from certain cases of mere reliance. I might, for example, know that you will be moved by the thought that I am counting on you because you fear my retaliation if you let me down. If I believe that you will be directly moved by fear and only indirectly moved by the thought that I am counting on you, our relationship is not, on my analysis, one of trust.

There are two ways to see that an expectation has to be added to the affective component of trust in order to have an adequate account: by considering unwelcome trust and by considering the ways in which a reliably benevolent person's actions and motives might yet fall short of the actions and motives that we would demand of someone we trust.

We do not always welcome trust. Sometimes someone's trust in us can feel coercive. When it does, we don't usually complain about the person's having an attitude of optimism about our goodwill and competence, or even about her displaying such optimism in her interaction toward us, for it is rare that we would find such an attitude unwelcome. (Although there can be such cases: as when, for example, we find it impertinent that someone has attributed goodwill to us with respect to a particular domain of interaction.) In the standard case, however, what we object to when we do not welcome someone's trust is that, in giving it, she expects that we will be directly moved by the thought that she is counting on us and, for one reason or another, we do not want to have to take such expectations into account, across the range of interactions the truster wants. (If we are morally decent, we do not find the trust common between strangers coercive, because what is demanded of us is minimal.) We would rather that the one trusting did not expect us to respond to her counting on us because we would rather not have her count on us. We may, for example, feel that we cannot live up to her expectations, or we may have reservations about what such expectations will amount to in a given case, or we may feel that too many people are already counting on us and that one more is a burden we would rather not have.

Perhaps not everyone will be convinced by this argument. It might be thought that we never object to someone's trust, as such, but only to their *entrusting* certain things to us. When someone entrusts something to our care they expect us to respond to the fact that they are counting on us. Cases of objectionable or unwelcome trust are always cases of unwelcome entrusting, as when, for example, you burden me with your secrets. Thus, having the expectation that another will be directly moved by your counting on them is part of entrusting but, for all that's been said so far, not part of trusting. (When I discuss Baier's account of trust, I'll return to the connection between trust and entrusting in more detail.) However, we can see that this objection cannot be right, for I can find your trust a burden even when you have not entrusted anything in particular to me. Moreover, since we can entrust where we don't trust (I might know, for example, that you will take good care of whatever I entrust to you because you wouldn't dare do otherwise), it seems that if entrusting *sometimes* involves the expectation that the other will be directly moved by the thought that we are counting on them, then that expectation must be part of our trusting rather than our entrusting.

The second consideration in favor of supposing that trust must involve an expectation as well as an attitude is that someone who isn't at all directly moved by the thought that you're counting on them but is, let us suppose, reliably benevolent toward you, is reliable rather than trustworthy. Suppose that the only operative motive in your interaction with me is concern about my well-being. Regardless of what I count on you to do, you do it only if it maximizes my well being, and if it does that, you would do it anyway, whether or not I counted on you to do so. I would be justified in having an attitude of optimism about your goodwill while refraining from seeing you as trustworthy.

It might be objected that it is only in cases where optimism about goodwill is grounded in perceived benevolence that we need also attribute to the truster the expectation that the other will be directly and favorably moved by the thought that she is being counted on. To demand it in all cases, or even in the majority of cases, is to make one's analysis overly narrow and vulnerable to counterexample. But this seems to me mistaken. Consider trust in physicians.[4] The objection asks, "Isn't it enough for me to count as trusting my physician if I view her as a person of integrity and competence who cares about the interests of her patients? Why must I also expect that she will be responsive to my counting on her?" The answer is that we hope that what the physician takes to constitute acting with integrity and takes to constitute the interests of her patients will be, at least in part, shaped by the expectations of those patients. And if a physician refuses to allow the expectations of her patients to shape her understanding of what, here and now, good medical practice consists in, her patients would not be justified in trusting her. (This explains why a physician might have reservations about having someone as her patient:

if she feels that she will have objections to living up to her patient's expectations, she will think it difficult to maintain the proper relationship of trust.) For this reason, it would be a mistake to think that the ideally moral are always properly trusted. While it might be true that the ideally moral are properly trusted by those who are themselves ideally moral, it doesn't follow that they are properly trusted by those who are not.

I have claimed that trust is composed of two elements: an affective attitude of optimism about the goodwill and competence of another as it extends to the domain of our interaction and, further, an expectation that the one trusted will be directly and favorably moved by the thought that you are counting on them. Our expectation is, in the typical case, grounded in the attitude of optimism. That is to say, we expect that the other will react favorably to our counting on them *because* we are optimistic about their goodwill. Our expectation is usually grounded in the very same evidence that grounds our attitude of optimism. Thus the attitude of optimism is central.

B. The attitude of optimism

We now have a sketch of an account of trust. But it remains a sketch insofar as we do not yet have a firm grip on what is meant by saying that trust is, among other things, an affective attitude of optimism about the goodwill of another.

According to one influential account of the emotions, held in various forms by Rorty, Calhoun, and de Sousa,[5] emotions are partly constituted by patterns of salience and tendencies of interpretation. An emotion suggests a particular line of inquiry and makes some beliefs seem compelling and others not, on account of the way the emotion gets us to focus on a partial field of evidence. Emotions are thus not primarily beliefs, although they do tend to give rise to beliefs; instead they are distinctive ways of seeing a situation. In resentment, for example, the object of resentment might be seen as a "manipulative exploiter."[6] Similarly, the claim being advanced here is that the attitude of optimism constitutive of trust is a distinctive way of seeing another. This way of seeing the other is constituted by a distinctive trusting cognitive set, which makes one's willingness to rely on the other seem reasonable.

The cognitive set constitutive of trust restricts the interpretations of another's behavior and motives that we consider. It also restricts the interpretations we will consider as possibly applying to situations and the kinds of inferences we will make about the likely actions of another. Consider the following exchange:

Iago: My lord, you know I love you
Othello: I think thou dost;
        And, for I know thou'rt full of love and honesty
        And weigh'st thy words before thou givest them breath,
        Therefore these stops of thine fright me the more;
        For such things in a false disloyal knave
        Are tricks of custom; but in a man that's just
        They're close dilations, working from the heart
        That passion cannot rule. *(Othello,* 3.3.117–23)

Othello trusts Iago and interprets his words and behavior in the light of his trust. Had Othello not trusted Iago, he would have been able to see Iago's speech and the very fact of his interference for what they were, malicious attempts to harm him. Trust restricts the interpretations we will consider as possibly applying to the words and actions of another. When we can—and sometimes even if doing so requires ingenuity—we will give such words and actions a favorable interpretation as consistent with the goodwill of the other. Trusting thus functions analogously to blinkered vision: it shields from view a whole range of interpretations about the motives of another and restricts the inferences we will make about the likely actions of another. Trusting thus opens one up to harm, for it gives rise to selective interpretation, which means that one can be fooled, that the truth might lie, as it were, outside one's gaze. Because we impute honorable motives to those we trust, and typically do not even stop to consider the harms they might cause if they have dishonorable motives, we are willing to rely on those we trust. The harms they might cause through failure of goodwill are not in view because the possibility that their will is other than good is not in view. What in the absence of trust would be taken to be a reason for jealousy, for wary suspicion, or for action to protect my interests will not be so taken when there is trust.[7]

It is because the one trusted is viewed through the affective lens of trust that those who trust are—usually cheerfully, and often on the basis of the smallest evidence—willing to risk depending on the one trusted. Someone might object that it is possible to have this distinctive way of seeing another without trusting her. You might see her in this way, but resist the appearance, and struggle to keep nontrusting interpretations in mind. We can see the force of this objection by considering a possible parallel with phobic emotions. If I have a phobic fear of spiders, I still fear them, even though, let us suppose, once I'm aware of my fear I make every effort to resist the patterns of salience and tendencies of interpretation that constitute fear.[8] If trust, on account of having an affective component, has features in common with emotions, it should be the case that there can be "phobic" trusting, but this, the objection continues, is implausible. To reply to this objection we need to consider the difference between trusting someone, however briefly, and having a relationship with that person that is predominately characterized by trust. In many circumstances, these will amount to the same thing, as, for example, when I trust a stranger in a momentary meeting: there is no relationship beyond the momentary that could be distrusting. Let us look at an example to see how this reply evades the objection.

Suppose that I have a friend who is particularly charming and particularly irresponsible. Time and time again she lets me down, and time and time again I forgive her and resume a relationship, promising myself that this time I will be more cautious, this time I will not count on her, this time I will remember to think of the ways in which I make myself vulnerable to her, and this time I will take measures to protect myself. I won't trust her again. For all my resolution, I might nonetheless find myself trusting her. It's true that whenever I become aware of doing so, I will resist the impulse and will once again be on my guard. At one extreme, I might only become aware of my having again trusted when I am again let down. I would say of myself that I find myself trusting her, even though, when I think about it, I'm aware that I shouldn't. Our relationship, for that time period, would have been characterized predominantly by trust. At the opposite extreme, my caution might undermine my tendency to view her with trust so that no sooner do I find myself viewing her that way than I call myself to attention and remind myself of all the reasons not to trust her: in this circumstance, I would not be willing to depend on her when the need arises. Here, I'm inclined to say that I don't trust her, although I fight the tendency to do so: I do not go far enough along with the patterns of salience and tendencies of interpretation that partly constitute trust for it to be the case that I trust her. Even when caution dominates, there is, though, the possibility of momentary trust—trust that is unnoticed and would be withdrawn as soon as it were noticed—and there will be momentary trust whenever I'm not quick enough to catch myself and reject the view of her that I have adopted. When I'm not quick enough at catching myself, my view of the other can give rise to the risk-taking behavior characteristic of trust. In this kind of case, our relationship is not one characterized by trust, but for all that, it can have moments of trust. Usually, when we say that A trusts B (within a certain domain), we mean that A's relationship with B (within the domain in question) is predominantly characterized by trust's distinctive way of seeing someone, and not merely that on occasion A sees B through the lens of trust. Thus, there is some truth in the claim that when I reject the appearances trust gives rise to, I don't trust, but this does not force us to say that trust requires more than a distinctive way of seeing someone, although a trusting relationship (which is usually what we have in mind when we say that A trusts B) requires a consistent pattern of such interpretations. This solution to the objection is preferable to saying that trust requires us to have an endorsed attitude towards another, because we are generally not aware of our trusting and seldom bring it sufficiently clearly before our minds to endorse or reject it.

C. Clarifying the distinction between trust and reliance

While trust is always a possible attitude to take towards a person, we sometimes rely on people instead of trusting them. So, for example, I can rely on someone to behave in a certain kind of way because I have evidence that it is likely that she will behave in that way out of, say, habit, fear, vanity, or stupidity. As Baier notes, trust is not a precondition for relying on someone.[9]

Trusting is not an attitude that we can adopt toward machinery. I can rely on my computer not to destroy important documents or on my old car to get me from A to B, but my old car is reliable rather than trustworthy. One can only trust things that have wills, since only things with wills can have good wills—although having a will is to be given a generous interpretation so as to include, for example, firms and government bodies. Machinery can be relied on, but only agents, natural or artificial, can be trusted.[10]

Some cases of reliance are not grounded in perceived features of a person's psychology at all. Sometimes we adopt a policy of not checking up on people because to do so would be too time-consuming or too expensive. It's better to allow a few people to cheat on the coffee sign-up sheet than to devise a cheat-free method for collecting the coffee money. Devising a cheat-free method would simply take more time and cost more money than it would be worth.

There are some additional things that need to be said about the difference between trust and reliance. Sometimes we rely on things because we have no choice but to do so; thus we can be forced to rely on something when we are unable to predict that the event on which we rely will occur. However, if we have a choice about the matter, we will rely on someone only to the extent that we would be willing to make a prediction that the favored outcome will occur. In section IV, we shall see that things are otherwise with trust: we can be justified in trusting even when we would not be justified in predicting a favorable action on the part of the one trusted. Our evidence for trusting need not be as great as the evidence required for a corresponding justified prediction. In this respect trusting is more like hoping than like predicting.

III Advantages of the account

As we have seen, trust is to be distinguished from reliance in that trusting requires an attitude of optimism about the goodwill and competence of another as it extends to the domain of our interaction with them, and, in addition, trusting requires an expectation that the other will be directly moved by the thought that we are counting on them. It still needs to be shown that this account is adequate as an account of trust. An adequate account of trust should be able to explain at least the following three fairly obvious facts about trust: that trust and distrust are contraries but not con-tradictories,[11] that trust cannot be willed,[12] and that trust can give rise to beliefs that are abnormally resistant to evidence.[13] Because my account places an affective attitude at the center of our understanding of trust, it is able to explain all these things.

Given that trust and distrust both involve attitudes, it should be the case that together they do not exhaust the possible stances we can take towards another's goodwill and competence. Optimism and pessimism are contraries but not contradictories; between them lies a neutral space. As a consequence, the absence of trust is not to be equated with distrust, for one may fail to trust without actively distrusting—one may simply not adopt any attitude at all towards the goodwill and competence of another. In between trust and distrust are found various forms of relying on and taking for granted which are not grounded in either optimism or pessimism about the other's goodwill.

Affective attitudes look toward features of the world that would make them justified and can no more be sincerely adopted in the fate of a known and acknowledged absence of such grounds than a belief can be adopted in the face of a known and acknowledged lack of evidence. Because trust involves an affective attitude, it is not something that one can adopt at will: while one can trust wisely or foolishly, trust cannot be demanded in the absence of grounds for supposing that the person in question has goodwill and compe-tence and will be likely to take into account the fact that one is counting on them. This is not to say that there can never be an element of decision in adopting beliefs or attitudes. We can, for example, *decide* that the evidence we now have is enough to support the belief, but we can't just decide to believe regardless of the evidence.[14] While trust cannot be willed, it can be cultivated. We cultivate trust by a selective focus of attention towards the grounds for trust and away from the grounds for distrust.

Trust gives rise to beliefs that are highly resistant to evidence. While affective attitudes can't be willfully adopted in the teeth of evidence, once adopted they serve as a filter for how future evidence will be interpreted. If I trust you, I will, for example, believe that you are innocent of the hideous crime with which you are charged, and I will suppose that the apparently mounting evidence of your guilt can be explained in some way compatible with your innocence. Of course this resistance to evidence is not limitless: given enough evidence, my trust can be shaken and I can come to believe that you are guilty. When my trust is shaken, I will come to see you in quite a different light: that certain shortness of temper that never seemed so important before, seemed always to be able to be explained away, now seems highlighted. I can come to see that, yes, you could have done what you are charged with, and, perhaps, even more strongly, that, yes, it is the sort of thing you would do. But in coming to see you in this way, without trust, I undergo a significant shift in the patterns of my attention with respect to your character and in my habits of interpretation of you, your character, and your motives.

If, as I have claimed, trust has an affective component and emotions are partly constituted by patterns of salience and tendencies of interpretation, it should come as no surprise that trust gives rise to beliefs that are highly resistant to evidence. For the same reason, trust and distrust have a tendency to seek out evidence for themselves and so to be, to a degree, self-confirming.

Bearing in mind these three facts that an account of trust ought to be able to explain, I turn now to Baier's account of trust in "Trust and Antitrust." According to Baier, trusting is a matter of *entrusting*. Trusting is analyzed as a three-place predicate: A trusts B with valued thing C.[15] Baier acknowledges that there are three difficulties with her account: It involves a degree of regimentation in that it may sometimes be difficult to specify exactly what is entrusted (p. 236). It might suggest a greater degree of consciousness and explicitness than our trusting relations typically display, so we need to guard against interpreting the model in this way (p. 240). And finally, it seems to overlook plain, non-goods-relativized, trust. But we might think that we should first trust before we entrust. (Baier herself notes this [p. 259] but thinks that we flatly rule out entrusting anything whatsoever to someone or some group of persons only when our interests are in complete opposition.)

I want to test an entrusting model against the three common-place facts about trust mentioned earlier. It turns out that, because the model leads us to focus on the disposition of cared-about objects at the expense of focusing on attitudes, it has problems explaining at least two of the three commonplaces; furthermore, with our attention drawn outward towards these objects, it is easy to lose sight of the crucial element of optimism about the goodwill of another. Trust becomes insufficiently distinguished from (mere) reliance.

It seems that one either entrusts valued thing C to B or one does not. If not entrusting is distrusting, then trusting and distrusting are contradictories. But it seems that while one has to either entrust or not, trust and distrust do not exhaust the options, and so trust and distrust are not to be equated with entrusting and refraining from entrusting. Explaining why trust and distrust should be contraries but not contradictories is thus at least a prima facie problem for an account that analyzes trust in terms of entrusting. There may, though, be a way to preserve this distinction within an entrusting model. Perhaps trust involves a positive handing over of the thing entrusted, and distrust involves a positive *refusal* to hand over, a deliberate *withholding* of, the good in question, or, perhaps, purposive action to *protect* the valued thing. Trust and distrust could then be seen as contraries, for there is room for a neutral position in which one neither hands over the valued good nor holds it close to oneself. How good a reply this is depends on what it is that is being entrusted to another. There are three stances to take toward, say, you and the family silver: I may lend it to you, lock it up when I know you are visiting, or take no special precautions over it. It is less clear that there are three stances to take toward one's own self when walking down the street, and so it's not clear that this reply is fully satisfying.

The second commonplace that an account of trust must be able to explain is that trust cannot be willed. Baier notes this fact: "'Trust me!' is for most of us an invitation which we cannot accept at will—either we do already trust the one who says it, in which case it serves at best as reassurance, or it is properly responded to with, 'Why should I and how can I, until I have cause to?'" (p. 244). But *why* cannot one trust at will? If trust is entrusting it seems that I should be able to entrust at will, simply by handing over the relevant good. I may not feel very comfortable about it, but unless a feeling is built into the analysis of trust, that seems beside the point. Entrusting is an action and actions are, paradigmatically, things that can be willed. If, however, trusting involves an attitude, and attitudes cannot be adopted at will, we have an explanation for why one cannot trust at will.

Put just like this, the objection is surely unfair. We must cash out the "trust" as it occurs in the entrusting model's "A trusts B with valued object C." Perhaps without a belief in the reliability of the goodwill of another we cannot trust but instead can only rely on them. Baier says that the difference between trusting and relying on is that when we trust we rely on the goodwill of others toward us, whereas we may rely on others' "dependable habits, or only on their dependably exhibited fear, anger, or other motives compatible with ill will toward one, or on motives not directed on one at all" (p. 234). So we are to view trust as entrusting on the basis of a belief about the goodwill of the other. Trust is the action in conjunction with the belief that specifies its reason. Such a belief would have to be based on evidence and so could not be summoned at will. However, when an entrusting model is adopted, the significance of confidence in the goodwill of the other easily falls from view. This is because we can entrust where we don't, on my account, trust. That goodwill drops out of the picture when we focus on entrusting is shown in Baier's discussion of the moral rightness or wrongness of trust relations. The cases she considers as trust relationships appear to lack this element of reliance on the goodwill of another: "Where the truster relies on his threat advantage to keep the trust relation going, or where the trusted relies on concealment, something is morally rotten in the trust relationship" (p. 255). I would suggest that in a situation such as this you haven't a morally rotten trust relationship, you haven't a trust relationship at all; instead you have a case of mere reliance. Optimism about goodwill is central to trust, but in situations like the one Baier

describes, there is no goodwill. Trust does not seem to be sufficiently distinguished from relying on. Nor should this surprise us
given that one can entrust where there is mere reliance. If I can rely
on another's fear, my ability to control the purse strings, or the
foolishness of another, I might be fully justified in entrusting them
with something I care about, for I can know that they will not dare
harm it or that it won't occur to them to do so. In such cases,
confidence in some other aspect of a person's psychology has
replaced confidence in her goodwill, but where this other thing is
sufficient to ensure adequate performance, I need not also depend
on her goodwill. This is not to say that relationships of reliance
aren't sometimes mixed or can't depend on both kinds of
elements.

Goodwill readily drops out of an entrusting model even when
we attempt to include it, as Baier does. This is because we are led
to focus on the disposition of cared-about objects rather than on
attitudes toward a person, whom we might, as a consequence of
holding such an attitude, willingly let get dangerously near things
we care about. One of the chief motives for adopting an entrusting
model—namely, that we be able to say what is in common and
what is different between the various forms of trust, ranging as
they do from trust in strangers to trust in intimates—can be
accommodated within a nonentrusting model provided that we
allow for variation in the domain over which the attitude extends.
This lets us keep "plain trust" (p. 259), as an attitude directed
towards a person and as explanatory of the kinds of risks we
might willingly expose ourselves to with respect to that person,
while yet being able to make the same kinds of distinctions that an
entrusting model can.

An entrusting model is silent about the third commonplace
a theory of trust should explain. And this is so even when such a
model is fully spelt out so that trust is entrusting on the basis of
a belief that the other has goodwill. The belief that another has
goodwill may lead us, in the first instance, to be doubtful about her
guilt. This is perfectly reasonable insofar as the evidence that supports the belief that the other has goodwill is also evidence for the
belief that the person couldn't have done such a thing—think of

character witnesses in criminal trials. However, as a belief of a perfectly ordinary sort, it should not be abnormally resistant to evidence, and it should not lead us to hold additional beliefs that are themselves abnormally resistant to evidence.[16] But the beliefs we form on the basis of trust *are* abnormally resistant to evidence and so, in general, is the optimism about the goodwill of another that grounds such beliefs.

I conclude that an entrusting model does not sufficiently bring out the affective component in trust. In particular, it obscures the importance of optimism about the goodwill of another.

IV Justified trusting

Given the usefulness of trust, should we say that a trusting attitude is the rational default position and that we should tend to approach the world with a trusting cognitive set? Or should we say that in the light of the harms to which we are vulnerable when we trust unwisely, the rational default position is one of distrust? Or, finally, should we say that the rational default position is one of neutrality?[17] Appropriate default stance is too sensitive to climate, and to domain and consequences as they interact to affect the expected disutility of misplaced trust, for there to be useful generalizations here. Further, for the individual truster, the appropriate default stance is linked to her assessment of tendencies in her own trusting and distrusting.

In climates in which there is strong motive to be untrustworthy, it would require more evidence for our trust to be justified than in climates where there is little incentive to untrustworthiness. A final verdict on whether a particular act of trusting is justified will have to step beyond that particular case to examine general features of the social climate we inhabit. Thus I take it that at the height of the Chinese Cultural Revolution, the justified default position was one of distrust, and that it took more evidence to be warranted in moving from this position than it would take to warrant justified trusting in a more favorable climate. During those campaigns, people accused of being counterrevolutionary were subject to public shaming, beating, and incarceration. At the time, there was strong motive for people to be untrustworthy. Informers were held up as model citizens, and anyone who displayed goodwill towards someone who became a target of the campaigns was in danger of herself becoming a target. In such a climate, showing goodwill towards others was dangerous. In contrast, in an ideally moral climate, the interests of each would be harmonized so that trust could flourish. The motivation to be untrustworthy would diminish, and there would thus be grounds for the expectation that those we encounter are trustworthy.

Domain and consequences interact to determine which default stance is justified and how much evidence we need to move from that default stance. If I am to have the depth of trust that would make it reasonable to entrust you with a secret of mine, then I'll want to have quite a bit of evidence about your character. If, though, I am to trust you not to attack me in the street, I may need no particular evidence about your character at all. This might seem to be a counterintuitive result, since surely it is worse to be attacked in the street than it is to be embarrassed by a confidence indiscreetly betrayed. However, domain is here signaling likelihood of performance. We are all aware of the lively pleasures of gossip and of the strength of character required to resist them. In contrast, it is not hard to refrain from harming a stranger on the street; that just takes basic decency, a trait that we can assume is widely shared, unless the climate is sufficiently bad. Once we hold domain fixed, consequences become of the first importance: of course I'm going to need more evidence of your trustworthiness before I willingly tell you a secret that, if spread abroad, would be damaging to me, than before I tell you a secret whose disclosure would be merely embarrassing. It is not, therefore, that one or the other of domain or consequence is always the most important; rather what is important is how they interact to determine the expected disutility of misplaced trust (or distrust).

While climate, domain, and consequences are variables determining which default stance is justified that extend across agents, the fourth variable determining the appropriate default stance is agent-specific. Some agents have reason to be distrustful of their tendencies toward trust in certain domains. When we believe that we are poor affective instruments, either in general or across a specific range of cases, we should distrust our trust, or distrust our distrust, and demand a correspondingly higher amount of evidence before we let ourselves trust or distrust in the kinds of cases in question. Consider responses to physicians. We can imagine someone with a tendency to find authoritative and avuncular physicians trustworthy and physicians who acknowledge the tentativeness of their diagnoses and the limits of their art untrustworthy. Given how sexism shapes what we take to be signs of competence, we should be wary of our tendency to trust when an etiology of that trust tells us it is as likely to be caused by mannerisms of privilege as by marks of trustworthiness.

Because climate, domain, consequences of misplaced trust, and appropriate assessment of the tendencies of our own trusting and distrusting affect how much evidence is needed before our trust can count as justified, the question of the rational default position has no general answer. However, there is still an important question to be addressed: Are there any instances of apparently justified trust or distrust where we would not want to say that the person would be justified in having the belief that the other was trustworthy or untrustworthy? If there can be such cases, then if we advocated an analysis of trust which made trust fully or partly constituted by a belief about the other's trustworthiness, we would be forced either to reject evidentialism or admit that the cases weren't justified after all.

There are two places to look for examples of trust leaping ahead of the evidence: when trust is governed by forward-looking or instrumental considerations, and when trust is governed by backward-looking considerations of evidence but our responses seem to outstrip the evidence. Let's examine the forward-looking cases first.

Earlier I remarked that trust cannot be willed but that it can be cultivated. We might want to cultivate trust towards people in general, towards members of a certain group, or towards a particular person. Moreover, it seems that we can sometimes be justified both in attempting to cultivate trust and in the trusting that is the result of such cultivation. If trust and distrust are partly constituted by patterns of attention, lines of inquiry, and tendencies of interpretation, it should be possible to cultivate them by controlling our patterns of attention, our lines of inquiry, and our interpretations. Thus, while trust cannot be directly willed, we can will to pay attention to the kinds of things that are likely to support, create, or extend our trust, and we can will to refrain from focusing on the kinds of things that are likely to undermine and limit our trust.

Sometimes we set about cultivating trust because we think that by trusting, and displaying our trust, we will be able to elicit trustworthy behavior from the other. When we do this our hope is that by trusting we will be able to bring about the very conditions that would justify our trust. It might be thought that we do not need to inquire whether attempts at this sort of bootstrapping can be justified, for we need never actually trust on the basis of forward-looking considerations—all we need do is act *as if* we trusted. To actually set about trying to trust is to do more than is needed. It is a mistake, though, to think that acting as if you trusted will have the same results as acting on the basis of genuine trust, cultivated in the hope of bringing about trustworthiness. Acting as if you trusted and genuinely trusting could have the same result only on the assumption that there is no perceptible difference between the behavior that would be produced from trust and the behavior that would be produced from acting as if you trusted. But this assumption is implausible in the kinds of cases where one is most likely to adopt this sort of strategy in the first place. Trusting in the hope of eliciting trustworthiness is a pointless strategy to adopt with those with whom we have infrequent contact. In such circumstances our strategic trusting could not bear fruit. Instead, it is the kind of strategy a parent might use with a child, or a lover with her beloved. But it is precisely the frequency of contact between the one who would trust and the one she would elicit trustworthiness from that makes it implausible to suppose that merely acting as if you trusted could, on each of many separate occasions, result in behavior indistinguishable from the behavior of one who genuinely trusts. If this is so, then we do need to ask when, if ever, bootstrapping is justified.

Bootstrapping is not always possible and not always reasonable. It won't be possible if we cannot find sufficient foundation in evidence for our trusting. Despite our attempts to control our patterns of attention and our interpretations, we might be unable to find enough to focus on to support our trust. Our attempts at giving positive reinterpretations of those aspects of a person that might otherwise have tended to support the hypothesis that she is untrustworthy have the feel of fantasy and wish fulfillment. They do not ring true. Whenever trust can be achieved only through a fantasy construction, our trusting is unlikely to elicit trustworthiness from the other, for if fantasy is required to see the other as trustworthy, it is highly unlikely that the other has the potential for trustworthiness.

In addition to cultivating trust in order to elicit trustworthiness from another, we sometimes cultivate trust in order to realize a conception of ourselves. So, for example, the rape victim whose trust in others has been shattered might set about cultivating trust because she sees herself as someone who is free-spirited and bold, and she does not wish to be the kind of person who is timid, protective of the self, and on the lookout for betrayal. She does not want her horrible experience to lead to a change in herself. The trust that results from willful cultivation can be rational. Provided that its cultivation did not require fantasy and distortion, it can be reasonable to view it as keyed to real and perceptible features of the agent's situation.

The second sort of cases involve flash intuitive assessments that do not seem to be based on evidence sufficient to support a belief. Let us consider an example taken from Greenspan's *Emotions and Reasons*.[18] I find myself feeling suspicious of a salesman, worried that he will harm my interests, worried that he is not trustworthy. Let us suppose, further, that the salesman has been recommended to me by a friend whose judgment in such matters I believe to be reliable. On the basis of this recommendation, I believe that the salesman is trustworthy, yet I find myself unable to help viewing him with suspicion. I continue to see him as untrustworthy, although I am not yet prepared to abandon my belief that he is trustworthy. I cannot articulate why I view him with suspicion, except to say that there is something creepy about him, something in his manner that I don't like. Finally, let us suppose, although I don't know this myself, that I am not, in general, a reliable detector of untrustworthiness. My suspicion would not track untrustworthiness across a suitable range of counterfactual circumstances relevantly similar to the present one. Thus, as the example is set up, if having a justified belief requires being able to give an account of what justifies that belief, I haven't got a justified belief. Similarly, if having a justified belief requires having a belief that tracks the truth across some range of counterfactual circumstances, I haven't got a justified belief. And if having a justified belief requires having a belief formed by a reliable process and the absence of undermining beliefs, I haven't got a justified belief, for my belief that the salesman is trustworthy appears to undermine my perception of him as untrustworthy.[19] Thus, it seems that I wouldn't be justified in forming a belief that he is untrustworthy on the basis of my seeing him as untrustworthy.

If we think that trust and distrust are primarily beliefs, it seems that—regardless of any of the variables mentioned earlier—we would have to say that my distrust could not be justified. But it seems to me that, especially if the stakes are high, I might still be justified in following through with the lines of inquiry and patterns of salience that are constitutive of distrust.[20] This is because emotions and other affective states often do represent the world in the way it is: those we are suspicious of often are untrustworthy.[21] I do not mean to claim that distrust would have to be justified in cases of this sort, only that even though we've *decisively* shown the belief that the other is untrustworthy is unjustified, we haven't decisively shown that distrust is unjustified. To do that we would have to step back and examine the other variables affecting the justification of trust, and they could well return the verdict "justified." This example better lets us understand the importance of the truster's assessment of the tendencies in her own trust and distrust: the metajustification in terms of the worth of following up on affective appearances would not be available to those with reason to distrust their distrust.

If there can be cases of the sort I have described, then an account of trust that makes affect central has an unexpected payoff: it lets us say that such cases can be justified without confronting the evidentialist thesis. It is beyond the scope of this article to argue the merits of evidentialism. It might well be that evidentialism is false—perhaps, for example, we can be justified in believing on instrumentalist grounds. But if, as I have argued, trust and distrust are not primarily beliefs, then trust and distrust cannot be used to unseat evidentialism.[22] Equally, though, evidentialism cannot be used to challenge our intuitions about when trust and distrust are justified.

Notes

I would like to thank the editors of *Ethics*, Judith Baker, and an anonymous referee for comments that greatly improved this article and for suggesting a new title. Lively discussions with Bennett Helm, Martha Nussbaum, Naomi Scheman, and audiences at Cornell University and UCLA helped considerably. Special thanks are owed to Allen Wood for a discussion of evidentialism and to Terry Irwin for helpful comments on numerous drafts.

1   Amélie Oksenberg Rorty, "Explaining Emotions," in *Explaining Emotions,* ed. Amélie Oksenberg Rorty (Berkeley: University of California Press, 1980); Cheshire Calhoun, "Cognitive Emotions?" in *What Is an Emotion?* ed. Cheshire Calhoun and Robert C. Solomon (New York: Oxford University Press, 1984), pp. 327–42; Ronald de Sousa, "The Rationality of Emotions" (originally published 1979), in Rorty, ed., pp. 127–52, and *The Rationality of Emotion* (Cambridge, Mass.: MIT Press, 1987).

2   The account I develop here is indebted to Annette Baier's account—in "Trust and Antitrust," *Ethics* 96 (1986): 231–60, and "The Pathologies of Trust" and "Appropriate Trust," delivered at Princeton University as the Tanner Lectures on Human Values *(Tanner Lectures on Human Values,* Vol. 13 [Salt Lake City: University of Utah Press, 1992])—most significantly in the following ways: (i) in maintaining a distinction between trust and reliance, (ii) in acknowledging the importance of the competence of the other (Baier, "Trust and Antitrust," p. 239, and *Tanner Lectures on Human Values,* pp. 111–12), and (iii) in recognizing that trust can be faked *(Tanner Lectures on Human Values,* p. 112). The difference in our positions will become clear in section III.

3   That trust involves discretionary powers is first noted by Baier ("Trust and Antitrust," pp. 236–40). However, I think she rather overstates the case in claiming that trust always involves discretionary powers.

4   Thanks to the editors of *Ethics* for this example.

5   Rorty, "Explaining Emotions"; Calhoun; and de Sousa, "The Rationality of Emotions" and *The Rationality of Emotion*.

6   For a discussion of the notion of cognitive sets and of the cognitive set involved in resentment in particular, see Calhoun.

7   Ronald de Sousa discusses *Othello* in the context of how control of perceptual focus can give rise to emotions and how jealousy affects our interpretation of situations (*The Rationality of Emotion*, pp. 195–6).

8   For a discussion of spider and other phobias, see Calhoun.

9   Baier, "Trust and Antitrust," p. 234.

10 It is a consequence of my account, though, that when we say nonnatural agents trust, our usage is analogous to our usage in attributing trust to a natural agent; but insofar as it is metaphorical to attribute affective states to nonnatural agents, the meaning is not precisely the same. (This is also true, though, when we attribute beliefs to nonnatural agents.) Sometimes government policies can enact something similar to the selective vision characteristic of trust, and the rationale for those policies can duplicate the expectation constitutive of trust. For example, a social-welfare agency might decide not to use surveillance methods to eliminate cheating, on the grounds that the number of cheaters is likely to be small and can be further reduced by a policy of not checking since that would make the recipients feel they were being treated respectfully, and they would respond positively to such treatment. Here, the government agency would have been expecting its clients to respond favorably to the fact that they were being counted on. The agency's policy would have mimicked the way optimism gives rise to selective interpretation in that the agency would have proceeded on the basis of the assumption that cheating was not something to be expected. Note that the rationale for the policy matters: it would not be correct to say that the agency trusts its clients if they simply thought checking up on them was cost-inefficient.

11 This is noted by Trudy Govier in "Trust, Distrust, and Feminist Theory," *Hypatia* 7 (1992): 16–33, 18.

12 This is noted by Baier in "Trust and Antitrust," p. 244.

13 This point is made by Judith Baker in "Trust and Rationality," *Pacific Philosophical Quarterly* 68 (1987): 1–13. Baker is concerned about the problem of reconciling trust with evidentialism, or the view that we should never believe anything without sufficient evidence. She claims that trust is "a kind of commitment, a state of the will" (p. 10). (If this were right, though, it seems trust should be able to be willed.) Trust still essentially involves beliefs, although it is to be assessed primarily for strategic rationality. She attempts to resolve the tension in saying that trust involves beliefs but is primarily assessed in terms of goal-directed, rather than truth-directed, rationality by pointing out the importance of trust for

friendship: "But if a result of becoming someone's friend, of one's trust, is that barriers to honesty are removed and the other person is open with us, then trust in their veracity will be merited and end-directed rationality will not be opposed to truth-directed rationality" (p. 12). If believing makes it so, then the belief is justified. But, of course, believing does not always make it so, and so strategic and representational rationality won't always be in alignment. My account, which places an affective element at the center of trust, is able to finesse the evidentialist objection. I return to the issue of evidentialism in section IV.

14   Of course, that we cannot adopt an attitude in the face of a known and acknowledged lack of grounds is not to say that our affective stances follow our beliefs in a timely fashion, nor that we don't sometimes find ourselves experiencing "spill-over" feelings, as happens, for example, with phobias.

15   Baier, "Trust and Antitrust," p. 236. For the remainder of this section, page references in the text are to this article.

16   In Baier's newer work on trust, the entrusting model is less emphasized, and she acknowledges that trust also involves an affective aspect, though she does not attempt a detailed account of it *(Tanner Lectures on Human Values,* pp. 111–12). For Baier, the affective aspect is not central in an account of when trust is justified. In section IV, I will claim that the affective aspect of trust is central for understanding when trust is justified.

17   Talk of default positions is compatible with the section III claim that emotions look to the world for evidence. Consider anger: we can admit that anger can't be willed but still inquire whether it is better to be irascible, placid-tempered, or something in between.

18   Patricia S. Greenspan, *Emotions and Reasons* (New York: Routledge, 1988). Greenspan argues that suspicion can be justified when one would not be justified in forming a belief that the other is untrustworthy. Her account of justification also stresses forward-looking conditions. However, she does not think that scepticism about our own capacity as an emotional instrument is especially undermining of the justifiedness of an emotion.

19   These three options are meant to exhaust the possible accounts of what makes a belief justified. The first is an internalist account and the others externalist accounts.

20   That is why this sort of example is best developed with cases of suspicion, since usually the costs of being wrong in our distrust are less than the costs of being wrong in our trust. But this is a generalization that admits of exceptions: there can sometimes be severe consequences of misplaced distrust.

21   In *Passions within Reason* (New York: Norton, 1988), Robert Frank presents an evolutionary argument for why emotions can have this role.

22   In "The Virtue of Faith," *Faith and Philosophy* 1 (1984): 3–15, Robert Adams claims that trust requires beliefs that go beyond the evidence.

Index